# STILL ON AIR

# STILL ON AIR

## Producing Television in Small Markets

Yvette J. Rowe and Livingston A. White

The University of the West Indies Press
Jamaica • Barbados • Trinidad and Tobago

The University of the West Indies Press
7A Gibraltar Hall Road, Mona
Kingston 7, Jamaica
www.uwipress.com

© 2018 Yvette J. Rowe and Livingston A. White
All rights reserved. Published 2018

A catalogue record of this book is available
from the National Library of Jamaica.

ISBN: 978-976-640-675-2 (print)
978-976-640-676-9 (Kindle)
978-976-640-677-6 (ePub)

Cover illustration by Nicholas Shelton.
Book and cover design by Robert Harris.
Set in Scala 10.5/15 x 27.
Printed in the United States of America.

The University of the West Indies Press has no responsibility for the persistence or accuracy of URLs for external or third-party Internet websites referred to in this publication and does not guarantee that any content on such websites is, or will remain, accurate or appropriate.

FOR ALL JAMAICAN PRODUCERS OF TELEVISION
AND THE PEOPLE WHO CONTINUE TO SUPPORT THEM

# Contents

Preface    ix

Acknowledgements    xv

Abbreviations    xvii

1. Before We Begin: A History of Television Programming in Jamaica    1

2. And Now the Details: Understanding Television in Jamaica    15

3. *Schools' Challenge Quiz*: Jamaica's Long-Standing Quiz Show    23

4. *Profile*: Presenting Personalities Persistently    37

5. *Hill an' Gully Ride*: Documenting Jamaican People and Places    46

6. *Entertainment Report*: Showcasing Jamaica's Popular Culture    57

7. Stay Tuned: Why They Continue to Be on Air    66

8. Coming Up: Shows Watched and Ones to Watch    90

9. Sneak Preview: Future Trends in Jamaican Television    124

10. Still Ahead: Possibilities and Recommendations    133

Appendix 1. Definitions of Some Typical Genres for Free-to-Air Television    141

Appendix 2. Some of the Longest-Running Shows in Various Countries    148

Appendix 3. Market Research Figures for Four Jamaican Television Shows  **152**

Appendix 4. Television Programmes Produced and Aired in Jamaica  **166**

Notes  **217**

Selected Bibliography  **235**

Index  **239**

# Preface

*Still on Air: Producing Television in Small Markets* offers a detailed analysis of four Jamaican television programmes (*Schools' Challenge Quiz, Profile, Hill an' Gully Ride* and *Entertainment Report*) by examining the various production elements that have contributed to their success. The book documents their historical, production and broadcast experiences and offers an analysis of the reasons for their longevity. The length of time on air can be an indicator of a show's success in certain contexts such as small markets for television. In this circumstance, this book interrogates these programmes' ability to sustain being on air in the evolving media landscape in Jamaica, and suggests ways in which local producers can create successful programming. The project represents an important work as it documents an aspect of the Jamaican television industry that has never before been given detailed attention. The work provides readers with insights into what is required to produce television programming that is culturally sensitive, affordable and responsive to audiences in small markets.

This book focuses on not only the history of television shows in Jamaica but also on the main issues affecting their production and presentation. The span encompasses the birth of local television in 1963, a year after independence, to 2015, over fifty years later. Gathering the information was a demanding task given the state of audio-visual archiving and documentation in the country. Therefore, the research methodology used relied heavily on oral histories, interviews with individuals associated with indigenous television production and programming who had personal knowledge of many of the programmes featured. One challenge presented by this method is the extent to which people are able to recall facts. While some interviewees kept detailed records and diaries and could produce documents, others could not always remember exact details. To deal with this, there was ongoing cross-referencing with other sources to ascertain the validity of the information gathered. This approach has been used in similar efforts on this subject. For example, in studying British television shows for his 2015 book *BBC and Television Genres in Jeopardy*, author Jeremy Tunstall conducted over 150 interviews with executive producers and various other television professionals.

The work presented here makes a contribution to the literature on television studies looking specifically at production in small media markets. Previous research on television in Jamaica has focused on issues relating to its development.[1] These studies have explored issues such as the management of television entities, the public versus private sector model of television in Jamaica, the policy framework governing the sector and the ratio of foreign to local television content. Other Jamaican works that have helped to document the history of Jamaican television have been autobiographical in nature. Former media manager and television producer Carey Robinson, wrote about his experiences in media in his 2012 book *Memoirs of a Jamaican Media Man*. Though not writing specifically about television, Alma Mock Yen's 2002 autobiography *Rewind: My Recollections of Radio Broadcasting in Jamaica* is important because it documents information about the Jamaica Broadcasting Corporation (JBC) that provided not only radio but also television services to the island. What is missing from the literature is an in-depth focus on the production processes that have led to the creation of local television content relevant for Jamaicans, as a response to concerns over the level of foreign media content.

In addition to searches of the newspapers regarding general matters of Jamaican television, specific searches of the television programme guides published in Jamaican newspapers from 1963 to 2015 were reviewed to ascertain the existence of over three hundred local television programmes produced during that period. Archive searches of Jamaica's daily newspapers provided additional information to substantiate statements made by interviewees. The video archives of the Public Broadcasting Corporation of Jamaica (PBCJ) and the Creative Production and Training Centre (CPTC) provided access to early versions of the shows examined in detail in this book. Television Jamaica (TVJ) also provided later editions of some of these

PREFACE

programmes. Some of the earliest copies could not be found because they were not in the archives, the quality of the storage medium had deteriorated, or they had been destroyed or recycled. This work therefore makes an important contribution by documenting information about many Jamaican television programmes for which no video copy currently exists.

While our research focused mainly on four shows, we also captured any information that could be accessed on other local programmes. These have been briefly described in chapter 8 to give an idea of the range of local programmes. Information about them was found in printed documents such as newspapers, annual reports or minutes of meetings. Other evidence was discovered through online searches of social-media platforms or by mentions in conversations between the researchers and producers who recalled some of their favourite local programmes. While every attempt has been made to acknowledge all multi-episode programmes created in Jamaica, some would have been omitted if they had not been properly documented or if there was no accessible historical record of their existence. Appendix 4 includes a list of television shows created in Jamaica, along with a brief description of each and its status at the time of this publication.

To be considered as a *Jamaican* television programme for inclusion in this book, the show had to

- be created by a production team involving Jamaicans even if the format originated elsewhere;
- include multiple episodes;
- address content that is markedly related to a Jamaican audience and a substantial amount of that content had to be recorded and produced in Jamaica; and
- be financed, at least in part, by a Jamaican source.

This book focuses specifically on programmes that have been shown on free-to-air television since its start in Jamaica in 1963. Based on Jamaica's 2011 census, 96 per cent of households have a television set and can therefore access these. Free-to-air or broadcast television has remained the main distribution mechanism for locally produced content even with the introduction of regulated subscription cable television services in the 1990s. In

## PREFACE

2015, the Broadcasting Commission of Jamaica estimated that only 17 per cent of households subscribed to cable services through one of their licensed cable operators. Local programmes which are only shown on subscription cable television were therefore not considered. To be reflected here, a show had to be airing on free-to-air television by the end of 2015, after enjoying a period of sustained broadcast.

Audience ratings, viewership figures, maintaining a loyal viewership, length of time on air and number of episodes produced are some aspects of a television show that can be used to evaluate its success. All these elements are not always relevant in various contexts and for different programmes.

Given the foregoing, the four longest-running local programmes that were still on air in 2015 are *Schools' Challenge Quiz*, which first aired in 1970; followed by *Profile*, which began in 1987; then *Hill an' Gully Ride*, which started airing in 1989; and finally *Entertainment Report*, which began in 1991. These shows originated during the JBC years and are now aired on TVJ. There have been other long-running shows and newer ones that have been on the air for over ten years that might in the future make the list. Those with potential for longevity and sustainability are also discussed in chapter 8 of this book.

The four shows in question represent different television genres. *Schools' Challenge Quiz* is a quiz game show. *Profile* is a talk show. *Hill an' Gully Ride* can be categorized as a factual programme while *Entertainment Report* exemplifies the current and public affairs genre. JBC, which was the first and the only television station in Jamaica for over thirty years, represents more than half of the history of the first fifty years of Jamaican television. It was a state-owned entity that received a subvention from the government but was also expected to earn money from advertising and sponsorship. Its aim was to educate, inform and entertain as a public broadcaster. In this book, we demonstrate that the four shows (table 1) began in an era when JBC attempted to fulfil this mandate, and how these shows managed the transition to private sector ownership after JBC was divested.

The book also presents a framework comprising seven factors which, if addressed, contribute to the successful production of television shows in small markets. It ends with a discussion of trends that have implications for the future.

**Table 1.** The Four Longest-Running Shows in Jamaica

| First Broadcast | Title | Free-to-Air Station | Status as at 2015 |
|---|---|---|---|
| 26 February 1970 | *Schools' Challenge Quiz* | JBC, SSTV, TVJ | Still on air |
| 22 February 1987 | *Profile* | JBC, SSTV, TVJ | Still on air |
| 13 January 1989 | *Hill an' Gully Ride* | JBC, SSTV, TVJ | Still on air |
| 15 November 1991* | *Entertainment Report* | JBC, SSTV, TVJ | Still on air |

*This is the earliest dated broadcast copy of the five-minute version of *Entertainment Report* found in the JBC archives at the PBCJ. The earliest copy of the thirty-minute version found had a broadcast date of 26 March 1993.

# Acknowledgements

The authors thank the following people for their support during the research phase of creating this book: Beverley Brammer, librarian at the Creative Production and Training Centre; Sheree Rhoden, librarian at the Gleaner Archives, and Jovan Johnson, who assisted with locating archived material about the shows; Kimberly Blackwin of the Jamaica Archives and Records Department; Nadine Shaw, research assistant of Market Research Services Limited; Simone Williams of Multimedia Jamaica Limited; the national librarian and CEO of the National Library of Jamaica, Winsome Hudson and her staff – in particular, Kirk Fellows, Demar Ludford, Michael Thomas-Hannibal, Bernadette Worrell and Paul Maxwell, audio-visual librarian of Public Broadcasting Corporation of Jamaica. These individuals were instrumental not only in finding copies of television programmes but also in verifying information about the shows. Don Dobson, information officer at the Broadcasting Commission of Jamaica, helped in verifying information related to broadcast regulations. The research could not have been completed without connections that were established with key informants. Hazel Bennett, retired historian; Claire Stewart and Kathryn Stewart, daughters of *Schools' Challenge Quiz* creator Hope Stewart; and Suzanne Francis-Brown, historian and museum curator, connected us with individuals who were able to share memories of their association with television programmes in Jamaica. Thanks to the staff of the Caribbean School of Media and Communication for their encouragement.

The following individuals guided us through their willingness to share their experiences and connecting us with others who could: Judith Alberga, Rohan Amiel, Don Anderson, Kishka-Kaye O'Connor Anderson, Patrick Anderson, Omar Azan, Jean Barnes, Andre Bidwell, Don Blades,

## ACKNOWLEDGEMENTS

Tricia Blair, Celia Blake, Mel Blake, Ian Boyne, Theresa Brodber, Kerlyn Brown, Keith Brown, Roy Brown, Kirk Buchanan, Jonathan Burke, Louis Burke, Zahra Burton, Keith Campbell, Leslie Campbell, Simone Clarke-Cooper, Helene Coley-Nicholson, Mary Collins, Aston Cooke, Lukkee Chong, Bill Cummings, Marie Cunningham, Saudicka Diaram, Chester Dowdy, Val Duffus, Hopeton Dunn, Raymond Edwards, Fae Ellington, Owen Ellis, Khadene Foote, Leonie Forbes, Marcia Forbes, Gary Ferguson, Kathy Gayle, Lois Gayle, Michelle Geister, Michael Gonzales, Archibald Gordon, David Graham, Claire Grant, Cordel Green, Joylene Griffiths-Irving, Dahlia Harris, Joan Andrea Hutchinson, Deborah Hickling, Pablo Hoilett, Ruth Ho Shing, Donna Hope, Dennis Howard, Chantal Hylton-Tonnes, Carol Ivey, Dionne Jackson-Miller, Bernard Jankee, Monica Johnson, Trevor Johnson, Arnold Kelly, Mark Kenny, Michael Kerr, Teddy Laidley, Aneiph Latchman, Pat Lazarus, Garnet Lewis, Lennie Little-White, Ealane Livingston-Smith, Allia McDonald, Sabrena McDonald-Radcliffe, Ali McNab, Gregory 'Asha' McPhail, Dervan Malcolm, Kenia Mattis, Laleta Mattis, Anthony Miller, Maizie Miller, O'Neil C. Miller, James Moss-Solomon, Gary Neita, Leo O'Reggio, Kay Osbourne, Tony Patel, O.C. Powell, Patrick Prendergast, Pat Riley, Adrian Robinson, Carey Robinson, Claude Robinson, Sadie Robinson, Tony Robinson, Shermain Robotham, Heather Royes, Sandra Rose, Melita Samuels, Sharon Schroeter, Susan Simes, Ray Smith, Franklyn St Juste, David Soutar, Marlene Stephenson-Dalley, Denzie Stephenson-Miller, Laurence Stewart, Mark Taylor, Carmeta Tate-Blake, Moya Thomas, Mark Anthony Thomas, Valentine Tyrell, Rosemarie Voodrouw, Alphonso Walker, Garth Walker, Milton Walker, Shane Walker, Shaun Walker, Ed Wallace, Oliver Watt, Marjorie Whylie, Jason Williams, Winford Williams, Elaine Wint and Lincoln Wynter. Thanks to all for their help.

# Abbreviations

| | |
|---|---|
| BCJ | Broadcasting Commission of Jamaica |
| BBC | British Broadcasting Corporation |
| CBF | Cultural Broadcasting Facility |
| CIN | Caribbean International Network |
| CPTC | Creative Production and Training Centre |
| CVM TV | Community Television Systems, Videomax and Mediamix Television |
| DVD | digital video disc |
| JBC TV | Jamaica Broadcasting Corporation Television |
| JIS TV | Jamaica Information Service Television |
| JLP | Jamaica Labour Party |
| NBC | National Broadcasting Company |
| NCB | National Commercial Bank |
| PBCJ | Public Broadcasting Corporation of Jamaica |
| PNP | People's National Party |
| RJR | Radio Jamaica Limited |
| SSTV | Super Supreme Television |
| TVJ | Television Jamaica |
| VOD | video on demand |

# 1

# Before We Begin

A History of Television
Programming in Jamaica

What makes a television programme successful in Jamaica? Before answering this question, it is necessary to describe the introduction and development of television in the country, which is best understood by assessing its evolution. Of the many local programmes created, some have been aired for varying lengths of time; some have been produced, aired and then shelved; others have never moved beyond the single pilot episode while some have never made it to the screen.[1]

In this work, we examine the production of four Jamaican television shows – *Schools' Challenge Quiz*, *Profile*, *Hill an' Gully Ride* and *Entertainment Report* – and present a framework for understanding why these shows are still being produced and maintain their viewership. This is intended to serve as a template for producing successful television programmes. We argue that if a programme contains certain elements, it is likely to be successful – that is, capture audiences and remain on air. We also briefly examine other shows that have not had a long run, with a view to strengthening our argument. We end the book with some ideas about the future of television programming in Jamaica.

Creating a television programme in Jamaica is not an easy task. Creating sustainable programmes is even more challenging and depends on a number of factors ranging from technical talent to consistent sponsorship. A review of the development of local television illustrates the complexity of the process for developing, producing and broadcasting shows. Regardless, productions like the four that we highlight in this publication remind us that it is possible to develop viable, relevant programming for audiences in a country such as this.

Despite its development challenges, Jamaica is known internationally for its reggae music, its track athletes and its tourist attractions. There is a perception that foreign investment in the country is low because of the crime rate and government systems that are not always transparent.[2] In the past, the country has earned from its bauxite, sugar and banana industries, but more recent foreign exchange earners are remittances from abroad and tourism.[3] It is not surprising that remittances are among the major contributors to the economy as there are many communities of people with Jamaican ancestry living in North America and the United Kingdom – about 240,000 legal permanent residents in New York, for example.[4]

Jamaica, the third-largest island in the Caribbean, is about 146 miles long and 51 miles wide. The capital, Kingston, is located to the southeastern part of the island. The population of 2.8 million comprises people of African, European, East Indian, Middle Eastern and Chinese descent. While English is the official language, many communicate using Jamaican creole. Having been a former British colony, Jamaica now has a parliamentary democracy

Table 2. Key Points in the Evolution of Jamaican Television

| Date | Activity |
| --- | --- |
| 1963 | JBC TV begins transmission |
| 1970s | Videotape begins to replace the use of film |
| 1980s | Unregulated cable television introduced |
| 1982 | Colour television introduced based on the US National Standards Television Committee (NTSC) system |
| 1983 | Early talks about divesting JBC TV |
| 1984 | Jamaica Film Commission established<br>CPTC established |
| 1986 | The Broadcasting Commission of Jamaica (BCJ) established replacing the Broadcasting Authority that began in 1959 |
| 1993 | CVM TV begins transmission<br>JBC TV makes a profit for the first time |

**Table 2.** Key Points in the Evolution of Jamaican Television (cont'd)

| Date | Activity |
|---|---|
| 1997 | JBC TV sold to RJR<br>JBC TV's name changed to SSTV<br>PBCJ Act passed in parliament |
| 1998 | SSTV's name changed to TVJ in October<br>Love TV begins transmission<br>Cable television operations legalized; approx. 40 licenses issued |
| 1999 | Emergence of local cable channels |
| 2003 | First talks of digital switchover led by BCJ |
| 2004 | TVJ moves operations to RJR at Lyndhurst Road |
| 2007 | PBCJ begins operating on a cable channel |

*Sources:* Carey Robinson, "The JBC-Television Story", JBC TV Supplement, *Gleaner*, 4 August 1993, 4; Carey Robinson, "30 Years of JBC–TV", JBC-TV Supplement, *Gleaner*, 4 August 1993, 4; "Cable Pirates at Large Broadcasting Commission on the Hunt", *Gleaner*, 16 August 2000, 1A; Brown, "Mass Media in Jamaica"; "About the Film Commission", FilmJamaica.com, accessed 30 August 2015, http://www.filmjamaica.com/; "Creative Production and Training Centre", JIS, accessed 30 August 2015, http://jis.gov.jm/agencies/creative-production-and-training-centre/; Mordecai, "State Policy, Global Trends and Regulation in Broadcasting"; Dunn, "Jamaican Media"; "JBC/RJR Merger: A Look to the Future", *Gleaner*, 10 June, 1997; "RJR Takes Charge of JBC", *Gleaner*, 13 June 1997, B5; "Super Supreme TV", *Gleaner*, 2 August 1997; "Public Broadcasting Corporation of Jamaica", Government of Jamaica, accessed 31 August 2015, http://opm.gov.jm/agencies/public-broadcasting-corporation-of-jamaica-pbcj/; Karen Blair, "Divestment and a New Day", *Gleaner*, 19 June 2011; Vernon Davidson, "Good Evening and Welcome to TVJ", *Observer*, 30 October 1998, 8; "Love 101fm/Love TV", 2005, accessed 20 August 2015, http://www.love101.org/love_tv.htm; "Subscriber (Cable) Television", BCJ, accessed 2 September 2015, http://www.broadcastingcommission.org/get_site_content.php?scid=13; "Steps to Digital Switchover", BCJ, accessed 2 September 2015, http://www.broadcastingcommission.org/get_site_content.php?scid=27; "RJR Annual Report 2004/2005", Jamaica Stock Exchange, 31 August 2005, http://www.jamstockex.com/attachments/2005-10/rjr-annual-report-year-ended-march-31-2005-doc-5792.pdf.url; "Public Broadcasting Corporation Begins Operations Next Financial Year", JIS, 22 December 2005, http://jis.gov.jm/public-broadcasting-corporation-begins-operations-next-financial-year/.

based on the Westminster model. There are two major political parties: the Jamaica Labour Party (JLP) and the People's National Party (PNP). The country gained its independence from Britain on 6 August 1962, and almost a year later, television was introduced.

The history of television in Jamaica is partly the history of the Jamaica Broadcasting Corporation (JBC). Its operations moved to a commercial model from one based on what has been described in the broadcast world as the "Reithian Model" (after director general of the British Broadcasting Corporation [BBC] Lord John Reith).[5]

The JBC operated the national public radio station which had been established in 1959. In November 1962, it obtained a licence which allowed it to extend its service to include television, which it began broadcasting in 1963. The ground breaking ceremony for the television studios at 5 South Odeon Avenue, Kingston, occurred on 31 January 1963.[6] The terms of reference for the JBC were: "for entertainment and relaxation; imparting objective news and information; the vitality of democratic institutions and values, free speech, the rule of law, respect for the individual, freedom of worship, the freedom of inquiry; the health of the community, the efficiency of its economy and its good repute abroad; the education of youth; sports; and the creative arts".[7] Table 2 outlines the evolution of Jamaican television.

On 21 June 1963, JBC Television announced that low-powered test transmissions would begin from its Half Way Tree studios on that day. The signal appeared on Channel 11 from 11:00 a.m. to 2:00 p.m. daily. The first official broadcast on Sunday evening, 4 August 1963, was planned to coincide with Jamaica's independence celebrations. It started with an opening ceremony in Studio C which included dignitaries of church and state, along with the station's management team.[8] After the success of this initial broadcast, regular programming began.

Author and journalist William Stanley-Moss, writing in the column "Teleview" in the *Daily Gleaner* of 6 August 1963, gave his description and assessment of the first day of broadcasting.[9] He noted that it began with speeches, and lamented the inability of the speakers to engage with the camera. After this came the programme *The Life of Riley*, an American television series,[10] followed by the documentary film *Festival*, from the Jamaica Information Service (JIS), depicting aspects of Jamaican life. This was followed by more speeches, and congratulations from home and abroad. Next on the schedule was what Moss described as a canned programme, *Panic*, which was a series from NBC TV. A live local programme called *Variety Showcase* then featured Jamaican entertainers such as Sonny Bradshaw and his combo, Ranny Williams, the Frats Quintet, Louise Bennett and a ballet performance from members of the National Dance Theatre Company. The final presentation was a BBC production of Shakespeare's *Richard II*. Moss concluded that "the evening's offering was satisfactory but not particularly inspiring. One cannot help feeling that it could have been better – but on the other hand it could have been a great deal worse."[11] Regular broadcasts started with five hours per day going from afternoon to evening, rising to seven hours. Morning transmission came in 1970 on Saturdays and Sundays.

Some of the earliest local television programmes produced by JBC TV and appearing in the 1960s included *The Verdict Is Yours* with Emil George, Harvey DaCosta and Frank Barrow; *Children's Corner* with Barry Davies and Erica Allen; *Brains Trust* with Bill Carr; *Round the World Quiz* with Adrian Robinson; *Country Calendar* with Carol Reckord; *Mirror* with Cynthia Wilmot and Beverley Anderson; and *Teenage Dance Party* with Roy Hall. During the 1970s, others appeared, such as *Romper Room*, *Ring Ding*, *Roundabout*, *Here and Now*, *Face-to-Face*, *In Person*, *Where It's At* with Alphonso Walker, and *Schools' Challenge Quiz* with Dennis Hall mainly hosting.[12]

There was a mix of local and foreign programming. Some foreign shows seen then included *The Avengers*, *Bonanza*, *The Beverly Hillbillies*, *Car 54*, *Dennis the Menace*, *The Dickie Henderson Show*, *Doctor Kildare*, *Dragnet*, *The Flying Doctor*, *The Honeymooners*, *I Love Lucy*, *Naked City*, *Perry Mason*, *Peter Loves Mary*, *Peyton Place*, *Robin Hood*, *Sea Hunt*, *Sesame Street*, *The Tom Ewell Show*, *The Twilight Zone* and *The Val Doonican Show*. A short Sunday afternoon broadcast included *Rejoice in the Lord* followed by sports programming.[13]

The JBC shows were supplemented by a number of local productions created by other entities. One such entity was the JIS,[14] the government information agency, which established a television unit in 1963 and produced programmes aired in time made available for government broadcasts, typically between 6:30 p.m. to 7:00 p.m.[15] In the early days of JIS TV, most content was broadcast live with occasional film inserts.[16] It produced *Life with the Littles*, one of Jamaica's first television drama series, described by former head of JIS Carey Robinson as a cross between a sitcom and a soap opera.¹⁷ This half-hour show imparted government information and other messages, such as how to complete an income tax form and facts related to the decimalization of the Jamaican currency.¹⁸ Other shows coming from JIS included *Dear Mama, Great Junction, Inside Story, Jack Mandora, Nightview, Onstage, Portraits, Reflections, Update* and *Walk n' Talk*.¹⁹ It still produces government based programmes which are shown each day in the thirty-minute time slots still allocated for this purpose on Jamaica's three free-to-air broadcasting stations, TVJ, CVM TV and Love TV.

Between the late 1980s and early 1990s, the government introduced macroeconomic policies of privatization, deregulation and commercialization that eventually led to an expansion of media.²⁰ This meant that JBC would no longer be the only terrestrial television broadcasting facility in Jamaica. Even in that uncertain period, it produced some of the most memorable television. The 1980s was marked by programmes such as *Creative Cooking, Enter the Dojo, Hill an' Gully Ride, Lime Tree Lane, Morning Time, Oliver at Large, Profile, Round Table Talk, Seen, Trails* and *Vibrations*. It seemed there was now a concerted effort to increase the local offerings and producers were eager to see their work on air. This enthusiasm continued into the 1990s. JBC presented programmes like *Claffy, Entertainment Report, Health Watch, Oliver, Perspective, Rappin', Thwaites and Company, Titus* and *Tuesday Forum*.

On 12 June 1997, the government divested JBC TV. It became known as Television Jamaica (TVJ) – a totally owned subsidiary of the Radio Jamaica Limited (RJR) Communications Group. There was an RJR interim management group that administered the transition. Between August 1997 and October 1998, the station was branded as Super Supreme Television (SSTV),²¹ but public reaction on the appropriateness of such a name led to its rebranding as TVJ. As much as it was no longer a government owned station, the inclusion of the word "Jamaica" in the name appeased those who were arguably saddened by the sale. The name "Television Jamaica" gave the impression that it would still be operated in the country's interest.²² TVJ continued producing some shows that had appeared on the former JBC TV. Though there was brief legal activity to settle who owned the copyright to some programmes, many of the shows that had dedicated viewership continued to populate the schedules. Some were still based on their original concept but were upgraded, giving them a new look. For example, *Morning Time* became *Smile Jamaica – It's Morning Time*.[23] There were new local programmes: *Deuces Wild, Man and Woman Story, So Me See It* and *Watch n' Win*. New foreign shows included *Absolutely Fabulous, King of the Hill, Law and Order, Mortal Combat, Special Ops Force* and *The Hughleys*.

As part of the sale agreement, the programming created at JBC TV up until 1997 formed part of an audio-visual archive established in June of that year. The archive houses the video and audiotapes of the former JBC and became the property of the Public Broadcasting Corporation of Jamaica (PBCJ) established in April 2006.[24] Not all programmes produced at JBC TV can be sourced here. The collection only dates back to the early 1980s because tapes containing previous recordings of shows and other useful video content were damaged, lost, stolen or recycled, with original content having been taped over.[25]

In the 1990s, two other terrestrial broadcast television stations emerged: CVM TV, which began transmission in 1993, and the National Religious Media Television Service, Love TV, which started in 1998.

CVM TV was established in 1987, when three production houses – Community Television Systems Limited, Videomax Limited, and Mediamix Limited – joined forces.[26] Its broadcast licence was only granted in 1991, as delays were experienced because start-up funding was difficult to obtain. Ironically, it was Claude Robinson, JBC director general from 1991 to 1997, who convinced his board of directors to lease transmitter facilities to them. Finally on Sunday, 28 March 1993, CVM TV went on air at 4:00 p.m.[27] The two-hour broadcast included a half-hour introductory programme detailing the station's plans and aims, and promos for programmes that were going to be aired. Local programmes appearing over the years include *Buzz, CVM at Sunrise, D-Wrap, Face-to-Face, The Golden Nugget, On Stage, Royal Palm Estate, The E-Strip* and *Traxx*.

Love TV provided local and international religious-themed programming such as *Catch the Fire* with David Keane; *Da Spot*, a youth programme; *Vantage Point*, a current affairs show; *Yes! Today*, a Saturday morning show; *Hour of Power*; *Methodist Connection*; *Miracle Revival*; and *Power of Faith*.[28]

The existence of three television stations did not lead to a substantive growth in local content. As this was comparatively more costly to create, they still relied on affordable foreign programming to fill airtime. Audiences also had access to foreign television offerings through cable services, when in 1997 the Broadcasting Commission of Jamaica (BCJ), the government agency with regulatory responsibility for electronic media, awarded licences to over forty subscriber service providers, more commonly called cable operators. This action represented the BCJ's attempt to regulate a sector that appeared in the early 1980s in various locales such as hotels and neighbourhoods, which installed satellite dishes and distributed programming from US satellites to hotel rooms and to residents willing to pay for the service.

As this increased the amount of imported material, operators were required by *must carry* legislation to carry at least two free-to-air channels, in addition to one for public service and educational shows.[29] In a sense, there were now more outlets for Jamaican programming, and local content also emerged on cable TV stations such as Hype TV, Music Plus, Reggae Entertainment Television and the Jamaica News Network. Channels featuring local parties, known at the time as "bashment" channels, also began to appear. Many of these were later classified as adult channels as they showcased unedited footage of individuals dancing in an explicitly sexual manner.[30] However, as this book focuses on free-to-air television for reasons which we will later outline, we leave the discussion of local programmes on cable TV for another publication.

Indigenous offerings for Jamaica's television screens originate from a number of traditional sources including the national television stations, production houses, independent producers, government broadcast houses and corporate entities. The broadcasting television stations – TVJ, CVM TV and Love TV – typically produce their own news, current affairs, sports and morning magazine programmes, and some advertisements.

Some material is independently created using facilities separate from the broadcast station. Airtime is then bought from the station with the support of a sponsor whose advertisements appear during commercial breaks and the completed programme is aired. This would not be possible were it not for corporate Jamaica's willingness to be involved, and for the many production houses providing technical support, in what has become a small television production community of close-knit individuals.

There are times when the staging of major live sports events requires the recruitment of additional staff to make productions possible.[31] Some of the independent producers would have previously worked with and learnt from others in the more established production companies and television stations. In an effort to maximize the benefits from scarce resources, production managers often borrow, share or rent equipment, as well as employ staff from different companies to organize an efficient production crew. It is not unusual to read programme credits and find a videographer who freelances for various productions.

Production houses in Jamaica that have provided programmes include Apex Productions, Cinecom Productions, the Creative Production and Training Centre (CPTC), Frame by Frame Productions, Jamrock Cultural Productions, Mediamix Limited, Phase Three Productions and Vidquip Limited, some of which have ceased operations. Video content which they have created that airs on television includes mainly advertisements and music videos. Those which have survived also participate in film productions and do corporate videos for private use. They also produce pilots for sitcoms, documentaries, game shows and other types of shows which are sometimes shelved due to the unavailability of financing for an entire series.

Educational programmes have also been a mainstay on Jamaican television as a result of the public broadcasting ethos associated with the early years of JBC TV. After its divestment, no institutionalized public service broadcasting entity existed in Jamaica until the passing of the PBCJ Act of 1997 and the establishment in 2007 of the PBCJ as a cable channel.[32] Before this, public broadcasting via television had existed in various guises depending on the ruling political administration. There was the Educational Broadcasting Service started in 1965 as a project of the Ministry of Education which became defunct in 1984. It aired twenty-minute programmes in the mornings on JBC TV focusing on science and geography.[33]

The CPTC was established in 1984 and would occupy the building where the Educational Broadcasting Service once operated. Set up to provide the necessary training and facilities to produce public service programming, its tagline was "Training the best, producing the best". Today, it operates as a limited liability company and, although partly owned by the government, has to be self-sufficient.

There were also the short-lived Cultural Broadcasting Facility (CBF) and the Public Broadcasting of Jamaica, created to promote the ethos of the then JBC TV in the latter part of the 1980s.[34] Under these entities a number of programmes were produced in the national interest such as the magazine show *Today in JA*, the teenage discussion show *Rappin'* and the programme on aspects of Jamaican rural life and folk history, *Hill an' Gully Ride*. These were aired on JBC TV in thirty-minute time slots labelled "Friday Special" and "Sunday Special".

Producers of Jamaican television are capable of creating an array of productions from news magazine programmes, half-hour comedies, talk shows and one-hour dramas to documentaries and music videos. However, these are not often produced and aired in a consistent manner. The more common locally produced shows telecast on a weekly or daily basis include news and sports coverage, news magazine shows and talk shows – arguably those which are relatively easier and cheaper or more feasible to produce. Within the news package, there are usually short features that are capable of being seen as stand-alone productions such as *A Ray of Hope, Inspire Jamaica, Health Report* and *Double Take*.

In the past, individuals producing local television programmes had been trained mainly outside of Jamaica, or had been allowed to develop their skills on the job. JBC TV provided training for most of its staff.[35] The establishment of an Institute of Mass Communication on the Mona campus of the University of the West Indies in 1974 (which later became the Caribbean School of Media and Communication) meant that there was now a locally based entity offering education and training opportunities in these fields. The CPTC, which had also provided training for television workers, launched the Media Technology Institute in 2005 to strengthen its programme.[36] The Northern Caribbean University and the University of Technology also began offering media and communication related training in the 2000s.

Though not the focus of this publication, a brief comment on the film industry of Jamaica is warranted, as there is a connection between the television, video and film industries. Feature films eventually appear on television and constitute the bulk of video content shared in various formats.[37]

The Jamaica Film and Television Association, established in June 2015, emerged out of the now-defunct Jamaica's Film Producers Association. It is a non-profit association representing the interests of members of the film and television industry in Jamaica. Arguably, the Jamaica Promotions Corporation's Film Commission established in 1984 contributes indirectly to the television industry as individuals working in television are exposed to opportunities to also work on film projects done locally, mostly by overseas companies.[38] Over fifty feature films have been shot on location in Jamaica since 1953. Jamaica grossed an estimated JA$1.5 billion in the 1990s from film productions done by foreign companies.[39] The Jamaica Promotions Corporation Film Directory, published around 1994/1995, revealed a listing of approximately seventeen production companies, which in addition to working on overseas film projects also helped to create local television productions. The filmjamaica.com website listed twelve production companies in 2015. Local films produced in the 1970s include *The Harder They Come, Rockers, Children of Babylon, Smile Orange* and *Countryman*. Since the 1990s, other Jamaican films have been produced such as *The Lunatic, Dancehall Queen, Third World Cop, Better Mus' Come* and *Ghett'a Life*.

## Market Research of Jamaican Television Audiences

One of the earliest efforts to understand Jamaican media audiences was in 1965 when Caribbean Research Limited, a local affiliate of Miami-based firm First National Research Company, did the first independent survey of radio, television, press and cinema. The study, sponsored by the Advertisers Association of Jamaica and the JBC, reported on radio listening and television viewing peaks.[40]

Prior to this, Marketing Advisory Services Limited, a research firm based in London, conducted radio listenership surveys for RJR beginning in 1962.[41] The fourth such survey was done by them in 1967,[42] and their last, in 1969, focused on radio, television, press and cinema. Thereafter, media audience research in Jamaica was done by a local affiliate of Cooper

Research and Marketing International, with offices at 25 Tobago Avenue in Kingston. In December 1970, they produced results of a study on television audiences in Kingston.[43]

It was not until 1973 that a local company, Market Research Services Limited, began conducting research on Jamaica's media audience. Their first two studies in 1973 and 1974 focused on radio only, and in 1977 they also included television. Following that, they did media surveys in 1979, 1981, 1984 and 1986, commissioned by the media and advertising sectors. Since then, they have done annual surveys between 1988 and 2000; then none until 2002; annually again from 2005 to 2009; then in 2012 and 2014.[44] Users of these studies have expressed concern about their currency, given that the fieldwork is most often done in the last quarter of one year and the results published in the first quarter of the following year. Despite the criticisms, the Market Research Services Limited media audience survey that is now known as the *All Media Survey* continues to be one of the main sources of media audience-share data in Jamaica and provides information to advertisers, media managers, programme managers, and sales and marketing personnel who all need to make critical decisions about creating television that can attract supporting advertising in a market such as Jamaica.

### Jamaica's Small Market for Television

According to a 2011 census conducted by the Statistical Institute of Jamaica, with a population of 2.8 million, 845,000 households had TV sets and therefore had the potential to receive the same or similar signals from terrestrial broadcasters. Given that the same census established that there were 881,000 households at that time, 96 per cent of them had television sets. While this is a high proportion, the actual number is low. It should also be noted that because of the island's topography, there are some sections that may receive weak or no signals at all, which further diminishes the potential audience for free-to-air television. Terrestrial broadcasters, however, continue to develop transmission infrastructure to provide access to the widest audience possible, and most households with television sets can access one or more signals.

BEFORE WE BEGIN: A HISTORY OF TELEVISION PROGRAMMING IN JAMAICA

The relatively small size of this market is even more obvious when compared to that in other countries. For example, in the United States in 2014, there were 116 million households with TV sets according to the Nielsen Company, the US-based TV audience measurement research agency.45 It has also been reported that in Canada, there were 13.6 million such households in 2014.46

With an area of just 4,213 square miles, geographic limits help to define the market size, so Jamaica's free-to-air television operating at the national level cannot feasibly be broken down into smaller geographically defined markets. However, it can be segmented according to demographic variables such as age and gender, and also according to time of day – such as prime-time, daytime or late-night – and in terms of programme content such as sports, news or children's programming. This type of market share information provides valuable data for producers and distributors in setting rates for advertising which is a major source of revenue.

Here we do not consider locally produced programmes for cable channels, but rather those for free-to-air television stations, otherwise known as broadcast channels.47 In this work we focus on Jamaican television defined as programmes about Jamaicans, created for Jamaican audiences and shown on channels associated with Jamaican broadcast entities. Shows that have been aired for over twenty-five uninterrupted years and which were still on air in 2015 are what we have classified as long-running.

In addressing long-running shows, broadcast television, which has been available for free in Jamaica for over fifty years, presents a better opportunity for a richer analysis than does cable, which only emerged in Jamaica in the 1980s and became regulated in the 1990s – just over thirty years ago. Further, as it provides mainly foreign material through a paid service to a relatively small audience share, we have excluded cable's local offerings from our scrutiny. According to subscription reports submitted by cable licensees to the BCJ in December 2014, only 18 per cent of households with television sets (or 155,000 households) subscribe to cable television services.48

Jamaica's television programming emerged out of a close-knit community supported by training institutions and production houses. Even in light of limited research on Jamaican's small television market, this chapter illustrates that Jamaican audiences have been able to access local television programming content since the introduction of the television in Jamaica in 1963. Despite the small market for television audiences in Jamaica, the local television industry has demonstrated that it is able to create programmes that can be sustained in such markets. This especially when there have been long-running television shows with guaranteed audiences such as *Schools' Challenge Quiz, Profile, Hill an' Gully Ride* and *Entertainment Report*. Indeed, it is possible – despite the limitations of the market and production resources – to create television shows that can maintain viewership.

# 2

# And Now the Details
Understanding Television in Jamaica

Any discussion of Jamaican television programming would be incomplete without an overview of contextual factors that can help deepen our understanding. There were political, economic, technical, regulatory and cultural forces that contributed to the evolution of television in Jamaica. Political interference, management challenges, limited production resources, the amount of local television content versus foreign content, increasing access to cheaper foreign content and limited research on audiences in a small television market were some of the main issues affecting the sector. Various scholars have offered explanations about how and why it evolved in the way it did in countries such as this, a former British colony.

The fact that television emerged a year after independence from Britain signifies that it had a role to play in shaping the country's independent identity and in helping to achieve its national development goals. Jamaica was newly independent and television was new to Jamaica – both Jamaica and television in Jamaica now had to forge their identities. Introducing JBC TV on the first anniversary of independence suggests that the medium was regarded as an important national institution with a public service mandate to educate, to inform and to entertain.[1]

Central to the establishment of JBC TV was nationalism, and the intent of the education imperative to use media to aid in national development and in the creation of national identity. Arguably, JBC was modelled on the BBC to develop a somewhat refined culture among Jamaicans and this determined the type of programmes that it aired at the time. As a former British colony, the decision to adopt this model was almost expected, but this choice presented challenges for the creation of a Jamaican national identity and has had an impact on the type of programmes subsequently aired on the station.[2] The practice of looking elsewhere for television programme ideas has almost characterized the nation's television industry from the start. It is not surprising that today many producers still look elsewhere to adapt ideas for local audiences. Of course, this is not always a bad thing, given trends in television format exporting. Instead of selling a programme, a production company will sell the programme format, allowing the buyer to adapt it to the particular environment but using the premise, scripts and characters. Some examples of format exporting include *Law and Order UK*, based on the US original; the game show *Who Wants to Be a Millionaire*; and talent shows *The Voice* and *The X Factor*, which have been exported to countries across the world.

Having been a British colony with a slave plantation system, independent Jamaica was characterized by structures of its past. According to Norman Stolzoff, "In spite of political independence from Britain in 1962, the foundations of the colonial system (the rigid class structure, racial hierarchy, European cultural hegemony) were still essentially in place."[3] The post-independent era of the 1960s was a time of hopefulness and prosperity. Politically, the country had just left the West Indies Federation, and newly independent, it attracted foreign investment especially in the bauxite industry. There was a push for representation of aspects of the local culture. According to Lloyd Bradley, in describing the mandate of the JBC, "The cornerstone of the new station's brief was to promote the indigenous arts and to reflect local tastes accurately."[4] Technically, local television content was mostly live from studio with some elements on film. The bulk of advertising was live because of the high cost of film and the lack of other means of recording. Output was affected by the cost of using film to produce programmes and by the limited access to few studio facilities. Despite the limitations, JBC TV managed to create television shows and the schedule reflected a mix of local and foreign programming. Audiences had varied reactions to this and expressed concern about the number of foreign shows compared to the local shows.[5]

AND NOW THE DETAILS: UNDERSTANDING TELEVISION IN JAMAICA

JBC TV's attempt to fulfil its mandate as public service broadcaster was challenged by interference from whichever political party ruled the country at a given time. Wycliffe Bennett, who served as general manager of JBC between 1968 and 1971 and again from 1976 to 1981, argued that traditionally the station would support the programmes and policies of the duly elected government, JLP or PNP, and was accused of being a "PNP station" by the JLP when the PNP was in office and being a "JLP station" by the PNP when the JLP formed the government.[6] The political manipulation mostly affected the newsroom while the programme and production departments managed to continue creating local television shows.

The 1970s in Jamaica was marked by capital flight, economic sanctions from the United States, and falling investments and revenues, which arguably resulted from the country's political leanings towards democratic socialism as well as the international oil price shock. By the mid-1970s, there was political violence that led to a state of emergency. The ruling PNP sought help from the International Monetary Fund which led to cuts in public spending. This meant that funding for JBC TV was now affected, and the quality and amount of local television programming and production suffered. Regular power outages interrupted viewers' ability to watch television. Technically, video was now emerging, so television productions could be pre-recorded, and the portability of the video equipment facilitated more field production. Despite this opportunity to improve local production, the television schedules were dominated by foreign content. In 1976, 73 per cent of JBC TV airtime depended on imported television programming.[7]

In the 1980s, Jamaica shifted politically to the right with the election of the JLP. A sense of austerity and adjustment prevailed. There was warming of relations with the United States which brought with it economic aid, market access and increasing foreign investment. Structural adjustment programmes with the International Monetary Fund continued. There was need to curtail spending in the public sector, including in the government-run JBC. Liberalization paved the way for privatization of certain entities formerly controlled by the government. There was now talk of establishing a second television station – no doubt to introduce competition to the sector. Television moved from black and white to colour and from PAL (phase alternate line) to NTSC (National Television Standards Committee) systems. JBC

TV now had satellite dish technology, allowing convenient access to international content. Some homes could also now access foreign content with private satellite dishes. Hotels offered foreign television channels to their guests using satellite and cable. Videocassette recorders gave consumers the opportunity to record, rent or purchase content for home viewing.[8] Video rental services emerged. With these satellite, cable and video technologies, Jamaicans developed an appetite for foreign content of their choice. Foreign content also continued to dominate the programme schedule of the sole national television broadcaster, JBC TV. In 1987, for example, 76 per cent of all programmes carried by the station originated from foreign sources, predominantly from the United States.[9]

The cultural imperialism thesis proffered by scholars such as Herbert Schiller was used as a framework for understanding how the foreign media output of one nation overshadowed that of another nation. In a detailed literature review of the cultural imperialism thesis, Livingston White noted that proponents of this notion argued that Western-produced content, especially from the United States, dominated the media of other countries that had limited resources.[10] There was a fear that Western values and images would erode indigenous culture.[11] Since the early days of television, the United States dominated the international market and offered low-cost programmes to broadcasters in other countries. Because these broadcasters could not afford to produce content of similar quantity and quality, they imported the low-cost US programming, which led to audiences developing an appetite, thus expanding the market for such products.

Jamaican media and communication scholars, such as Aggrey Brown, have reconsidered the cultural dependency thesis to suggest that its conceptions are limited and that it constitutes a "misdiagnosis of the situation" as "no nationality has a monopoly on creative imagination".[12] Citing Jamaica's international successes in reggae music, Brown has implied that local creators have the potential to meaningfully participate in the global flow of media content. Even so, the lack of a supporting policy environment to encourage local television production meant that foreign material would still compete with attempts at creating indigenous content.[13]

The period from the late 1980s to the 1990s represented an interesting turn for local television. Some key events occurred that were emblematic of the turbulent and changing times that would affect it. In 1988, Hurricane Gilbert damaged transmission facilities at JBC TV and affected power supplies across the island. Television broadcasting service became limited and viewership was affected, but JBC TV eventually recovered. There was a state of emergency limiting population movement for security reasons.[14]

In 1989, the country had a general election resulting in a change of government. In 1991, the JBC Act was amended. There was restructuring to ensure that there was equal representation from political parties on the board of directors. The general manager who served for three years was now a director general who would hold that office for six years.[15] That appointment and the reconfiguration of the board of directors were both significant. It was now recognized that using the JBC as a political tool was counterproductive. Any political pressure was absorbed at the level of director general and not allowed to affect the newsroom or any other part of the entity.[16]

The 1990s was an era of liberalization for Jamaican television media that led to more competition. Two new television stations were introduced. CVM TV started broadcasting in 1993, with assistance from JBC which leased them spare transmission facilities. Love TV started in 1998. JBC was sold to RJR in 1997 and the legal framework for the PBCJ was established then. In the late 1990s, cable subscription service licences were issued, representing the government's attempt to regulate a sector that began informally. Jamaicans continued to be exposed to a mix of foreign and local television content, now via terrestrial and cable services.

In the 2000s, access to digital technology expanded. Quality equipment was now available at lower prices. There was increasing access to personal and mobile smart devices. Terrestrial television stations faced increasing competition for advertising from online and cable content providers. Media entities merged in the face of competition as telecommunication companies expanded their services into cable television. Though Jamaica continued to struggle with political leadership issues, rising debt and falling exchange rates, the country strengthened and diversified its international relations with various world powers. Audiences had more choice in terms of where and how they could access a range of television services using various devices. They could watch at home or on the move. While local producers now had more opportunities to serve local viewers, there was still more foreign content on free-to-air stations. Nickesia Gordon, in a study published in 2008, has argued that though there was an overall increase in local content on Jamaican television stations, moving from approximately 25 per cent in 1994 to 34 per cent by 2007, foreign programming occupied more than 60 per cent of Jamaican television.[17] This is not surprising because foreign content continued to be cheaper.

Foreign television shows are usually more affordable for Jamaican stations than producing an equivalent local programme with similar production values. Television producers operating within large markets with efficient distribution networks are likely to have recovered their production costs and made profits through on air advertising, syndication and licensing fees before offering the programme outside of their domestic market. Therefore, a show developed in a large market can be shared in foreign markets at lower rates. Jamaican broadcast stations can choose to pay these lower rates for foreign content rather than producing more costly local programmes.

In a small market like Jamaica, producers have to consider what type of television show is feasible to produce. When considering types of shows, we may want to look at genres in television. What is a television genre? A genre is a particular form or category determined by a set of attributes. The word identifies categories in various types of art forms including film, literary works, painting, music and television. A television genre describes a set of styles or structures that guides both the creation of content by the producer and the reception of such content by an audience.

As such, genre is an important concept in any discussion on television programmes because it not only plays a role in production but also contributes to the reception of the show. When audiences are told that a television programme represents a particular genre, they may expect certain elements to be present. In fact, their reception of the programme – the extent to which they enjoy or do not enjoy the show – will be determined in part by how much the show incorporates characteristics of that genre. Also, a producer who is attempting to remain true to a genre can ensure that certain structures are incorporated into the production. With both producer working to meet certain standards and audience anticipating certain elements, it is possible that some genres may work better in certain cultural contexts than in others. It should also be noted that all shows within a genre may not enjoy similar levels of success.

One production may fit into several genres, blending elements from two or more to form a sort of hybrid genre or cross-genre. Also, genres are not necessarily fixed as they can evolve over time to generate subgenres or totally new ones. Some may become unpopular, or gain wider appeal; others may develop or transform into something more feasible to produce, based on changes in television technology, channel characteristics, transmission or dissemination trends.

A particular show may fit into one or more categories, and though not exhaustive, here are some examples of genres generally used to describe free-to-air television programmes: animation, charity, children's, comedy, current and public affairs, drama, educational, entertainment, factual, infomercial, magazine, music, quiz and game shows, reality, religious (or inspirational), sports, social advocacy, talk show and weather. For definitions of these and examples of their subgenres, see appendix 1.

## What Is Successful Television?

There are many elements that can be used as a measure of a television show's success. These include audience ratings, viewership figures, maintaining a loyal viewership, length of time on air and number of episodes produced. Other aspects such as level of promotion, scheduling in particular time slots, good writing and a strong production team have also been mentioned as contributing components. However, ensuring that all these are present does not guarantee success. It also depends on how they are combined and the particular context in which the show is being produced. Within small markets, where keeping a show on air can be affected by limited resources, remaining on air for a long time arguably becomes a key marker of accomplishment. In fact, Burbank has argued that longevity is synonymous with success in television programmes.[18]

A successful programme garners viewers and is one with which advertisers or sponsors want to be associated. Audience figures can bolster marketing efforts to get and keep programmes on the air. Even for stations that do not rely on advertising support, successful programmes are important as the aim is to get viewers, and those that work deliver that. Not every successful programme needs a "mass" audience. A great deal will depend on the station's target, the time of broadcast and whether or not the station or the programme is aimed at the mass, at a niche market or at a minority audience. Viewership for a successful programme in prime time will be different from that of one in a different time slot. Daytime shows such as soap operas and others aired during the day may be perceived to be successful with very different viewing numbers. Programmes may do well in a particular time slot or for a particular station or market.

Despite the various pressures – political, technical, economic – that have affected Jamaica's television industry, producers have managed to create a range of genres for their audiences. Considering the broad range available, certain genres seem to have a better chance of being produced here than others. Determining what is good television is subjective and depends on which perspective is being considered. Given the local historical and political context, with its public broadcasting mandate, the government of the day might consider good television to be that which promotes national development goals. From an audience perspective, it might be that which engages and delivers information and entertainment. From an economic perspective, television stations and producers might define successful television as that which will attract and keep an audience that advertisers would pay to target. Creating successful television – television that is fit for purpose with that purpose being to keep viewers and attract advertisers – is a possibility, despite the limitations of a small market and other production resources. Several elements contribute to a successful show, such as audience ratings, viewership figures, length of time on air, number of episodes produced, good writing and a strong production team. Longevity is a good measure of success in certain circumstances and markets. The four shows we consider here – *Schools' Challenge Quiz*, *Profile*, *Hill an' Gully Ride* and *Entertainment Report* – exemplify what it means to produce successful television in the Jamaican context.

# 3

# *Schools' Challenge Quiz*
Jamaica's Long-Standing Quiz Show

On Friday, 13 February 1970, JBC TV's mobile unit set up at the Manning's School in Savanna-la-Mar, Westmoreland. The team was there to record the first episode of a new programme called *Schools' Challenge Quiz*. In this first episode, Manning's School and Rusea's High School from Lucea, Hanover, competed against each other with the home team winning. The show premiered on Thursday, 26 February 1970, on JBC TV.[1]

*Schools' Challenge Quiz* was the brainchild of Hope Stewart (née McIntyre). She came up with the idea for the show at a cocktail reception hosted by JBC board chairman Ivan Levy in late 1969. Stewart felt that JBC TV needed more programming that supported education. During the cocktail discussion, she suggested a quiz show for schools.[2] The JBC chairman asked if she could do it. She answered "yes" and took up the challenge.[3]

At the time, Hope Stewart was the wife of JBC's assistant general manager, Laurence "Laurie" Stewart. When she began working on *Schools' Challenge Quiz*, she worked on the Mona campus of the University of the West Indies as a part-time lecturer. Between attending St Andrew High School for Girls in Jamaica and the St Hugh's College at Oxford University in the United Kingdom, she had taught briefly at the Manning's School.[4]

In preparation, one of the first things she had to do was to generate the many questions that would be needed and have them carefully checked. Her links to the university community helped, as she set up a team of writers

**Table 3.** Schools Participating in the First Season of *Schools' Challenge Quiz* in 1970

| Date of Match | Teams | Date Aired |
|---|---|---|
| **First round** | | |
| 13 February | *Manning's* vs Ruseas | 26 February |
| 2 March | Camperdown vs *Munro* | 5 March |
| 10 March | DeCarteret vs *Manchester* | 19 March |
| 12 March | *Jamaica College* vs Wolmer's Boys* | 12 March |
| 16 March | *Cornwall College* vs Mt Alvernia | 26 March |
| 18 March | *Servite Convent* vs York Castle | 2 April |
| 8 April | *St Hugh's* vs Calabar | 9 April |
| 13 April | Morant Bay vs Titchfield | 23 April |
| 16 April | Kingston Technical vs *Kingston College** | 16 April |
| 27 April | *Hampton* vs St Elizabeth | 7 May |
| 30 April | Alpha vs *Priory** | 30 April |
| 4 May | *Wolmer's Girls* vs Clarendon College | 14 May |
| **Quarter-finals** | | |
| 11 May | *Jamaica College* vs Servite Convent | 28 May |
| 20 May | Cornwall College vs *St Hugh's* | 21 May |
| 22 May | *Manchester* vs Priory | 11 June |
| 26 May | Munro vs *Kingston College* | 4 June |
| 29 May | *Hampton* vs Wolmer's Girls | 18 June |
| **Semi-finals** | | |
| 25 June | Manchester vs *Hampton** | 25 June |
| 26 June | *Jamaica College* vs Manning's | – |
| 30 June | *St Hugh's* vs Kingston College | 2 July |
| 7 July | Finals | 9 July |

*These shows were broadcast live. Winning teams are in italics.
Source: "The Early Years," *Schools' Challenge Quiz* 2004 35th Anniversary Supplement, *Gleaner*, 11 May 2004.

to support her own efforts in creating the quiz questions, which were set out on index cards. Bernie Chin, a television director at JBC TV, helped with the format of the show. There were three main segments – an alternate questioning section, a speed section and a buzzer section – a format which has remained at the core of the show. Another task for Stewart was contacting schools to ensure their participation. A few principals felt it would be a negative experience for their students but this did not stop Stewart, who had the support of many, including the station's general manager (Wycliffe Bennett) and his assistant (her husband, Laurie Stewart). Over thirty schools expressed a willingness to enter and twenty-four schools actually agreeing to compete in the first season.[5] Of this number, twelve schools would advance to the quarter-finals and six to the semi-finals, resulting in a three-way final match, a natural outcome given the number of schools involved. Being a good record-keeper, Stewart had noted most of the dates for the recording and airing of the first season in her diary (see table 3).[6]

The first series was recorded mostly on location at competing schools for broadcast later on Thursdays. JBC TV also used the programme to expose areas around Jamaica by creating features introducing the schools. The first show was done in the parish of Westmoreland at Manning's School in Savanna-la-Mar. A portable set was designed by George Rodney and carried to each location.[7] *Schools' Challenge Quiz* went around the island for the first season, and then went into studio fully the year after that.[8]

A typical programme included the match and a feature about the school and its surroundings. The buzzer/light system used by quiz team members in the final section of the match was designed by engineer Rupert Bent. Bill Cummings worked on the show as part of the team. Oval Lue and Martin Darien were the engineers on the mobile unit. One of the challenges for this team was the Ampex two-inch helical videotape recording system they were using, which suffered problems in high humidity.[9]

The fourth match of the first season, between Jamaica College and Wolmer's Boys', turned out to be the first live broadcast of the show. On Thursday, 12 March 1970, this match was transmitted live from the Jamaica College school grounds located at Old Hope Road, Kingston. A member of the Jamaica College team remembers that week being filled with activity – there was a match for the Sunlight Cup cricket competition, a hockey game and the *Schools' Challenge Quiz*. Two members of the quiz team were also on the hockey team. They remember playing the hockey match at the school on that Thursday afternoon and rushing to get ready for the live quiz show. When they arrived in the room, still somewhat sweaty from the hockey match and full of competitive spirit, they saw the Wolmer's team in school blazers looking cool and calm. The two teams were allowed to play a practice round in preparation for the live broadcast. Wolmer's won that practice round but they were not so lucky in the actual competition when the live broadcast began. Jamaica College emerged the winners and advanced to the next round.[10]

The first quizmaster was the Reverend Philip Hart. Erica Allen, who had been working at JBC since 1960, substituted for Reverend Hart when he could not do the show. In addition to producing each programme, Hope Stewart also initially did the refereeing. Having achieved what she set out to do – which was to add some educational value to the JBC TV output – Stewart stood down after the first year. She had had her hands full with work and a young family.[11]

After what appeared to have been a successful first season, which ended in July 1970, there was a decision to produce the show in the studio in subsequent years. This was driven in part by the challenges associated with recording on location in its first year. During the 1970s, shows were broadcast live from the studios with schools travelling to Kingston to participate. They would receive a stipend and help with transportation. Some teams would stay in Kingston overnight on recording days and return home early the following morning in time for the start of classes.[12] Dennis Hall was the main quizmaster and Ruth Ho Shing produced the shows.

In the early part of the 1980s, the show continued live after JBC's evening newscast. Later, an increasing number of queries regarding questions and answers extended the live show's transmission beyond its usual thirty minutes and ultimately affected programme schedules.[13] Pre-recording which began later in that decade presented the producers with the best solution to this problem, as it allowed time for issues to be resolved. Dennis Hall continued as the main quizmaster while the show was produced by a team assigned based on the station's roster. Lois Gayle coordinated the show in the 1980s and early to mid-1990s.

As it continued to grow in popularity with increased interest from sponsors, the producers ensured that it maintained its educational integrity. At the time, the JBC was the main sponsor and the winning team received the JBC *Schools' Challenge Quiz* trophy. Later, an increasing number of sponsors gave additional trophies. After retiring some of these, most of the prizes included scholarships and educational items.

Over the years, there was a marked improvement in the quality of the prizes demonstrating how the show grew in popularity. For the very first season in 1970, the winning school received a clock and the team members received gift vouchers.[14] In the late 1970s, in addition to other trophies and scholarships, there was a prize trip to Canada.[15] In the 1980s and 1990s, there was the prize trip for the winning team from British West Indian Airlines, the Trinidad and Tobago–based airline operating in the region from 1940 to 2006 that served and connected Caribbean destinations.

Michael Gonzales had been the captain of the Calabar High School team in 1984. In 1989 he worked in the newsroom at JBC TV and was invited by Lois Gayle to help with writing questions.[16] He focused on questions on the arts for about three years and during that time also did some judging. In the early 1990s, Donat (Don) Bucknor, senior producer and director at JBC TV, asked him to become the official coordinator of the questions for the arts, and in 1993/1994, he became the producer. At the time, the show was still pre-recorded and was shown at various times. At one point, it was aired as early as 5:00 p.m. – a decision which many felt had a negative effect as the show appeared to lose audience share in that time slot.[17]

When JBC was sold to RJR in June 1997, the new station had the option of continuing the programme, which it did. In fact, for RJR it was an easy choice because viewers made it clear that this was one show that should continue despite the change of management.[18] In a poll, it was at the top of the list of shows that should be continued.[19] It was now seen as the nation's programme, having been on the air for over twenty-five years.

Gonzales, who was producer in the years leading up to the JBC sale, was asked to remain in that role. It went back to being a live show for a few years, appearing after the station's nightly newscast on Tuesdays and Thursdays. Although now a TVJ property, it was still broadcast from the JBC studios at 5 South Odeon Avenue. Then, in July 2004, when RJR opened its state-of-the-art digital television studios at 32 Lyndhurst Road (dubbed the RJR Broadcast House), the operations moved there and continued from that location in 2005.[20] The season started in either January or February and ended by May. Critics felt that the series ran too far into the school year and would affect contestants' preparation for their final regional examinations.[21] This was not a new complaint. There had always been a concern about how it affected quiz team members – most of whom were in their final year at high school and needed to study for examinations. As a result, a number of changes were made to the show for the 2006 season.[22]

The programme began airing at 6:30 p.m. and now, in a prime-time slot before the station's major evening newscast at 7:00, the producers could not let the show overrun. Pre-recording on Mondays ensured that queries could be addressed beforehand and could be resolved without affecting the broadcast schedule.[23] The season was shortened, starting in January and ending in March. The number of shows per week increased from two to six with one per day from Mondays to Fridays at 6:30 p.m. and one on Saturday mornings at 11:30. Eventually, the six shows were shown over five days – one show from Monday to Thursday and a doubleheader on Friday. Rules were also revised after a comprehensive review. An appeals panel with representation from the station, the judges and the schools was created to resolve any major issues. Schools were allowed up to three queries per show.

The changes helped to strengthen the show's appeal. The fact that the series ended in March meant that it coincided with Jamaica's major national Inter-Secondary Schools Association track and field championship – Boys and Girls Champs. Some schools prided themselves on competing in both the Quiz and Champs in the same year – a "QUAMPS" double.[24] In 1974, 1975 and 2009, Kingston College achieved the QUAMPS double and Calabar achieved it in 1989 and 2012. The victories in 2009 and 2012 were significant because both competitions in those years culminated in the month of March. The influence of *Schools' Challenge Quiz* on schools and on other high school competitions goes beyond aiming for the QUAMPS double. Schools have been known to go the extra mile in preparing for the quiz competitions.[25]

There are *Schools' Challenge Quiz* clubs and camps with practice matches during coaching periods. Entire communities have rallied around the win-

## SCHOOLS' CHALLENGE QUIZ: JAMAICA'S LONG-STANDING QUIZ SHOW

ning team upon their return home. Principals have noted improvements in school spirit when their team wins a match.[26] At the primary level, students have used the results of the various matches as a guide when selecting their high school. Members of quiz teams have gone on to pursue successful careers. The show boasts an impressive list of alumni. On occasion, some have returned to play in the *Schools' Challenge Quiz* Masters Match episodes.[27] Quiz alumni have also coached teams at their alma maters.

With such widespread appeal, the show easily attracted sponsorship. It continues to be funded by advertising and sponsorship with some sponsors providing prizes. Sponsors that have been associated with the programme include various companies operating in Jamaica such as Lasco, National Commercial Bank (NCB), Freshhh, Wata, Kingston Bookshop, Coca Cola, Nestle, Nabisco, Sherwin Williams, Digicel, Megamart, Colgate-Palmolive, Air Jamaica Express, BWIA, Kingston Hireage and Wholesale Liquors, Mall and Tropical Jewellers, and the Students' Loan Bureau, among others. Prizes have continued to include scholarships, trophies and trips to destinations in North America such as Toronto and Atlanta. Sponsors have been creatively incorporated into shows, sponsoring elements such as the quiz countdown timer and the viewers' question answered by text message. Producers have carefully managed various sponsorship opportunities to ensure commercial content does not overwhelm the programme.

After Reverend Philip Hart served as quizmaster for the first season of the show, Dennis Hall became the first quizmaster to host the show for over twenty years from 1973 to 1994. Marlene Stephenson-Dalley is another long-standing host of the show, having started in 1996.[28] Other presenters who have alternated with these main quizmasters included Erica Allen, Barry Davies, Robert Pickersgill, Nadine Campbell-Brown, Helene Coley-Nicholson, Winston Williams, Cordel Green, Errol Lee, François St Juste, Dervan Malcolm, Devon Yetman, Anika Jackson, Jean-Paul Menou, Kalando Wilmoth and Yvonne Chin. The quizmaster plays an important role in the show, having to articulate questions in a timely manner and immediately acknowledge correct answers while moderating the general flow of the questioning. The individual also has to be familiar with discipline-specific technical terms when phrasing scientific questions, and also fluent when asking foreign language questions. While the show is enhanced by the personality of the quizmaster, it is the team members who are the focus.

Over the years, the programme has benefited from the input of JBC and TVJ staff as well as freelancers in the roles of quizmaster and production personnel. There is a core team of about seven or eight people and that rises to around twenty-nine when the programmes are recorded. There is also a marketing team handling giveaways, prizes and promotion for the show. Memorabilia, including a souvenir magazine featuring aspects of the programme's history, is also created to augment the promotion.

Pre-production includes set design, set building, set dressing, wardrobe, make-up and lighting design. Writing and checking questions, contacting schools, making bookings, scheduling matches, assigning crews and hosts, scripting links, and catering were other activities done before production. The recordings feature a small studio audience comprised of mostly students and teachers of competing schools. Other participants include quiz team members, judges, coaches, the timekeeper and the quizmaster. It is a switched studio production with the director, vision mixer, audio technician and teleprompter operator all in the control room, while on the studio floor there are camera operators and a floor manager.

The programme is recorded live in front of an audience. Five shows are recorded on a Monday starting at around 10:00 a.m., with the first one edited for broadcast later that day and the others for later in the week. The recorded programme is transmitted from master control at the station's Lyndhurst Road studios and repeated the following day after the station's morning magazine show *Smile Jamaica* at 8:30 a.m. Live-stream and archived programme content is available on the Internet and can be accessed on TVJ's site. DVD copies of the programme are sold by TVJ.

*Schools' Challenge Quiz* is known for its distinctive studio set that in the first season was transported to the school locations for the recordings. The use of split-screen technology allows the audience to see both teams on screen in the rounds where questions are open to both. In the 1980s and 1990s, a two-tier set was used to achieve this effect. Before then, teams sat at desks set at an angle on either side of the quizmaster. These desks carried the name of the school and the names of team members. After the sale of JBC to RJR, there were new configurations. Now, with the help of technology, the two teams sit on either side of the quizmaster in the studio and a split screen is used to show both teams in a single screen, adding to show's visual appeal. The theme song may have changed over the years, but other audio cues have remained constant. One is the sound of the buzzer in the final segment of the show and the other is the sound of the desk bell signifying the end of a section. Timekeeper Carol Ivey operated that bell for years and would describe it as one "ting" for the end of the first and second rounds and then "ting ting ting" for the end of the entire match. At times, some matches were so closely contested that the desk bell would be rung more than three times, to clearly signify what would turn out to be a resounding close to a match, complete with energetic applause from the studio audience.

In a second-round match transmitted on TVJ in February 2013 between St George's College and Wolmer's Boys' School, the scores were eighteen to Wolmer's and twenty to St George's with ten seconds left on the clock.

> **Quizmaster**: Bible knowledge – which woman's son was raised from the dead by Elisha.
> *Buzzer sounds.*
> **Quizmaster**: And this will be Wolmer's Boys'.
> **Wolmer's Team**: The Shunammite woman.
> **Quizmaster**: Correct. Biology – what is the more popular name . . .
> *The desk bell rings signalling the end of the match.*
> **Quizmaster**: Is that the final bell? Oh, goodness! There is a tie. And we are not quite at the end of the match. We're on 20-20 and what that means is that we will ask the questions until the first correct or incorrect answer comes. Spanish – What is "la libreta"?
> *Buzzer sounds.*
> **Quizmaster**: George's
> **St George's Team**: The notebook.
> **Quizmaster**: Correct!
> *The sound of the final bell is drowned out by the cheering from the studio audience.*
> **Quizmaster**: Our winner . . . our winner . . . is George's . . . St George's College!

Over the years, the grand final shows have been transmitted live in a special extended programme format. This special broadcast has been shot on location, in some cases at the Pegasus Hotel in Kingston, to accommodate the large number of people who wanted to be present. This became problematic because the size of the audience affected the level of concentration by both competitors and the judges. In 2008, TVJ brought the final match back to the studio to create the controlled environment needed to conduct the broadcast without any interference.[29] In order to accommodate the fans and not compromise the live competition, tiered seating was set up in the TVJ back-lot where supporters of both teams could watch the game on a large screen and cheer as loudly as they wished. The show featured live links from presenters roaming among them. Sometimes production crews were also sent to capture footage of supporters watching the live programme at the schools, and this, too, would be integrated into the final production.

*Schools' Challenge Quiz* was born out of a desire to support local programming and to deliver educational content. The programme has an inbuilt appeal, given that there are those who will watch because it is a local programme or because they are associated in some way with the participants as parent, teacher, schoolmate or alumni, or because they are attracted to the content and the format.

The programme resembles other quiz shows such as Britain's Granada Television series *University Challenge* and the US *College Bowl* on which the former was based. *It's Academic* is another long-standing quiz competition for high school students in the United States.[30] The similarities between the local *Schools' Challenge Quiz* and some foreign quiz shows include specialist and general questions, questions open to both teams, the loss of marks for wrong answers and the use of buzzers or bells to signify a team's decision to respond to a question. *Schools' Challenge Quiz* is the longest-running seasonal programme on Jamaican television and is longer running than some well-known international quiz and game shows such as *The Price Is Right* which began in 1972, *Wheel of Fortune*, which begain in 1975 and *Jeopardy*, which begain in 1984. *University Challenge* began on 21 September 1962 but went off air in 1987 until it was revived by the BBC in 1994.[31]

Though there may have been changes over the years to aspects of the competition and the production, the overarching format of *Schools' Chal-*

*lenge Quiz* remains the same. In each episode, two teams answer questions as teams or as individuals in a number of rounds. The team with the highest score wins and goes on to the next round, until the grand season finale where the two top teams compete for the title, trophy and prizes.

There are three sections in each match. In the opening section of six minutes, teams answer questions alternately. If a team does not answer, the opposing team has a chance to answer. Teams gain one point for a correct answer within the allotted time and no points are lost for incorrect answers. Section two is also six minutes and is the speed round. Each team receives questions open only to them for one minute before the next team also gets one minute. Each team has a total of three minutes to answer questions. There is no penalty for wrong answers and contestants are allowed to "pass" on a question. The final segment is the buzzer section, which runs for four minutes. Teams answer as many questions as they can in the time. Teams must press the buzzer first for the opportunity to answer and must wait to be identified before responding. Correct answers are worth two points, but if teams answer incorrectly or do not answer, they lose two points.[32] The sections are punctuated by commercial breaks and after the final section when the winner emerges, there is another commercial break before a return to the studio for the final handshake between team captains and the wrap up by the show's quizmaster.

While it may be the longest-running seasonal local programme in Jamaica, it began in a time far away from the technological advances present today. This has not stopped the production from embracing the new technology, including availability online, and social-media profiles on Facebook and Twitter. The show can be accessed using apps such 1Spotmedia, the RJR Communications Group media division that provides live-stream and video-on-demand (VOD) services. User-generated content is shared on other social-media platforms such as Instagram, under various hashtags including #schoolschallengequiz.

However, even though this may be a winning combination for the TV station and sponsors, how has it been able to stay on air for so long? One important factor is that it began on JBC TV and was continued on TVJ, the station that emerged from the purchase of JBC by the RJR Communications Group. PBCJ is the holder of some of the archives of the JBC, and as such became responsible for the archived content of the programme. Episodes aired on JBC TV up to 1997 can be sourced at the PBCJ where records indicate that the earliest available episode is dated 1988.[33]

The programme has led to spin-offs and competing shows with a similar format. Executive producer Michael Gonzales was walking across the TVJ parking lot when he met then-chairman Milton Samuda, who said he wanted a junior quiz competition.[34] In 2003, *Junior Schools' Challenge Quiz* debuted. It ran from September and was conceptualized to have a format similar to the senior quiz but with the "face-off" – a feature not present in the senior quiz. Michael Gonzales came up with the idea for individual students from each team to go up against each other to answer questions on mathematics, science, social studies and language arts. Another spin-off is *Schools' Challenge Quiz Access*, which trades on the popularity of the original show and provides information and highlights of the current season of the parent programme. The high school choir competition *All Together Sing* also runs on TVJ and began in 2004.[35] *KFC Quiz*, a similar and competing programme, ran for a few years after starting in 2002, and was hosted by former spelling bee champion Jody-Ann Maxwell. It was a quiz for ten- to thirteen-year-olds.[36]

Despite the longevity of *Schools' Challenge Quiz*, it has had its detractors. Some complain that the show is elitist, profiling only a few bright students, while others have lamented the obvious lack of preparation on the part of some students who perform below expectations during the competition.[37] Others have expressed concerns about the nature of the questions – one critic noted that the show's questions about religion focused only on Christianity and ignored other religions.[38] Other faultfinders have complained about quizmasters' ability to pronounce foreign language words and those in questions about the sciences.[39] Those sensitive to gender issues have wondered why males and not females tend to dominate the competition.[40] It is not unusual to see letters to the editor of the country's major newspapers documenting the range of criticisms.[41] Some have tried to be constructive too – suggesting ways the show could be improved to handle the relatively large number of schools entering the competition and the need to respect students' time to focus on preparation for other scholastic activities.[42] Loyal viewers have also complained about the resolution of scoring inconsistencies and errors in judges' decisions.[43] Over the years there have been challenges to the results and teams are prepared to protest even when limited to only three queries per show, according to updated rules. However, scoring errors are usually resolved within the match, as was the case in an episode transmitted in February 2013:

> **Quizmaster**: And the scores, well, they have changed, one extra in each instance. Wolmer's Boys' now on twenty-two and St George's now on sixteen. The question "Whose constant states the ratio of energy to frequency is equal to 6.63 times 10 to 34 joules per second?" And the judges will accept the answer given. Max Planck's constant. And of course an extra point for St George's as well. "A firm bought a typewriter for $950 which depreciates in value by 40 per cent per year; what was its devaluation after one year?" And the answer did in fact come just before the bell. So that's one for each team.

To some, it may be seen as just another television quiz show, but it is taken very seriously by those competing. This is not a new phenomenon, as a big challenge came at the end of the show's first season. The St Hugh's High School team initially lost their semi-final match to Kingston College when their answer to a physics question was not accepted as correct.[44] As one team member recalled, they were asked, "What do you call a packet of energy?" She responded "proton" but the expected answer was "quantum". Feeling cheated out of its victory, the St Hugh's team returned to school, researched the question and discovered its answer was also correct. Team members challenged the judges' decision and ended up in the final match instead of Kingston College.[45] St Hugh's High went on to win the season's three-way finale, after knocking out competing teams Hampton School and Jamaica College, to be the first winners in a quiz show that would become a high school tradition.

Some schools that initially refused to participate in the show have gone on to compete and have performed well. Featuring twenty-four high schools in the beginning, *Schools' Challenge Quiz* has since expanded to include up to seventy-eight over the course of its existence, becoming one of the longest-running television shows in Jamaica.

### *Schools' Challenge Quiz* at a Glance

| | |
|---|---|
| Title | *Schools' Challenge Quiz* |
| Genre | Quiz and game show |
| Created by | Hope Stewart |
| Presented mostly by | Dennis Hall, Marlene Stephenson-Dalley |
| Country of origin | Jamaica |
| Original language(s) | English |
| Number of seasons | 46 (as at 2015) |
| Number of episodes | Between 21 and 78 episodes per season |

**Production**

| | |
|---|---|
| Location(s) | Mostly studio; sometimes on location at schools |
| Running time | 30 minutes |
| Camera setup | Multi-camera |
| Production company | JBC TV and TVJ |
| Distributor | JBC TV and TVJ |

**Release**

| | |
|---|---|
| Original channel | JBC TV (1970–1997) |
| Other channels | SSTV (around January–May 1998); TVJ (as of 1999) |
| Original release date | 26 February 1970 |

# 4

# *Profile*
Presenting Personalities Persistently

On Sunday, 22 February 1987, *Profile* premiered on JBC TV. The programme opened with a graphic showing the title and host's name – "Profile: An interview programme with host Ian Boyne" – while announcer Dennis Hall introduced the show in a voice-over over the static title screen.[1] Next, viewers saw a two-minute feature on the show's first guest Carlton Alexander, then-CEO of GraceKennedy. Then the show moved to the studio where Ian Boyne and Carlton Alexander sat across from each other. A green carpet covered the floor, the backdrop was simple with a blue lighting pattern on the studio's cyclorama, a microphone stood between the seated guest and host, and Boyne began: "Mr Alexander, your rise to success has been spectacular. You moved from being billing clerk to chairman and chief executive of one of the most powerful companies in Jamaica, the Grace, Kennedy Group of Companies. Can that experience be duplicated by young people today or was it just for your time?" He continued asking questions about success, career and life.[2] This was the first of over fourteen hundred interviews that would be aired on Jamaican television on Sundays for over thirty years.

The show was created to feature the rags-to-riches and success stories of individuals mainly with Jamaican roots. Ian Boyne wanted to show viewers that they too could pursue successful lives like the guests who appeared on the show. It was meant to inspire viewers. It was the ultimate human-interest programme and fed Jamaican's curiosity about how others achieved their success. There were stories of struggle – the typical "walk barefoot to school" story, the sort of overcoming-obstacles tale that characterized some guests who appeared on *Profile*.

In an interview with Jamaican author and academic Peter Muir aired on Sunday, 19 April 2015, Muir shared his story:

> **Ian Boyne**: So you were scarce for food sometimes?
> **Peter Muir**: There wasn't enough food. There was no clothes. We wore, ahm, we used to wear some Salvation Army clothes.
> **Ian Boyne**: Salvation Army clothes, you used to wear?
> **Peter Muir**: There was not enough food. We were hungry a lot.
> **Ian Boyne**: So as a brown boy growing up, you were living like the regular poor black boys around town.
> **Peter Muir**: Of course. I even went to elementary school barefoot.
> **Ian Boyne**: Yes.
> **Peter Muir**: Because there was no shoes to wear. Not like there was a Sunday school shoes.
> **Ian Boyne**: You had a Sunday school shoes?
> **Peter Muir**: No no.
> **Ian Boyne**: Not even a Sunday school shoes?
> **Peter Muir**: I didn't have any shoes.
> **Ian Boyne**: None at all, not even a Sunday best?
> **Peter Muir**: Not even that [*chuckling*].
> **Ian Boyne**: Things were that hard.

Before the creation of *Profile*, Ian Boyne had worked as a journalist and newspaper columnist at the now defunct *Jamaica Daily News* and was still at the *Gleaner*. His columns appeared in the "In Focus" section of the *Sunday Gleaner*. Boyne wanted to do a television show that explored the human condition. He felt that if he could create a programme that could motivate and give people hope, there would be a place for that on television.[3] Boyne used his networking skills to introduce the concept to JBC TV. He was press secretary to several ministers of government and this enabled him to use his connections to convince JBC to let him present his idea. Then-minister of information Olivia "Babsy" Grange helped him set up an interview with JBC general manager Gloria Lannaman to discuss the proposed programme. They decided to give it a try but only under certain conditions. As was cus-

*PROFILE*: PRESENTING PERSONALITIES PERSISTENTLY

tomary at that time, all producers of new programmes were allowed a set period of three months to establish the viability of the show.[4] Additionally, he would have to find a media personality to co-host. However, the person he had proposed did not accept the terms of engagement and so Boyne became the only host of his show.

The probationary three months went well and, after the period, the programme continued on air, developing into one of Jamaica's well-known personality interview talk shows for television. In the early years it comprised a feature on the guest in addition to the studio interview. The feature would reveal aspects of the guest's life at home with family and at work with colleagues. However, owing to the cost of going on location, the feature was eventually dropped and the whole programme was done in studio.

The only major change in the show's history occurred in 1997, ten years after it started. When JBC was sold to the RJR Communications Group, *Profile* was aired on a station branded initially as SSTV and then later as TVJ. This did not affect the show much; for host Ian Boyne it was business as usual. He continued to apply the same approach – focusing on conversations with successful individuals.

It continued to be shot in the studios of the former JBC until the new entity moved its operations to the purpose-built studios of TVJ in 2004. The change in location was not obvious to the viewer because the set remained basic. But the show was not about the set; it was about the guests and their stories.

The set for *Profile* remained simple and efficient for many years. A typical show would begin with a simple graphic of the show's title and a theme song reminiscent of a 1970s-style disco soundtrack. Viewers would then see the profile of the guest and the host in silhouette, sitting on chairs on a platform. The lights then came up, revealing them in front of a plain backdrop erected by joining about seven standing panels made of fabric stretched over wooden frames. These were accentuated with coloured lighting and shadows of foliage. Occasionally, there would be a small centre table with glasses of water for two. The set remained like this for most of twenty-five years.

There were periods when the background changed – sometimes there would be a shelf with ornaments. Other times there would be real plants. At times guests were seated on chairs on a rug instead of a platform. It was not until 2015, some years after its twenty-fifth anniversary, that there was a major set change. The new set had bigger chairs, a larger centre table, a rug, shelves and a flat-screen television showing the title of the show, all in front of a solid wooden backdrop made to look like the wall of a room. In keeping with the name of the show, the lighting design maintained the creation of a silhouette of the guest at the start.

Having a simple set was probably one of the best production decisions made by the producer. The show did not rely on the visual appeal of the set; instead, it relied on the guests and their stories. For television, there were many opportunities for exploiting the visual elements that could be associated with the guests, such as showing cutaways of them in their everyday lives. This was done for a while but could not be sustained. For a long period during the show's history, from beginning to end, all viewers saw were the host and his guest talking, interrupted by commercial breaks.

Because of this, *Profile* has been criticized for being a "talking heads" show – a term used to describe a programme that does not fully demonstrate the visual potential of the medium. It was able to defy this tenet of television because it distracted the viewer with a good story, which saved the show. Even though the talking-head format is often considered boring, Boyne felt it could work based on the strength of the conversation with the guest, and watching someone tell their story for thirty minutes was sufficient for the Jamaican audience who did not miss the cutaways and other visuals. Sometimes the story extended to a two-part episode. Sometimes it was so compelling that viewers did not want to look away.

In an interview with Jamaican athlete Shelly-Ann Fraser-Pryce that was aired on 28 October 2012, she shared her story:

> **Ian Boyne**: Shelly, in 2007, we didn't know you. Let's talk about your life before 2008 because there was a 2007, right? What was happening then, and how did that prepare you for 2008?
> **Shelly-Ann Fraser**: Right, there was a 2007 and I must say that it prepared me well for 2008. In 2007, I made the national team to go to Osaka for the World Championships. Now this time I came sixth, which would make me a reserve on the relay team. So I just went with the mind-set that I was going to enjoy the atmosphere, the races and everything that came with being at one of these World Championships. I was really excited to go and everything. I

was also nervous too because I was twenty years old and did not know what to expect. Now, while I was there, I was called upon to anchor the relay team and I was, like, "Are you serious? I don't want to run! I'm just here to come and watch. I don't want you to put me out there with all these big stars and next thing something happens!" After that, I went to one of the training sessions and some of the girls on the team were really cruel to me. They were like telling me, "Make sure you don't drop the baton! Hold it in your hand tight!" This made me even more frightened than anybody else. I was now left with the task of carrying home that stick which means that if anything should happen I will be blamed. So I started to cry and everybody was laughing at me. But I was dead serious – I didn't want to run! It was all good that I was getting the experience but I was really so nervous. Of course, my coach heard that I was crying.

**Ian Boyne**: Stephen Francis

**Shelly-Ann Fraser**: Yes. Stephen heard I was crying and so he came and was asking me why I was crying and so I told. And he was like, "Don't worry about it. Next year, you're going to run leave all those girls."[5]

In terms of technical production, there was a production crew that has remained committed to the show over the years, including Louis Burke, Clevans Wilson, Ruddy Matherson, Zed Dawkins, Everald Harrow and Richard Prince. Dean Stewart and Radcliffe McBean have edited the show. Melissa Pinnock and Cameka Smith have worked as make-up artists for the show. Denise Kirlew was responsible for booking and scheduling guests.

During his time as host, Ian Boyne never missed interviewing a guest during the regular Sunday evening time slot and his persistence enabled the show to remain on air as a favourite among Jamaican audiences.[6] Since the start in 1987, he has been seen on Sunday afternoon television with a range of personalities from Jamaica and abroad, from all walks and stations in life. Remarkable individuals would appear, including public figures, politicians, entrepreneurs, entertainers, academicians, religious/spiritual leaders, international celebrities and other high achievers. Just as it has attracted a wide range of guests, the show has also attracted sponsorship from several companies including, among others, Jamaica Broilers, NCB, Sagicor, Jamaica Money Market Brokers, Gas Pro, Lasco Distributors, Shirlhome Chemicals and Guardian Life.

**STILL ON AIR**

Though media surveys attest to its popularity, as may be seen in appendix 3 which shows some of the associated figures, there have been mixed reactions on social media. Generally, *Profile* is seen as being motivating and inspiring. On Twitter, comments have included @chsAnthony, who described it as "my favourite series on TVJ", in a tweet on @televisionjam. On the other hand, Gary Lewis (@slidemongoose) says the show seems too driven by academics. He says it "seems to only interview people who have a Masters or Doctorate". There have also been criticisms of the interviewing style. What could be seen as the host's honest effort to fill airtime for a reticent guest has been viewed by critics as a tendency to talk a lot, giving guests little time to speak for themselves. Despite this, Boyne has received awards for the programme and for being a top journalist in his field.[7]

The appeal of the unadorned, unchanging format may centre on the show's simplicity and the opportunity the audience gets to hear about people from different circumstances who have a story to tell. It is the ultimate human-interest programme; fairly static and word-driven rather than visually driven in a world of the visual, and yet it works. Why this has survived in a place where similar shows such as *Round Table Talk* and *Tuesday Forum* have come and gone may be because of the range and calibre of the guests that Ian Boyne has been able to attract week after week over the decades.

Within the television talk show genre, there are several formats that could be followed. There are talk shows that are moderated by a single host who may interview one or more guests. Then there are those with several consecutive guests or a panel of guests. Any of these may have a studio audience. Other talk shows will feature more than one host interacting among themselves as well as with a number of guests. In Jamaica, some examples of talk shows over the years include *The Diana Wright Show*, which had a studio audience; *Round Table Talk*, featuring a host with a panel of guests; *Tuesday Forum, Thwaites and Company, Our Voices, Man and Woman Story* and *Man Talk* – none of which were still being aired at the time of this publication. Others still running include *Impact, All Angles* and *The Susan Show*.

There have been times when Boyne interviewed more than one guest at the same time. But more typical is the one-on-one format which allows for greater focus on the guest and the story. The show is pre-recorded as live-to-tape mostly on Fridays. There is minimal editing for time, commercial

## PROFILE: PRESENTING PERSONALITIES PERSISTENTLY

breaks and preparation for subsequent broadcast. Though *Profile* appeared at 3:00 on Sunday afternoons in the past, eventually it became established in the 6:30 p.m. to 7:00 p.m. time slot, with a rebroadcast on Mondays at 9:30 a.m. The Sunday evening slot was established since it was aired on JBC TV, the national television station at the time. This time slot was and still is good as viewers could watch the show and stay with the station for the major evening television newscast – an interesting juxtaposition, as the positive vibes of the success stories countered the less positive items of the news reports.

In its early years it was promoted in the print media alongside the TV schedule, with a synopsis of the upcoming programme and a brief background on the next guest.[8] More recently, the show's promotion on TVJ has featured Boyne doing a stand-up link to camera in front of the updated set, giving a preview of next interview, sometimes including a clip from the show.

One of the most memorable moments for the show's host was the interview with Una James, mother of Washington-area sniper Lee Boyd Malvo, in June 2003 that appeared over two episodes. This had a ripple effect as Ian Boyne ended up being featured in other news media in the United States. Content from this interview and some background on the programme made the front page of the *Washington Post* on 24 June 2003, in an article headlined "Mother Warned Malvo of Demon" by staff writer Marcia Slacum Greene. The American news programme *Dateline NBC* bought the exclusive rights to the interview and excerpts appeared on other NBC shows such as *The Today Show*.[9] He was also interviewed by Fox Network, CNN and the Associated Press.

Producing a show like *Profile* means selecting guests who fit certain criteria. For example, credentials had to be verified. On one occasion a guest lied about his qualifications and this was only discovered after the show had aired.[10] In addition to being a success, one had to be able to articulate responses to Boyne's questions. His preparation involved a pre-show pep talk to get his subject comfortable with speaking on camera.

While hosting *Profile*, Boyne appeared on other television programmes. In 1998 he began hosting JIS TV's *Issues and Answers*. In 2002, he hosted a radio programme called *Religious Hardtalk* on RJR 94FM.[11] Two years later, this was transformed into a television programme aired on Tuesday nights. That he is associated with three television programmes has never been an issue for his audience. They recognize his role as host in the three programmes, all of which are different. *Profile* has also been seen by audiences outside of Jamaica. It has appeared in the line-up on the Caribbean International Network (CIN), the cable station with outlets in Miami and New York.

Given *Profile*'s challenges – the emphasis on talking, the lack of cutaways – it is remarkable that it persevered to earn and maintain its place in a prime-time slot on Jamaican television. But there was nothing else like it and audiences accepted it. For many, watching *Profile* is almost a sacred Sunday afternoon ritual, and appearing on the show became a mark of distinction, validating successful guests and inspiring ambitious viewers.

PROFILE: PRESENTING PERSONALITIES PERSISTENTLY

*Profile* at a Glance

| | |
|---|---|
| Title | *Profile* |
| Genre | Talk show |
| Created by | Ian Boyne |
| Presented mostly by | Ian Boyne |
| Country of origin | Jamaica |
| Original language(s) | English |
| Number of seasons | N/A; year-round |
| Number of episodes | Approximately 1,400 (as at 2015) |

**Production**

| | |
|---|---|
| Location(s) | Mostly studio; on location features about guests |
| Running time | 30 minutes |
| Camera setup | Multi-camera |
| Production company | JBC TV and TVJ |
| Distributor | JBC TV and TVJ |

**Release**

| | |
|---|---|
| Original channel | JBC TV (1987–1997) |
| Other channels | SSTV (circa August 1997 to October 1998); TVJ (as of November 1998) |
| Original release date | 22 February 1987 |

# 5

# *Hill an' Gully Ride*
## Documenting Jamaican People and Places

On 13 January 1989, a feature entitled Hill an' Gully Ride that lasted for nine and a half minutes premiered on JBC TV during a thirty-minute slot called "Friday Special" that aired at 6:30 p.m.[1] This is how it began:

> Starting with the Public Broadcasting of Jamaica stinger, a Caribbean flavoured instrumental, a pink hibiscus flower appears right of screen against a white background; a hummingbird comes into frame and puts its beak into the flower; the letters PBJ [Public Broadcasting Jamaica] emerge from the flower as the bird flies away. This is followed by the CPTC logo and the sound of children singing "Hill an' Gully Rider". A panoramic view of Jamaica's hillsides is next, then a brook, a sugar mill in Trinityville, St Thomas powered by a donkey, more hillsides, with a superimposed animated Jamaican country bus moving across the bottom of the screen with the words "Hill & Gully Ride".[2]
>
> Meanwhile, a female voice says, *"Hill an' Gully Ride takes us on a trek through Jamaica to places on the map we've never heard of or visited and will uncover the stories and legends behind these interesting place names."* The title shot cuts to Monica Johnson standing next to a CPTC-branded vehicle. She continues, "Look here, for example". The camera moves to a close up of the Middlesex, Clarendon section of the Jamaican map. "Here is Kupuis spelt K.U.P.U.I.S. and Danks, both found in the parish of Clarendon. You've never heard of them? Stay on board." She enters the vehicle. "Let's go, Roy." So begins the programme's journey across the country . . . a journey that would continue for more than twenty-five years.

## HILL AN' GULLY RIDE: DOCUMENTING JAMAICAN PEOPLE AND PLACES

The host asks for directions along the way. Various residents give their version of the origins of Kupuis, including farmer Joseph Dillon and historian Sydney Clarke. Then Warren Juno gives his story about the origins of Danks. Monica Johnson also weighs in on other stories about nearby place names such as Morgan Valley. Daisy Thompson, a retired teacher in Chapelton, shares some history of slave plantations in Clarendon. Cutaways are shown during the storytelling. A.G. Thomas, other Chapelton residents, other teachers, farmers and older citizens also share stories about living in that parish.

Monica Johnson wraps up the show. "If you live in a district with an intriguing name and an interesting story behind it or you have more information on how the places got their names, tell us about it. If you call us, we will come." She invites viewers to write to CPTC, 37 Arnold Road, Kingston 5.

Then the *Hill an' Gully Ride* theme begins and the credits run over a sunset – Camera, Leighton DaCosta; Sound, Andre Bidwell; Script, Monica Johnson; Graphics, Gary Ferguson; Editor, Shawn Kennedy; Production Assistant, Teddy Laidley; Producer/Director, Monica Johnson; Assistant Executive Producer, Jean Morant; Executive Producer, Jean Barnes. A CPTC Production for PBJ.

CPTC was established in 1984 and in its early years, there was much experimenting and brainstorming in an effort to create new shows. Though the first episode aired on a Friday, for most of its first year, *Hill an' Gully Ride* was a short feature in a half-hour slot called "Sunday Special".[3] It became a half-hour programme on 31 December 1989 with a feature on Lionel Town, Lawrence Tavern and Glengoffe. Then, the credits read "Produced by the CPTC for JBC/CBF".[4]

The show was created to respond to the need for more indigenous programming that would allow Jamaicans to see themselves on television. It was conceptualized by Jean Barnes, Bernard Jankee and Monica Johnson and emerged when Jean Barnes was executive director of CPTC from 1987 to 1990. Before that she had worked with JIS TV and was involved in programmes such as *Life with the Littles*.

*Hill an' Gully Ride* was proposed as a feature that would look at the history behind place names in Jamaica. The idea was to explore these, as many were creative and lyrical and offered insights into Jamaica's economic and social history. The creators were partly inspired by a column in the Jamaica tabloid newspaper the *Star* called "Historical Notes", which highlighted and explained the origins of some place names. Myrnelle McIntosh was credited for compiling the column from 2 November 1982 to 16 January 1996.

One proposition was to name this feature "The Land of Look Behind" – an appropriate name given the show's intent, and the fact that "Look Behind" is the name of a district in the Cockpit country in the parish of Trelawny.[5] *The Land of Look Behind*, however, was also the title of a book written by Mona McMillan in 1957. As the story goes, she was looking at a map and saw an area identified as the "District Known by the Name of Look Behind".[6] Later maps referred to the place as the "District of Look Behind".[7] This name was also the title of a 1982 documentary about Jamaican reggae music by Allen Greenberg and a 1985 anthology by Jamaican writer Michelle Cliff.[8] Clearly the name was already associated with other publications and media products and the team needed to be original.

In searching for an appropriate name for the show, production assistant Teddy Laidley remembers visiting the CPTC's library and listening to a "Music and Youth" record produced by Wycliffe Bennett. According to the album's cover, the song "Hill an' Gully" was performed by students of the St Catherine High School under the direction of teacher Ken Neale.[9] It is a famous traditional Jamaican folk song sometimes referred to as a work song and other times as a play song. The call and response which used to be sung by workmen building new roads, refers to the uneven topography through which these roads had to be constructed, and is evocative of the pitfalls that beset anyone traversing the mountains and valleys on horseback:

> Hill an' gully rider . . . Hill an' gully (x2)
> An' then you ben' down, low down . . . Hill an' gully (x3)
> Hill an' gully rider . . . Hill an' gully (x2)
> An' then you come right up now . . . Hill an' gully (x3)
> Hill an' gully rider . . . Hill an' gully (x2)
> An' then you come and ketch you back now . . . Hill an' gully (x3)
> Hill an' gully rider . . . Hill an' gully (x2)
> An' if you tumble down you bruk you neck . . . Hill an' gully (x3)
> Hill an' gully rider . . . Hill an' gully (x2)
> An' then you bend down low down . . . Hill an' gully (x3)
> Hill an' gully rider . . . Hill an' gully (x2)
> An' then you come right up now . . . Hill an' gully (x3)[10]

## HILL AN' GULLY RIDE: DOCUMENTING JAMAICAN PEOPLE AND PLACES

It was first decided to name the show *Hill an' Gully*. But because the programme would involve travelling to various locations in Jamaica, the word "Ride" was eventually included to represent the idea of a journey throughout the countryside. Over the years other renditions of the song – performed by Harry Belafonte and Orville Manning – have been used as the show's theme. In a later version of the programme, the show is introduced by a voice-over: "*Hill an' Gully Ride* takes you on a picturesque ride to places all over Jamaica; some little-known, others very familiar. We'll meet the people, find out how places got their names and just generally become better acquainted with our country. So sit back, relax and take the *Hill an' Gully Ride*."

Thinking about it, the name is rather fitting because this television show involves travelling the terrain of Jamaica to feature aspects of the island's sociocultural history. For most of the show, people tell stories about their lives and their communities. These narratives are usually in response to questions posed by the show's producer. The show, like the song, involves call and response. Questions are called out and responses are real-life stories.

The CPTC was housed in the Caenwood Centre in the Ministry of Education complex at 37 Arnold Road, Kingston. It is not surprising that it was now producing this show, having its studios in what was formerly the home of the Educational Broadcasting Service. But though *Hill an' Gully Ride* was undoubtedly educational and informative, one could not miss the entertainment value in listening to Jamaicans relate stories about their lives in their native tongue.

The first programme was about the communities of Danks and Kupuis in Clarendon. Other memorable communities were featured over the years. There was Animal Hill in Lucea, Hanover – a place where early twentieth-century residents had surnames like Hogg, Mare, Steer, Lyons, Fox and Wolfe.[11] There was Amiel Town, St Mary, where a number of people had the last name Amiel; and Rat Trap, Westmoreland, named because of an abundance of rats in the area.[12] Places with natural geographic features such as Mayfield Falls in Westmoreland, Nonsuch and Hope Bay Caves in Portland were other locations visited.[13]

Since it began there have been more than thirteen hundred episodes of *Hill an' Gully Ride* produced. Carey Robinson, a long-standing producer of the show, will tell you he has been to almost every community in Jamaica. Robinson began working on the show in December 1989, shortly after Monica Johnson and Teddy Laidley left CPTC. They helped to build the foundation of this show, having been involved in the long process of moving from concept to the actual episodes for the first year. When Robinson joined the team, he was no stranger to television. He was former general manager of JBC, serving twice from 1971 to 1973 and 1987 to 1988. He had also worked for the JIS TV and Film Unit. By the time he came to CPTC, he had had many years of media experience. What some people may not know about him is that he is a passionate historian and the author of historical texts and he has created television productions focusing on Jamaica's history, such as *A Tale of Freedom* (1996), *Spirit of Freedom* (1995), *Stepping Stones* (1995), *Flashpoint '38* (1988) and *Living Treasures of Jamaica* (1988). He wrote, directed and produced the first full-length docu-drama filmed in Jamaica – *Time of Fury* (1965).

In the first few years of *Hill an' Gully Ride*, there were on-camera presenters. When it began in 1989, it featured a presenter who appeared on camera, on location, and during its run four presenters have been featured. The first one was Monica Johnson, then later came Jonathan Burke, Celia Blake and Sonia Holman. However, the practice of having a host on screen was short lived. For the more than twenty years that the programme has been produced by Carey Robinson, though he has worked with presenters, he has favoured an approach where the narrator is heard but not seen. At CPTC this has earned him the nickname "Phantom". When Monica and then Jonathan served as presenters, they would go on location. The others, Celia Blake and then Sonia Holman, did not. Instead, they did stand-up links on camera, usually under a tree outside the studios of CPTC. "Stand-up" refers to the practice of a presenter speaking to camera, also known as a "piece to camera" or PTC. A "link" is commentary done on camera or as a voice-over that connects various elements of a show by introducing features or items. The linking script was written by Carey Robinson. Viewers did not seem to miss the host though, and except for this variation from the original format, the programme maintained its style for many years.

In the early years, the production team would decide on the places to be visited. As the show became popular, they had no shortage of requests from communities hoping that they would be featured. The team would then travel to these locations around Jamaica and occasionally abroad.[14] Sometimes the simple act of asking for directions would lead the producer to feature another community on the way to the original destination for the shoot.

In an episode aired on 15 August 1993, Congo Hill and Joe Hut in the parish of Trelawny were featured. Carey Robinson asks Lucie Edwards for directions to Congo Hill:

> **Carey Robinson** (*off camera*): This road will take you to Congo Hill?
> **Lucie "Miss Girlie" Edwards**: Yes when you go up to the wall, the long wall, then you turn over the field and go over and turn up . . . yes is up there.
> **Carey Robinson** (*off camera*): And you find the spring up there?
> **Lucie "Miss Girlie" Edwards**: Yes under a little rock bubbling up. Nuh care how time dry, you get water but it far for we to go, but we have to go there to get the drinking water. Yes. Me going up to ground where me buying yam fi go to market.
> **Carey Robinson** (*off camera*): Ground?
> **Lucie "Miss Girlie" Edwards**: Yes, me going up to a field where we buy yam from.
> **Carey Robinson** (*off camera*): To buy the yam up there, to take it to market?
> **Lucie "Miss Girlie" Edwards**: Yes.
> **Carey Robinson** (*off camera*): Which market you going take it to?
> **Lucie "Miss Girlie" Edwards**: Falmouth.
> **Carey Robinson** (*off camera*): How you going get there?
> **Lucie "Miss Girlie" Edwards**: We have truck up there. The same yard where we going fi the yam now, is there the truck is.
> **Carey Robinson** (*off camera*): Coming today?
> **Lucie "Miss Girlie" Edwards**: It is there right now.

A historian at heart, Robinson was able to ask questions to capture stories of what it was like growing up in Jamaica. One common question was "How did you survive?" Interviews were interspersed with cutaways of scenes in the community – the random dog, the passer-by, the trees. While viewers would never see the producer asking questions, they became familiar with his voice. On a shoot in Llandewey, St Thomas, one fan of the show exclaimed as she saw Robinson in real life, "You are the man behind the voice. You never show your face but I know that voice asking the questions." The show was not about Carey Robinson – it was about the people of Jamaica. Robinson was never seen on screen.

Over time Jamaicans grew to accept this, and the show became a staple in their lives – Sunday dinner of rice and peas and chicken followed by relaxing and watching *Hill an' Gully Ride*. The show is now aired at 6:00 p.m. on Sunday with a repeat on Tuesday mornings. Previously it could be seen as early as 11:00 on Sunday morning on JBC TV.

The programme's long-serving crew members included Brian "Johno" Johnson and Rohan Amiel, who did camera; Andre Bidwell, who managed sound; and Garnet Lewis, editor; and production assistants would book the crew and arrange transportation. In the beginning there was a driver, sound recordist, videographer, producer, production assistant and sometimes presenter. Over the years this team got smaller and consisted of a driver trained to do sound on location, a cameraperson, producer and production assistant with an editor at CPTC. Even more recently, this has been further reduced to the producer, a driver/sound person, a cameraperson and, on good days, a production assistant.

The CPTC underwrites the cost of production and provides facilities and personnel. Shooting on location takes one day, usually a Friday, as the production budget does not allow for overnight accommodation. Crew members on the shoots would sometimes have long walks over uneven terrain in isolated areas to get the shots needed. Editing is done over two and half days between Mondays and Thursdays in the following week, during which time a linking script is also written and recorded so that the programme is ready for broadcast on Sunday.

The technical elements of the production include a one-camera location shoot, scripting links, recording narration, editing and dubbing. Such is the appeal of the show that community members are often reluctant to speak until they realize that the team is from *Hill an' Gully Ride*. By the end of the shoot, these same people insist that the crew leaves with produce – yam, bananas and coconuts – as is typical in rural areas. The gifts are from those people featured on the programme or others who had had the opportunity of hosting the team for a day, appreciative that their stories are being told.

## HILL AN' GULLY RIDE: DOCUMENTING JAMAICAN PEOPLE AND PLACES

On this programme, real people are the stars rather than celebrity presenters or well-known personalities. It has even inspired viewers to write about the show. Seaforth Primary School teacher Sadie Robinson wrote a poem called "Hill an' Gully Ride". Tafanyah Mitchell, a student at the school, was awarded a gold medal for performing it at the St Thomas parish finals of the Jamaica Cultural Development Commission Festival competition in 2013. Here is an excerpt from the poem, written in Jamaican dialect:

> Go fresh up yuself and a don't waan hear a soun.
> A today di Hill an Gully ride people dem suppose to come
> Git up! Hurry up! Go do weh mi sey yuh fi do. Run. . . .
> . . . Alright walk good, memba watch yuh step.
> Mmmm, mmmm, yuh nasty up back yuh shoes.
> Yuh dweet agen. Yuh step back inna di same dooo-
> Nuh worry bout dat though, safe journey back to town
> Heh, heh! Mi ago de pon TV wen Hill an Gully come roun.

The show's popularity extends beyond Jamaica and reaches not only the Jamaican diaspora but also other markets as far away as Europe.[15] It has been included in the line-up on CIN's cable channels in New York and Miami and there have been requests from locations such as Spain.[16] Subtitles would be required for non-English-speaking audiences. There is also the story of a prison in a Caribbean island where unofficial recordings are shared with the prisoners, many of whom get upset when an episode is not shown.[17]

There have been similar local travelogue-type programmes reflecting elements of the *Hill an' Gully Ride* format. *Nyammings* features a host travelling around the country interviewing people who cook while talking about their culinary experiences. *Two Sisters and a Meal* also travels the island as two real-life sisters interview people while cooking. *Hidden Treasures* explores places of interest for locals and visitors. *Wat a Gwaan* and *Weh Yuh Seh* conduct vox pops. While it cannot be definitively argued that these may have been inspired by *Hill an' Gully Ride*, it is clear that the travelogue format has a place on Jamaican television.

*Hill an' Gully Ride* has a strong audience following. According to the *All Media Survey 2012*, approximately 76 per cent of those who view free-to-air television between 6:00 and 6:30 p.m. on Sundays watch TVJ. In other words, of the 296,000 people watching free-to-air between 6:00 and 6:30 p.m., 226,000 viewers watch TVJ (see appendix 3 for additional audience figures).[18] However, Carey Robinson notes that there was a time when its future was in doubt.[19] There was some controversy over ownership and origination of the programme, with some who regarded it as a CPTC product commissioned by JBC/CBF and others who believed it was a JBC/CBF product owned by them. This was quickly resolved and in 1997, when JBC TV was divested, the show continued to be produced by CPTC and aired on the new TVJ now managed by the RJR Communications Group. While the show remains popular with audiences, production support is nevertheless usually predicated on the management at the facilities with which it is associated.

The programme has always had a time slot on a Sunday. Advertisements are included in the TVJ broadcast and it is also seen on CPTC's cable channel. Sponsors over the years have included Shell, the Electoral Commission of Jamaica, Lasco and, for some episodes, there was an arrangement that saw sponsor GraceKennedy travelling with the show on location. Sponsorship has always been a challenge. However, CPTC gets some sponsorship through its marketing arm Jamvision, which also sells DVDs of episodes.

For most of its time on air the show's formula has remained basically the same. The main identifiable change was the shift in later years to a focus on the memories of older – often centenarian – people in the community, departing from the original intention. The show now featured talk about life at various points in the country's history, from pre-independence to the present. Centenarians and others who despite their age could vividly recall interesting facts and tales about growing up in Jamaica would tell stories with family members gathered and listening. In later years, the producers would also get requests to document the histories of ageing people.

Feedback about the show is shared online and on social media. The show has had its own Facebook page since 2014. People have commented on the show using the hashtag #hillangullyride. On 24 May 2015, @shawnii tweeted "bay ppl weh ova 100-y-o come pon Hill and Gully Ride enuh"[20] (translation: Only people over one hundred years old appear on *Hill an' Gully Ride* you know).

In an episode of the show aired on Sunday, 26 October 2003, Connie Webster, or Aunt Connie, of Port Royal, born in 1903, celebrated her birthday. Surrounded by family, she talks about her first grandchild:

> I brought her up from a baby. Right up. I had to look after her all the time. I had to be working and looking after her all the time. . . . As I told you before I was born 1903 and we had an earthquake in 1907. Well I was only four years old you know. I went to the bathroom and when I went to the bathroom, I just feel it was going around, falling, falling and I started to scream and come out of the bathroom and said "Mama, mama, shaky shaky dah come." And she lift me up and carry me outside.

Fast forward.

> **Carey Robinson** (*off camera*): Where you used to do your shopping?
> **Connie Webster**: In Kingston. I used to take the ferry go to Coronation Market and I go to store. When mi go to Coronation, the wages was very small you know, with the big hamper basket you get it full of things. Yam, cocoa, any kind of foodstuff. Coming on to the cloth. The material was so cheap. You could get a farthing, pound, shilling and pence in those days. A farthing per yard lace, a four pence per yard cloth. When I can afford a boy, I pay a boy to take it from the Coronation Market to the ferry, if not, I put it on my head and carry it down to the boat.
> **Carey Robinson** (*off camera*): You had good balance man.
> **Connie Webster**: Strong balance.

Carey Robinson narrates as a cutaway of a photograph of Ms Webster meeting Prince Charles is shown: "One of Connie Webster's favourite memories is of the day she met Prince Charles at the historic St Peter's Anglican Church."

> **Connie Webster** (*remembering the meeting in 2000*):[21] He wanted to see all the citizens. When he came to me him say I was made to understand that – I was much younger – that you are approaching one hundred years. Him say my grandmother is one hundred now and she is going strong. I am the only citizen in Port Royal that touched a hundred this morning. What a wonderful thing!
> **Carey Robinson**: You must be eating a lot of fish, Miss Connie.
> **Connie Webster:** Yes . . . yea mon.[22]

**STILL ON AIR**

The show pauses for a commercial break. No doubt, the viewers who would continue to watch would obviously have grown to appreciate the value of *Hill an' Gully Ride* in documenting Jamaican oral histories.

Carey Robinson has served as the show's producer for over twenty-six years. In the interest of succession planning, the CPTC has explored future production possibilities. Management seems confident that it can continue when the composition of the production team changes. For some, its secret is the fact that it contains "unfiltered stories of Jamaican success".[23] The show is positive and represents the good in people, showing them at their best.

---

*Hill an' Gully Ride* at a Glance

| | |
|---|---|
| Title | *Hill an' Gully Ride* |
| Genre | Factual |
| Created by | Jean Barnes; Bernard Jankee; Monica Johnson |
| Presented mostly by | Carey Robinson, narrator |
| Country of origin | Jamaica |
| Original language(s) | English and Jamaican Creole |
| Number of seasons | N/A; year-round |
| Number of episodes | Approximately 1,300 (as at 2015) |
| **Production** | |
| Location(s) | On location across Jamaica |
| Running time | 30 minutes |
| Camera setup | Mostly single or two camera |
| Production company | CPTC |
| Distributor | JBC TV and TVJ |
| **Release** | |
| Original channel | JBC TV (1989–1997) |
| Other channels | SSTV (circa August 1997 to October 1998); TVJ (as of November 1998) |
| Original release date | 13 January 1989 |

# 6

## *Entertainment Report*
Showcasing Jamaica's Popular Culture

"Hello, I'm Anthony Miller." This is how one of the earliest archived episodes of *Entertainment Report* opened. It was aired on Friday, 15 November 1991 as a five-minute feature in the JBC TV *Nightly News*.[1] This feature looked at local and international entertainment stories. The episode included a story on the unveiling of Sandra Foster's wardrobe for the Miss World Pageant 1991, an in-studio interview with dancehall artiste Tiger and a review of a food festival at the Jamaica Pegasus Hotel.

Since the 1980s, there was a trend of including an entertainment feature in the Friday night newscast of JBC TV. It represented light news and was meant to be a sort of kicker, that offbeat story typically used to mark the end of a newscast. In the early days, the Friday night entertainment kicker would be the responsibility of the individual who worked the weekend shift. It was ad hoc and the particular type of entertainment content was dependent on the available resources. Over time, feedback from viewers led to the development of a regularly scheduled, named and packaged feature with both local and international entertainment stories.[2]

Miller was an employee of JBC who worked as a news producer. His work schedule often included Friday evenings which meant that he would be responsible for the entertainment kicker. While working on the five-minute feature in the newscast, Miller says, he saw an opportunity for a change from his role in the newsroom.[3] The feature had potential and could be expanded. Sponsorship could provide the resources to help develop the short feature into a full programme, but sponsorship was never allowed in the newscast.[4] The five-minute feature continued for 1992 and eventually became a half-hour programme by 1993.[5] By this time, Anthony Miller no longer worked in the JBC TV newsroom. He was now a freelance producer.

The earliest archived copy of a half-hour edition of *Entertainment Report* that could be accessed was transmitted on 26 March 1993 on JBC TV. This was confirmed by the TV programme schedule appearing in the *Star* newspaper.[6] It is a thirty-minute programme that has been aired on TVJ since 1997 when RJR acquired JBC TV. It consists of approximately twenty-four minutes of content and six minutes of advertisements and is now a co-production between Miller Productions and TVJ.

As a former news producer, Anthony Miller brought his journalistic sensibilities to the production, planning and execution of the show. Arguably, the show's strength lies in its well-practised entertainment journalism. As a half-hour, fast-moving, edgy entertainment magazine programme, one of its main elements is the hard-hitting interview – warts-and-all coverage of entertainment events and personalities.

Its inception and development coincided with the rise of what some describe as the then renegade culture of dancehall music and was the first show on Jamaican television to give voice and coverage to emerging dancehall artistes.[7] Dancehall music, the leading popular youth culture music in Jamaica, was and still is a major part of the programme. But even from its beginnings, the show also highlighted other areas such as fashion, food, film and fine arts.

When the programme moved to half an hour in 1993, it was produced using the facilities of the CPTC because JBC TV did not have the necessary resources to create such a demanding show. CPTC provided cameras, studio and editing facilities along with office space and production assistant services. Acting as executive producer, it also administered quality control for the programme on behalf of JBC TV.[8] The show was aired on JBC TV on Friday nights with the credits stating that it was produced by Miller Productions and CPTC for JBC TV. After the sale of JBC TV in June 1997, the show continued on SSTV under the same joint venture arrangement between CPTC and Miller Productions.

In 1999, about two years after RJR bought JBC TV and had time to review the production arrangements surrounding this show, the programme was invited to be produced in-house at the newly branded TVJ. The show maintained its identity as a popular Friday night television show despite the changing station ID of the channel on which it aired.[9]

Having accepted the invitation to return to TVJ, it was now produced by Miller Productions and TVJ. The station aired it and provided all the technical production facilities along with some additional production assistants and office space, while Miller continued to write, produce and direct the weekly programme. The show is transmitted by TVJ and the programmes are housed by the station. Copies of the show before 1997 are in the archives at PBCJ and at CPTC.

The programme has been aired on Friday evenings during its run. It has been scheduled at various times, appearing mostly at 8:30 p.m. with some seasons being shown at 9:00 p.m. Regardless of its specific timeslot, the show has always enjoyed the prime-time slot after the Friday night newscast on TVJ. On occasion, it has been moved to accommodate special programming and events. As is customary with other local programmes, the show is repeated on the station at other times during the week. Repeats of *Entertainment Report* can be seen as late as 11:00 on Monday nights.

The show is pre-recorded, edited and aired on Fridays. During the week, some features and interviews are shot on location. Sometimes interviews are done in studio. On Thursdays, the studio links are shot against a chroma key background and a virtual set inserted during editing.

It was for financial rather than creative reasons that Miller took on the role of both host and producer and through the years brought in occasional hosts from CPTC, TVJ and elsewhere.[10] In 2005, *Entertainment Report* hired Denise Hunt, its first full-time paid host, allowing Miller to concentrate on producing and writing.[11] She left after eight years and, following an open-call audition to find a new host, the job went to Kerry-Ann "Kiki" Lewis, who left after some months. The show continued for a while with voice-over instead of a host. Since leaving, Denise Hunt has returned as a visiting host to do short stints on the show.

The concept has remained virtually unchanged over the intervening years. Miller has noted that no specific show or format was copied when *Entertainment Report* was being created. Instead, it emanated from ideas about what a production team wanted to see in a good quality entertainment show. It retains a format that sees four to five main items presented during the programme. The story treatments range from voice-overs, location or studio interviews, or packages linked by an in-studio host. The items and links are pre-recorded and edited into the final programme package. Occasionally the show's links have been presented on location.[12]

The producer takes on the task of going out on location with the camera crew, conducting location and studio interviews, and subsequently writing most of the link scripts and stories. Segments of the show are written by reporters and guest producers while production assistants help with booking guests and making logistic arrangements for covering stories. The focus is the entertainment scene and while most of this material is gathered within Jamaica, *Entertainment Report* producers have travelled to Europe, the Caribbean and North America to cover stories.

Though Anthony Miller has undertaken several production roles for the show, being producer, writer, director, interviewer and sometimes presenter, others have joined the team from time to time. Over the years, Judith Alberga, Tami Chin, Denese Gascho, Deborah Hickling, Yvette Rowe, Sharon Schroeter and Scott Wilson have been among those who have worked on the show as either guest producers, reporters or presenters. Other crew members include camera operators Rohan Amiel, Ian Guthrie, Tallawah Levy, Gregory "Asha" McPhail and Leavan Rainford; sound, Andre Bidwell, Michael Edwards and Neville Spence; production assistants Carlene Airey, Hertha Beckman, Carlene Davis, Dannielle Gordon, and Erica Wilson; graphics, Debbie Powell; editors Sean Irving, Greg James, Michael Kerr, O'Neil C. Miller, Shane Walker, Shaun Walker and O.C. Powell.

Editing is done in the station's digital editing suites by a small team which shares responsibility for most segments, compiling the show for broadcast and repackaging for CIN TV and for uploading to the online environment. Shaun Walker, one of the show's editors, concentrates on creating fast moving, quick cuts on main features that are a trademark of the show. O.C. Powell, another editor, has been responsible for editing some segments and overseeing the technical quality, including sound and colour correction. He feels that what makes the programme stand out from others is the technical superiority, partly a consequence of the recent investment that the RJR Communications Group has made in digital equipment that allows for high technical production quality.[13]

Production involves shooting during the week with a heavy emphasis on variety and a high number of shots. Editor Shaun Walker says that having many shots of high quality and a variety of angles and perspectives is imperative to creating the fast moving edgy style for which the show is known. This style emerged in the early years when editors and camera operators experimented with limited equipment to create a visual style that resonated with the entertainment theme. One particular innovation used was the white flash between edits.

In addition to its visual appeal, *Entertainment Report* is known for its witty and pointed way of saying what needs to be said. The journalistic style has been greatly appreciated eliciting both positive and negative reactions. At times the show has drawn the ire of those it covers. Artistes have been known to refuse to cooperate with the programme because they are unhappy about what they regard as negative reports about them. Witness an interview with Jamaican reggae artiste Konshens transmitted on 26 December 2013:

> **Konshens**: You know me woulda waan do over di interview yah from top.
> **Miller**: Hahahaha.
> **Konshens**: Me woulda love do it over from top. You see you, over the years, you is a very intimidating brother with how you ask question. You know why?
> **Miller**: Hahahaha.
> **Konshens**: You want people fi just deh pon dem Ps and dem Qs.

Miller could be said to be the driving force behind the programme. While there have been guest producers, there is not much evidence to suggest that plans are being put in place to recruit or train a successor who can handle the programme in the way Miller has done over the years. The programme has a set format, but much of its success comes down to the hand of production and writing – marshalling of all the elements including planning, pre-production, research, interviewing, directing shoots, writing and editing.

The show began in the era of analogue technology. It was shot on tape and compiled using linear editing. The introduction of digital editing systems resulted in the use of non-linear editing and recording on camera cards. It has benefited from technological changes and made use of the new technology to enhance its product. In early years, the programme links were sometimes presented in front of a live backdrop of the CPTC's production suites. Later this moved to a virtual set with the use of chroma key. More recently, virtual sets have included a motion graphic representation of the programme's initials, *ER*, added in post-production.

While the show is not aired live, it does try to keep abreast of developments in the entertainment industry. This has sometimes led to the need to reshoot links or re-edit content at the last minute to get the latest breaking news into the package. Crew members report that there have been nerve-racking moments when the first part of the show has been on air while subsequent segments were still being edited.

Work on the programme starts in the days and weeks before broadcast. Monday is dedicated to agenda setting, discussing story ideas and setting up shoots and interviews. Tuesday is the main shooting day with location shoots, and these extend into other days and the weekend depending on the coverage needs. Wednesday is the main day for logging of tapes and scripting the programme and its links. Thursday is studio production and a main editing day. Programme links are recorded in the studio and any in-studio interviews are also done then, with either the presenter, producer or production assistant. The links shoot requires the studio and a studio crew including the studio director, studio camera and sound. The links are recorded on digital card or to the hard drive in the master control. The studio session also includes a control room crew and studio camera operator. Other support services include make-up and wardrobe for guests, presenters and contributors.

The lead segment can be anything from four to eight minutes and may be presented as voice-over, wrap or interview. This item is followed by others that may or may not be part of a theme. The host in the studio introduces and links the items in the show. The rest of the show continues with a number of features. Among the programme features have been the top ten, new faces, video debut and picks from the archives.

The top ten is often sponsored and over the years various mechanisms have been used to compile the list, including using charts from another media organization or a research entity. In its early years, the show would produce a music video for a song from the artiste(s) interviewed on the episode. Sometimes a new music video produced elsewhere would be featured. *Entertainment Report* also highlights other topics including plays, social commentary, travel and events.

The programme is supported by advertising and sponsorship. It has had many sponsors over the years with Lucozade, NCB, AT&T, Digicel, Red Stripe, Courts and KFC among them. It also features advertising breaks within the programme and, at times, has included sponsor tags at the beginning and the end of the show. Head of Marketing for one of the sponsors has noted that his company knows that there is a great deal of convergence on Friday nights as people tune in to catch up with the latest in entertainment in Jamaica.[14] The producers have had to manage the relationship with marketers to ensure that they do not feel that sponsorship gives them the right to influence the show's content.

*Entertainment Report* has had some limited success in the international market. It was and still is one of the TVJ programmes that is packaged for delivery on CIN, a cable station with outlets in Miami and New York.[15] The show has been seen on European satellite station BskyB (British Sky Broadcasting).[16] A spin-off show, *ER2*, was occasionally aired on Saturday evenings in the early 2000s. The spin-off often centred on personalities or themes and consisted of material previously broadcast which had been reworked or repackaged.

The show has a presence on social media with its Facebook page and Twitter posts. It is uploaded for online viewing at other times and streamed live by TVJ online and via mobile apps. Also uploaded unofficially by others, it is available for viewing on YouTube as whole episodes or excerpts. While some appreciate the fact that it sometimes focuses on social issues such as politics, poverty or homelessness, some critics on Twitter have suggested that such content does not belong in an entertainment show. Regardless, many others applaud the show for being socially responsible. Miller's *Entertainment Report* feature on the Manatt Enquiry (Commission of Enquiry to investigate the Jamaican government's dealing with US law firm Manatt, Phelps and Phillips in the extradition of Christopher "Dudus" Coke) won a Caribbean Broadcasting Union award for best news feature in 2011.[17] Indeed, a show about entertainment can report on serious news matters.

**STILL ON AIR**

This excerpt was taken from an *Entertainment Report* twenty-first anniversary special transmitted on 26 December 2013.

> **Commentator Annie Paul**: I always particularly enjoy those moments when Anthony goes beyond the entertainment scene and reaches into the political culture of the country. And lampoons it or satirizes it.
> *Up audio of a dramatic instrumental television theme accompanying shots of leaders arriving at the Jamaica Conference Centre.*
> **Anthony Miller**: The main men in the Manatt spectacle arriving for their long-awaited showdown . . . Bruce Golding, prime minister . . . the witness with most at stake . . . . K.D. Knight, attack attorney . . . the voice of those with the most to gain. . . . Two titans squaring off over an extradition delayed. . . . Who paid? Or who didn't? And who did what and when? All against the backdrop of lives lost and people asking why. . . . A full house at the Jamaica Conference Centre but no one expecting full disclosure.

The programme has received a number of Press Association of Jamaica awards. Yasmin Peru, entertainment writer, describes it as giving a good analysis on any given topic pertaining to entertainment.[18] Cultural analyst Donna P. Hope says she tries religiously to watch each week, usually live on TVJ, but sometimes watches repeats online. She says in the early stages one could recognize the way that *Entertainment Report* integrated what was happening in dancehall into the programme and that that had had an impact on the growth of the show and its success.[19] Miller asks the tough questions, draws out the answers and brings out what is important to the fans. Many people involved in popular culture believe that having an interview with him is very important for one's career.[20]

For thirty minutes every week, on a Friday night, Jamaican television audiences get some insight into the country's entertainment industry. The sounds and scenes of dancehall. Close-ups with caution. Exposure from many angles. Clashes and controversies. The question that stumps the guest. The reluctant response. The crying diva. The prima donna. Light-skinned carnival revellers. Dark-skinned dancehall doyennes. A bashment uptown. A soiree downtown. A deejay's rhyme gone sour. The no-show at the stage show. Displeased fans. The struggling artiste. A career comeback. The big break. Runway models falling for fashion. Catwalk catastrophe.

## ENTERTAINMENT REPORT: SHOWCASING JAMAICA'S POPULAR CULTURE

Fine dining connoisseur. Celebrity chef. From fish back to lobster bisque. Social blunders. The latest dance move. Witty words, poignant puns. Commentary punctuated with fast edits and creative camera work.

And that's our show.

### *Entertainment Report* at a Glance

| | |
|---|---|
| Title | Entertainment Report |
| Genre | Current and public affairs |
| Created by | Anthony Miller |
| Presented mostly by | Anthony Miller; Denise Hunt |
| Country of origin | Jamaica |
| Original language(s) | English and Jamaican Creole |
| Number of seasons | N/A; year-round |
| Number of episodes | Approximately 1,200 (as at 2015) |

**Production**

| | |
|---|---|
| Location(s) | Mostly on location; in-studio interviews/links |
| Running time | 30 minutes |
| Camera setup | Mostly single camera |
| Production company | JBC TV, CPTC and TVJ |
| Distributor | JBC TV and TVJ |

**Release**

| | |
|---|---|
| Original channel | JBC TV (1991–1997) |
| Other channels | SSTV (circa August 1997 to October 1998); TVJ (as of November 1998) |
| Original release date | 15 November 1991 – earliest archived copy found |

# 7

# Stay Tuned
## Why They Continue to Be on Air

If I am bright, I can be on *Schools' Challenge Quiz*;
If I am a success, I can be on *Profile*;
If I get to be one hundred years old, I can be on *Hill an' Gully Ride*;
If I "buss", I can be on *Entertainment Report*.
—Anonymous

Why do television programmes stay on the air? We present an analysis to address this question in the context of Jamaica with its small market for television. Not every programme is destined to be on air for a long time. Some, by their very nature, would not be. For example, a short mini-series may only need to be aired for a limited period.

We are working with the assumption that longevity is a mark of success for any television programme. Producing a long-running show means one has been able to maintain the interest of an audience, to attract and keep sponsors, and to keep up with any technological changes that affect production values. We propose a framework of seven factors, which, if observed during the creation and production of a television show in a small market, could lead to its success on air.

These factors are based on an analysis of elements which have contributed to the success of four long-running shows in Jamaica – *Schools'*

*Challenge Quiz*, *Profile*, *Hill an' Gully Ride* and *Entertainment Report*. They are: people, funding, technology, production, content, routine and relevance. Successful television shows involve using funding and technology to produce content that is relevant and routinely accessible by people.

## The People Factor

This deals with the human element of television production, as it is made by people for people. The process involves a range of individuals working in front of the camera as well as behind the scenes. A typical production will involve a team of individuals – non-technical and technical personnel. The term non-technical personnel describes those who function as executive producers, producers, directors, writers, assistants and talent; while technical personnel work as vision mixers or switchers, camera operators, lighting directors, technical directors, floor managers, audio technicians, character generator operators, video editors, props managers, or in wardrobe, make-up or scenery.[1] There are usually other people who, despite not being directly involved in production, play a supporting role in ensuring that the production gets made and seen. They have roles in merchandising, marketing and sales, distribution, promotions, and public relations. The number of people on your team will depend on the budget and the size and complexity of the production. Television studies authors such as Dan Weaver and Jason Siegel, in their 1998 work *Breaking into Television and Film: Proven Advice for Veterans and Interns*, listed key production roles for various types of television shows, demonstrating the wide range of individuals who can be involved. Gerald Millerson, in his *Video Production Handbook* published in 2004, has argued that "successful productions usually depend on teamwork: each member of the team contributing their individual expertise and experience".[2] The people factor is therefore an important one when it comes to creating television shows.

Another group to consider is the audience who would consume the programme. They comprise the market and may be geographically located in one area or across national boundaries. The four long-running shows featured in this book have succeeded because of their connection with people. The shows are all about people. There are the guests on the shows on

*Entertainment Report* and *Profile*, participants sharing in a game activity on *Schools' Challenge Quiz* or talking about themselves on *Hill an' Gully Ride*. These shows allow Jamaicans to see themselves – long understood to be the basis for the success of local programming. Brazilian and Latin American television scholar Joseph Straubhaar reminds us that "many local audiences would like to see programming in their own languages, addressing their own cultures".[3]

However, it is not just about seeing themselves in programmes in their own language, reflecting their own culture – it is also about seeing themselves in different ways. In other programmes, such as news and current affairs, which are usually sensational, Jamaicans see themselves in a mostly negative light. The long-running shows we have featured offer a balance between negative and positive, conveying Jamaicans in a mostly positive light. Each show in this group taps into elements of the real life of Jamaican people.

The people behind the scenes are integral to the genesis and continuation of the shows which have succeeded, because they have crew members who have remained committed to seeing the productions completed. There are also individuals who bring something extra to the programme. The four producers, Boyne, Gonzales, Miller and Robinson, have certain skills that they have honed over the years. During his time as host, Ian Boyne was a journalist who was well read and well connected and could ask intelligent questions. Michael Gonzales is a lawyer who understands the fair-play and integrity imperatives of an educational game show. Anthony Miller is a journalist who can write a good script about what some may think is a very superficial topic, entertainment. Carey Robinson is a historian who understands the context in which guests tell their stories.

Each show had a beginning which involved pressure from programme managers which they had to withstand in order to stay on air. The producers will attest to the fights in which they engaged.[4] It was not enough to just be good; one almost always had to do more. Everyone involved has had to go over and above the call of duty, including exploiting connections and being committed to overcoming any opposition faced within a difficult production environment.

Even though the producers we highlight are outstanding, the shows are not about them. They fight or work behind the scenes and they may appear in front of the camera but they are still not the stars. Although important personalities have been associated with them from time to time, the shows are ultimately about the people.

It is probably risky to do a show in Jamaica that is personality-based, where there is heavy reliance on the presenter to carry it. Audiences can hate the show because they hate the personality associated with it. One must focus on people and allow the host to play a supporting role, connecting with the people on the show. There is a distinction to be drawn between a show which is personality-driven and one where the host works to link the show.

Dennis Hall served as the *Schools' Challenge Quiz* quizmaster for over twenty years. After his death in 1994, the show continued with other personalities hosting. It has changed quizmasters and the show remained on air, indicating that the programme is about the schools and students, not the quizmasters. Anthony Miller, the initial host of *Entertainment Report*, was followed by Denise Hunt, who was the programme's first paid permanent host – a position she held for eight years. Miller occasionally had guest hosts. Regardless, the show remained on the air. For *Hill an' Gully Ride*, Carey Robinson has never shown his face. The camera focuses on the guests, who are the real stars of the show. This is the exemplar because there is no longer a visual host. For *Profile*, Ian Boyne's role was to engage in conversation and ask questions of the guest, who is the real star of the show.

Having said that, these four long-running shows have grown to be associated with particular individuals, and these individuals are intimately involved with the shows and have created systems that can and have worked despite all the limitations. Of course the programmes become so associated with these people that one wonders what will happen when they are not there. For the shows to continue without them proper succession planning must be in place, along with continued support from marketing and sales teams. Producers have managed to balance the sometimes competing interests of production activity and marketing opportunities. Care has to be taken to ensure that the essence of the programme is not compromised in the pursuit of marketing support. If not managed properly, marketing personnel can sometimes try to take over elements of the production, making decisions that are rightly the responsibility of the producers. Marketing personnel offer good support but they should not be allowed to take over the production. The four long-running shows have managed to balance the need for marketing support with the need to maintain good production values.

The takeaway here is that people are at the heart of every aspect of the production, from its conception to its marketing to its viewing. A producer needs to assemble a team of committed people who can make a production work for the people or audience who will appreciate seeing themselves reflected in the programme. The team should be led by a producer who is either well versed in the area of production or who is willing to learn about the business of television production and who understands the content of their show.

### Takeaways

- Ensure your production team is committed to the programme.
- Emphasize positive human elements that connect with the audience.
- Employ producers who understand their role in keeping the show on air.

### The Funding Factor

The funding factor relates to the financial or business aspect of the production. John Ellis, a British professor of media arts and former television producer, in reflecting on television production in 2004 indicated that "financing a production often determines its most intimate details." Ellis described the nature of television finance as being complex and outlined various funding models that have been used by television producers.[5] In a small market like Jamaica, when it comes to funding, one has to consider costs associated not only with production but also with marketing and distribution. Producing television shows is a highly creative endeavour but in order to create successful shows, producers must also understand the business of television. Funding television shows depends on a number of issues such as the size of the market and the complexity of the programme.

Generally, the complexity issue affects all producers. A half-hour talk show with a guest and host done in the studio is likely to cost less than a half-hour magazine with content created both on location and in studio. Within Jamaica, the small size of the market is a challenge. An audience from a population of over 2.8 million viewers pales in comparison to television markets elsewhere that could amount to a billion local viewers, not including international sales to overseas markets.

Given this context, there are two main funding models used in Jamaica for financing programmes broadcast on free-to-air stations. The first model involves producers buying airtime from a television station and then getting their own sponsors. These sponsors invariably get advertising in the show either through an actual advertisement shown during a break or in promos, or through product placement or endorsements of the sponsor's services or products. In this first model, the producers do all the work – finding funding, conceptualizing and producing the show and paying for airtime.

The second model involves a joint venture between the producer and television station. In this model, the marketing department of the station sells advertising space for the show. There could also be an arrangement where the producer is paid a flat fee for producing the show and given a percentage of the advertising revenue. The four long-running shows have employed both these funding models through negotiations with the broadcast entities.

But a third model is emerging in the Jamaican market. A corporate entity underwrites a branded show and is the key sponsor with their brand occupying a prominent space – for example, *Digicel Rising Stars*, *Tastee Talent Trail*, *Magnum Kings and Queens of the Dancehall*, *KFC on the Verge*, *Scotia Teller* and *NCB Capital Quest*.[6] Additional income can be earned from texting to vote for aspects of some shows that allow for this kind of audience involvement.

One must consider a range of costs when seeking to produce a show. The actual budget can vary greatly and it is often difficult to provide specific figures. A typical budget would include costs for pre-production, production, post-production and promotion. Pre-production costs include personnel, script, equipment and facilities. Production costs would cover personnel, equipment and facilities, talent, art (set, make-up, music) and transportation. Post-production includes graphics, effects, personnel and facilities. Additionally there would be costs for insurance, miscellaneous expenses and taxes. Promotional activity would involve its own set of costs which could be borne either by the producer or by the station airing the programme.

Some producers are able to give a per-programme cost for their show or a cost for the entire series, which usually includes several episodes. In some cases, contra-deals are struck between sponsor and station, making it even more difficult to isolate the real cost of the show. Some final costings do not involve overheads as these are absorbed by either the production or broadcast entity. Within some shows, all the real costs may not be counted as a producer or production team members can fulfil many roles, but may only be paid for one. If this multi-tasker were to be replaced, the production might need to engage more than one person to complete the same set of tasks. It may seem like a saving to have a do-it-all producer or to have team members doubling up. However, if the do-it-all team member disappears, the show's continuity may be compromised if there is no budget for the real costs associated with the personnel for those tasks. For *Entertainment Report*, the producer has played multiple roles by also writing, presenting and reporting – all for the same episode of the show. On *Hill an' Gully Ride*, the sound and video operator sometimes takes on the role of driver.

In addition to ignoring hidden costs associated with multitaskers, another area often underbudgeted is marketing and promotion. Apart from a programme schedule that may announce a show's airtime and the occasional promotions run by the broadcast house, and on even fewer occasions merchandising – a t-shirt and cap here, or a branded item there – there usually is not much other promotional activity surrounding shows. Some producers or broadcasters offer copies of programmes for sale in branded packaging. TVJ, the station that airs *Schools' Challenge Quiz, Profile* and *Entertainment Report*, sells DVD copies of episodes on demand, and copies of *Hill an' Gully Ride* can be bought from the organization that produces it, CPTC.

Production and broadcast entities continue to search for creative ways to earn income from their shows. Programmes have been packaged for retransmission on cable channels locally and abroad in the effort. In recent times, there have been attempts to monetize televised content via the Internet using online platforms. Current episodes of *Schools' Challenge Quiz*, *Profile* and *Entertainment Report* can be seen free online by local viewers, or at a cost by overseas viewers, using an app called 1Spotmedia. Archived episodes are available at a premium cost. They are also promoted on social media and the web pages of the broadcaster. The advent of online advertising has increased the earning potential of shows but this also incurs costs for regular and efficient management. Rebecca Rowell has described, for example, how a platform like YouTube has expanded its partner programme to include producers who generate video content as well as commercial broadcasters. These partners realize their income-generating potential by earning money from advertising on the platform.[7] In Jamaica, critics have argued in the past that online content from national broadcast stations is not always uploaded in a timely manner – sometimes there is a two-week delay to seeing content already aired. With apps that now charge for such content, paying viewers are likely to expect and appreciate content uploaded within a reasonable time after its first broadcast.

Jamaican television managers will tell you that it is always cheaper to buy an overseas programme than a locally produced show. The overseas programme guarantees a profit when local advertising sales are made in what usually is a fairly good product capable of attracting an audience.[8] Not so with the local show which invariably has high production costs to recover, thus increasing the value of the show and decreasing the possible profit margin. In this situation, television stations in Jamaica cannot afford to make money from advertising alone so they also sell airtime to producers willing to pay for it or they make a deal. The four long-running shows made it on air initially because they were good ideas that were supported – financially and otherwise – by the broadcast entity while in their infancy. Eventually deals were made to ensure they remained on air. What is clear from this is that a producer's ability to negotiate a good financial deal with a broadcaster – with careful attention to issues such as ownership and budgeting – is key to sustaining a television programme on air in Jamaica.

## Takeaways

- Budget completely by including all associated costs.
- Understand the various aspects of the television business.
- Find creative ways to earn from the productions.

## The Technology Factor

Technology has been conceptualized as the physical or intellectual tools that extend the individual's capacity to relate to their environment.[9] Technology is particularly important in limited resource environments – a characteristic of the Jamaican television industry.

Television is technology driven. It is used at all stages in the production and consumption of television content – from conceptualization, production, editing to transmission, distribution and consumption. Examples of technology used in television include tools that support the writing of scripts, such as typewriters, word processing hardware and software; equipment that captures images and sounds such as cameras; audio devices, lighting, editing systems, recording media and hardware; transmission technology such as microwave links, towers, and outside broadcast units; television receiving devices such as television sets, computers, phones and game consoles; and consumer recording units. Technology continues to evolve and this has implications for television programmes and production. Millerson underscores the importance of technology in television production and has noted that while people may not know the inner workings of specific pieces of television equipment, they should know what can be achieved with such equipment.[10]

In the early years of Jamaican television, equipment was very costly to acquire and maintain which at times could affect the technical quality of the programmes created. However, access to this type of technology expanded creative production possibilities. Though *Schools' Challenge Quiz* struggled in its first year with video, which was very susceptible to humidity, it was this technology that allowed some episodes to be recorded on location around the island. In the 1980s, video continued to be used in television production in Jamaica. However, it was now of higher quality and was smaller and more portable with the half-inch U-matic tapes and then later quarter-inch Betacam and Digibeta systems. U-matic three-quarter-inch video cassettes, and Betacam, a half-inch professional videotape cassette system developed by Sony, recorded at higher speeds and higher quality. Digital Beta, also known as Digibeta and introduced as an alternative to the analogue beta, was available in Jamaica but was not in wide use.

This is the technological context in which *Profile, Entertainment Report* and *Hill an' Gully Ride* were created. The improved portable equipment meant going on location with an operator carrying a camera on shoulder, with a cable connected to a large recording machine on a strap over the shoulder of an assistant, requiring them both to move in unison and negotiate terrain to gather shots. This was a typical experience for the crew on *Hill an' Gully Ride*. Producers would benefit from the arrival of the camcorder and Betacam systems that were smaller and even more easy to use. Camera operators for *Entertainment Report* were now able to experiment with creative shots and angles. *Profile*, being shot in studio, would have benefited from any advances in cameras, studio facilities, master control and recording systems.

Developments in videotape technology influenced editing. *Schools' Challenge Quiz* began using open-reel videotape, which was difficult to edit precisely. Editing was done in a linear manner as shots were arranged one after the other in the order that they would be seen. This was a time-consuming process. The advent of compact video-cassette systems which were more robust meant that editing could be faster and more precise, allowing for more complex assembly of material. This development contributed to the fast-paced editing style that would become characteristic of *Entertainment Report*.

Up to this point, television production systems were still analogue. With the development in digital technology, superior quality equipment got smaller and more affordable in Jamaica. Digital technology led to a fuller integration of computers in production. Processes were now non-linear so one could work anywhere in a project; non-destructive, in that original footage remained intact; and lossless, where material could be copied without any reduction in quality. A number of special effects procedures, which previously had to be subcontracted or done on special equipment, could now be handled more efficiently. As Millerson has indicated, digital technology has transformed television programme making – not only in terms of improved quality of sound and picture but also in terms of the additional efficient production processes that were now becoming possible.[11]

Not to be left out are the audiences who continue to use technological developments to access and interact with television content. The television set had been the main piece of technology that allowed audiences to view content, usually in one location. Advances in that hardware have resulted in smaller and more portable television sets. There have also been increases in the platforms on which television broadcasts can be viewed including mobile telephones, game consoles, computers, tablets and outdoor electronic display boards. Alongside these, there are what could be called supporting technologies that have helped the viewer to engage with television in different ways. These include devices and media for recording such as video home systems or VHS, digital video discs or DVDs, digital video recorders, Blu-ray, computers and smart devices that allow the viewer to capture content and view at a later date. There have also been developments that allow for downloading and streaming once the content is made available online for access either officially or unofficially.

Though broadcasters still provide scheduled programming, viewers have been able to use technology to access content outside of the predetermined schedule. This has been labelled time shifting. At another level, the technological development has continued to facilitate interaction. The television set on its own has been criticized as a one-way form of communication. Now supporting technologies allow viewers to participate in programmes. In the early days, postal and telephone systems allowed audiences not only to contact their shows with feedback, but also to participate in programmes. With email, texting and social media, audiences have been allowed to interact more immediately with their programmes through second screening – using the screen of a smart device to interact with other viewers and producers while watching content on another screen. With these technologies, audiences have the power to decide how and when they watch broadcast content. Producers need to recognize this and use it to their advantage.

*Schools' Challenge Quiz* has used cell phone technology to enhance viewer interactivity for the show. Audiences are invited to text answers to a viewers' question posed during the show for prizes. *Hill an' Gully Ride* has been made available on DVD to viewers at a cost. *Entertainment Report* and *Profile* can be viewed online using the broadcaster's app 1Spotmedia, which allows access to both free and premium content. This means viewers can watch the show outside of its regular broadcast time. Social-media networks have allowed for online discussions about these four shows, at times led by the viewers and not the producers.

The latest equipment does not necessarily result in a better show. The technology will only go so far. But producers still need to understand the medium of television and how the technology can extend their ability to create a product appropriate not only for the visual medium, but also for viewers who have more control over how they access content. With the rapid changes in technology, one always has to make choices regarding what type of equipment to acquire and when. This is important because producers could invest heavily in the wrong equipment. The four shows have been produced across different technological eras. This suggests that they have managed to survive the challenges of those periods and so they should be able to adjust and keep up with technology as it changes in the future.

## Takeaways

- Know your technology and what it can do for your production.
- Use technology as a tool in support of an already well-conceived production with a good concept.
- Understand how technological advances will affect how your audience accesses and views your show.

## The Production Factor

The production factor affects all that is involved in making a programme idea into a final product. A television show starts with an idea, but it is the production process that brings this to fruition. It requires efficiently dealing with available resources by carefully planning the three main phases, pre-production, production and post-production. John Ellis has identified up to five stages of production in television: finance, pre-production,

production, post-production and marketing.[12] More importantly, Ellis's work reinforces the idea that the production component is an important factor in creating a television programme. In this work, we incorporate his finance and marketing stages into the pre-production and post-production phases respectively, which aligns with Millerson's support for the notion of three phases.[13]

During the pre-production stage, decisions are usually made regarding the financing of the entire production process as well as securing guests, crew, equipment, facilities and transportation. This is also when any necessary research is done and scheduling determined for the entire production. Depending on its style and genre, some shows may require a full script at this stage, or merely a partial script, while others may prepare one during shooting or after, for narration. Usually designs for lighting and set are done in pre-production. Theme music may already be established for the series but any additional music or sound design may be planned at this stage. Decisions about location or set, wardrobe, make-up, contributors, actors and hospitality, if needed, are also made and logistics surrounding these are confirmed.

Production begins with setting up in studio or on location, dressing the set, and establishing the lighting, make-up and wardrobe needs. When that is done, video and sound are captured. During the production, the producer may acquire content such as images and sound to help in completing any preliminary scripting. In order to do this successfully programme makers need to plan not only what is to be acquired but also how it will be used in production.

Based on their formats, *Hill an' Gully Ride* and *Entertainment Report* would need to acquire sufficient footage to build their visual stories and appropriate cutaways to enrich specific moments in the show, such as on-location interviews. *Profile* is different as it is a studio interview with few cutaways, and it is therefore up to the director to create visual interest by switching between shots. The onus is on the host to engage the guest to elicit the most interesting stories for the audience's visual imagination. *Schools' Challenge Quiz* is formulaic. The audience knows what it will see – team members and a quizmaster, but the real visual appeal in this show is the reaction of the team members to answering correctly or incorrectly –

that look of victory on the faces of the winning team and the look of defeat on those of the losing teams.

Post-production involves logging, editing, audio mixing, special effects, graphics, quality control, dubbing, uploading and preparing for online and other distribution, repackaging, and marketing promotions. In this phase, the amount of work is dependent on the type of production and the success of the production phase. It is always important to remember that there are three stages and producers should pay attention to all of them, even if the type of programme may suggest that more effort is needed in one. *Profile* and *Schools' Challenge Quiz* are done in a studio, recorded as live, so editing is likely to be minimal "topping and tailing" which is adding the opening montage and credits, end credits and possibly commercial breaks.

Pre-production and production phases were the most demanding for *Schools' Challenge Quiz* when it was live, as it all depended on properly planning production and execution to ensure it would go out without any glitches. *Hill an' Gully Ride* is demanding in all phases because it is reality based. Everything has to be captured as it happens and the producer must know what the story is. It is also heavy on post-production. *Entertainment Report* is also demanding in all phases. It relies on a lot of shots to make the programme what it is.[14] It involves capturing events live. This requires a strong production team who can see the story and capture it as it is happening, and also be able to interpret and package it for an audience.

An important element of post-production is ensuring that the programme is viewed before the show is aired. Here any egregious aspect of the show should be revised. Potentially slanderous content should be identified and addressed in these review sessions. After the show has aired, it is also useful to do an editorial and technical review in which the work is evaluated with a view to improving subsequent episodes.

### Takeaways

- Create an efficient system that works for the specific production.
- Invest time and effort in each phase of production.
- Conduct regular reviews after transmission or release.

## The Content Factor

The content broadcast during television programmes has been a central concern for those associated with television – from policymakers and programme managers to viewers.[15] Various Jamaican researchers, such as Salmon, White and Gordon, have given consideration to what it means to create more local television content as opposed to foreign content, in a market like Jamaica.[16] With more opportunities to create and distribute such local content, the discussion must advance to what type of content should be produced. As with the people factor, the content factor partly relates to the human-interest element of the show. The content should relate to, describe or portray the experiences or emotions of individuals and should also be balanced. There might be content that audiences can connect to at the human-interest level, but one should go further to focus on the essence of the story that would be familiar to the intended audience. A programme might have general human appeal but above that there is the specific cultural appeal that only the intended audience would understand and appreciate. While making that connection, one must be careful not to reinforce stereotypes but instead aim for a balanced portrayal of the content or story being told.

The four shows have remained on air because they tell stories about Jamaican people that have high human-interest value. Successful television shows are about effective storytelling. There are self-contained stories, completed within a single episode. There are stories that continue with follow-up in subsequent episodes, where the content is sometimes almost episodic, so viewers can follow a story until it reaches its denouement.

During *Entertainment Report*, the story is about the drama of celebrity, music, lifestyle and popular culture. It uses television storytelling – quality shots and sharp editing of specific creative camera angles and movement. The shooting style is edgy but competent and suits the style of the show, as do other elements such as the quality of sound bites and music featured. In addition to the visual storytelling, there is also a well-written script with literary elements that complement the visual. This includes well-chosen words, a bit of irony, double entendre, a particular matter-of-fact intonation in the narration – usually done by Anthony Miller and occasionally done by others under his supervision.

For *Hill an' Gully Ride*, the story is about the history of Jamaica and its people. The show allows guests to tell their story. Carey Robinson asks questions and the guests respond with their stories about people, history, events, and community. The fact that we do not see him puts the focus on the interviewees. Some might think that an unseen interviewer is indicative of poor production. However, audiences have grown to accept it and understand that it is about the story being told. *Hill an' Gully Ride* is also about the "ride" or the journey of the story, which is sometimes augmented by a written voice-over narration.

On *Profile*, guests tell their stories about overcoming struggles to be successful. The story is a familiar one but guests have idiosyncratic ways of telling the stories of their journeys on the road to success. Boyne in his role as host guides this story and draws out those elements that he knows will satisfy the curiosity of the audience. On *Schools' Challenge Quiz*, there is a story of quiz team members competing to be victorious. Each match is a story of a game being played. Though the audience knows the structure of the game, there is always the element of suspense and drama in finding out who will win. It is the ultimate story of victory and defeat. Again, these shows remain on air because they convey content that is appealing to an audience. It is all about a simple story – ranging from life in entertainment to living in Jamaica, and making it successful on a quiz show or in the game of life.

## Takeaways

- Employ the language of television in creating your content.
- Show the story you are telling for television.
- Highlight not only the human experience but also the cultural specifics in your content.

## The Relevance Factor

This is related to the content factor, but it goes further to focus on how a programme is adapted to its context and culture so that it is accessible to audiences. Patrick Barwise and Andrew Ehrenberg in their 1988 publication *Television and Its Audience* have argued that along with scheduling a programme on a particular channel at a particular time of day, it is the appropriateness of the content that determines how many people actually watch.[17] Chalaby, in discussing the production of international television formats for national audiences, illustrates how such formats can be adapted and made "locally relevant" thus ensuring a successful show.[18] Ellis has also argued that the need to adapt successful formats for local conditions have long been a crucial aspect of any television industry.[19] The television programme must therefore be relevant for its audiences; also, it must be relevant for the set of skills of the team who will produce it and for the resources available for its production. It makes no sense trying to do a multi-camera scripted drama production when all that is available is a single camera and no scriptwriter. When Hope Stewart started *Schools' Challenge Quiz*, though it was based on *University Challenge* which had competitors from tertiary-level institutions, she must have recognized that the show could not be created in Jamaica with universities because the country did not have enough universities to sustain such a competition. The compromise, therefore, was a quiz show for high school students. Stewart adapted the concept to the Jamaican context.

*Profile* appeals to Jamaicans because it is reminiscent of one of Jamaicans' favourite pastimes – sitting on a veranda to talk and inquire about other people's business. Boyne has taken this aspect of Jamaican culture and elevated it to a show and he has done it in a tactful way as he asks the questions that give the answers to feed viewer curiosity. In a similar way, *Hill an' Gully Ride* also feeds our curiosity about other people's business. But it goes further, tapping into that cultural practice in Jamaica of "going to country". Almost every Jamaican living in an urban area can trace their family lineage back to a rural past. Many have taken the road trip through hilly interiors and valleys to reconnect with that part of their family. Jamaicans always look forward to a trip away from home and therefore would naturally appreciate trips across Jamaica with *Hill an' Gully Ride*.

*Schools' Challenge Quiz* feeds an audience's desire to judge schools based on their performance in the quiz competition. The show remains relevant for Jamaicans who value education and the ambitious drive to acquire knowledge to be better. *Entertainment Report* is relevant to Jamaica as it understands the music industry here and the way it reflects our class structure. The programme allows viewers to see the ways in which different groups of Jamaicans entertain themselves.

On the production side, these producers have managed to create shows in a feasible manner given the limited resources available. Contra-deals are negotiated to cover costs related to production where, for example, instead of a cash payment a company will barter a service or product in exchange for advertising or on air acknowledgement. In some situations, instead of paying accommodation for a television crew, a deal is made between the hotel and the production entity where, for example, advertising is exchanged for rooms.

Though aired Monday to Friday during its season, *Schools' Challenge Quiz* is pre-recorded on a single day to reduce the costs of having to mount the set and manage arrangements for accommodating schools. The set is mounted once a week and six shows are created making the best use of the studio space and crew. This approach is relevant given the limited resources. With challenges to the judges' decisions and scores, the producers have adapted by establishing strict rules to respond to and manage this situation that had the potential to compromise the integrity of the show. There is no documented report of a cheating scandal on the show since its time on television.

*Entertainment Report's* budget does not always cover being able to stay the entire duration of a stage show that goes from after midnight to sunrise. As such the producers have adapted to this situation by a reliance on the willingness of crew members to work beyond the end of their shifts to be able to get the full story. Crew members understand the nature of entertainment and recognize that work will extend beyond regular work hours. Naturally, schedules associated with this programme are extremely flexible to accommodate the vagaries of the entertainment business. It takes a dedicated crew to report to work for a 10:00 p.m. call to capture footage of an artiste scheduled for a midnight appearance who does not take the stage until 6:00 a.m. Returning without the footage because of the late appearance is not an acceptable excuse in this business of reporting on entertainment.

Production for *Hill an' Gully Ride* is done on a set day. The trip out of town is done in a single day because there is no budget to pay for overnight accommodation. This means the production is feasibly created within the limited resources. The crew is efficiently managed as individuals multitask. Sometimes, the soundperson doubles as the driver to the location. *Profile* was never able to maintain producing features on the guests and so the producers have had to make the show work with just the interview in studio. The emphasis on making the guest tell stories without the need for cutaways has helped the show.

In all these situations, the producers have had to find creative ways to make their shows work and adapt to the limited production resources and the unpredictable conditions of the television business and life in general. As seen, compromises are made based on circumstances, and decisions result in a final product that remains relevant to its cultural context.

## Takeaways

- Adapt your concept to your context.
- Make the best use of available resources.
- Adjust production elements to meet quality expectations.

## The Routine Factor

Routine is a regular pattern of actions completed in a particular time. In the context of television, there is a production routine, there is a broadcasting routine, there is the routine in the show itself and there is the audience's viewing routine. Successful routine is based on time management and it is worth exploring how the four shows have coped. Producing a regular television show presents an opportunity to establish a system or routine for meeting broadcast schedules. Ellis has termed this the "routinization" of television which offers advantages such as efficiencies in the production process.[20]

In terms of a production routine, all the shows have established schedules for producing each episode. *Schools' Challenge Quiz* is seasonal and during its season, the week's games are pre-recorded on a single day. This allows time for minimal editing to complete the show for airing throughout the week. *Profile* is pre-recorded as live-to-tape on a single day with time to do minimal editing for broadcast on the following weekend. Millerson defines "live to tape" thus: "The show is recorded as if it were live using the production switcher to intercut between picture sources. The resulting live-on-tape version requires little to no further editing and is ready for transmission. A technical advantage of this method is that the entire show is an original first generation recording, without the deterioration in picture quality that subsequent editing can introduce."[21]

For *Entertainment Report*, shooting is completed over one or two days, followed by logging then scripting. Links are recorded and editing happens over the course of the week with more attention being given to this area in the two days leading up to broadcast. As the show aims to be current, the content aired on Friday is usually gathered during the same week of broadcast. *Hill an' Gully Ride* has a particular day for shooting, two to three days are reserved for editing and a day for scripting and voicing. This routine ensures the show is ready for broadcast on Sunday.

Being live or pre-recorded affects the show's production routine. *Schools' Challenge Quiz* was live for about two decades of its early existence, but later it became a pre-recorded production. When a show is live, the routine is affected as more emphasis is placed on the pre- and production phases. Once it is live on air the pressure increases, but when the show is done, most of the work is over. With pre-recorded shows, there is the opportunity to work up until the eleventh hour to meet broadcast deadlines.

In terms of a broadcast routine, these four shows have been established in certain time slots. The time at which a show is scheduled for broadcast can have an impact on its popularity. The time slot can make or break a show. Assigning the right time slot is important, but even more important is keeping that time slot, making it easy for audiences to establish a routine in watching the show. This supports the notion of appointment television or the idea that audiences make themselves available to watch a show at a particular time. These four shows benefited in the past from this audience behaviour, though this is slowly changing as content can be accessed at any time on different platforms. Programmes have died because they were put in wrong slots and moved around without much notice. Some shows grow into their slots and have made the slot a prime one because of what it has become – a successful show with a guaranteed audience.

*Entertainment Report* has always enjoyed a Friday evening slot. It is the perfect time for partygoers to see the latest news in entertainment before they go out for their own recreation later that night or over the weekend. *Hill an' Gully Ride* and *Profile* have been established as Sunday afternoon television. *Schools' Challenge Quiz* is now established as a weekday show in the slot leading up to the main newscast of its broadcast station. They were not always in these time slots but in more recent times, this is where they have become established. Any change from these times would require extensive promotion and possible justification from station management.

There is also a routine in the shows themselves that is exemplified in their formats. It is a routine that the audiences know. The shows have identifiable sections. *Schools' Challenge Quiz* has three sections and there are about three commercial breaks. *Entertainment Report* involves a first segment with one or a number of stories covered in different treatments, followed by the top ten and then a final story. The music video was a regular feature but not anymore. *Hill An' Gully Ride* has about three segments interrupted by commercials. The segments build through the show as a story is being told. *Profile* has a similar structure with about three advertising slots breaking the interview sequence.

All these shows are thirty minutes long now, but they all did not start like this. *Entertainment Report* and *Hill an' Gully Ride*, for example, began as short features in other programmes. Over time, based on their potential for growth, they were expanded to thirty minutes. By exploring shorter formats that could expand into longer versions, over time the shows have been able to develop a following and interest from an audience. It is risky to start a long show and not be able to maintain the content demands of its length. *Schools' Challenge Quiz* and *Profile* started as thirty minutes, but they had to prove that the show could work within that timeframe. Here we note that a show can start out with a particular timeframe and work, or it can start as a shorter product that can only expand later if proven to be successful with viewers. The four shows have remained on air because they have managed to create routines that facilitate the ongoing production of each episode.

A few words should be said about "seasons" as they relate to the timing and routine of local productions. The word "season" in television is used interchangeably with series and describes a period of programming – for example, thirteen weeks with thirteen episodes.[22] It can be more or less than thirteen, and some seasons can be split into smaller units. The length of the season is usually determined by a number of factors including time and resources available for creating the shows within the seasons, as well as the available space on the broadcast programme schedule and audience viewing habits.

Media studies specialist Landon Palmer has suggested that the season is considered a contractual term which guarantees an audience watching a programme for a set period of time, assuming those audiences are committed to the show.[23] A season in television was largely a trade term used to describe a show's longevity, the order of the episodes and to denote the terms for green-lighting and contracting the production team and talent.[24] It became an evaluative term as some shows were given a season to establish their popularity and if they did well, then subsequent seasons could be produced. Seasons underscore the routine and ritual of television. The season can help to determine the development of the story line of a show. Imagine a season finale where the plot line develops into a cliff-hanger and leaves viewers wanting more, thus making them look forward to the next season. Of all the four shows, *Schools' Challenge Quiz* is considered a seasonal television show aired in the first quarter of the year from January to March. *Entertainment Report, Profile* and *Hill an' Gully Ride* appear all year round and are not considered to be seasonal.

Seasons are also related to weather patterns. George Barnett et al., in describing seasonality in television viewing, have argued that many new television seasons premiere in the fall season in the United States because this is the time when it starts getting colder and audiences return inside to watch television after being outside in the summer months.[25] This conceptualization of seasons does not readily apply to Jamaica because the country does not experience distinct weather patterns such as fall, winter, spring and summer. Seasons, if used at all in Jamaica, are not bound to the calendar year or weather patterns, but recently the term is being increasingly used by more producers to describe a set of programmes that can be aired over a period with no established time for the start.

## Takeaways

- Understand the routine of your show.
- Maintain production routines to achieve outcomes efficiently.
- Create an established time for releasing your show on various platforms.

## Conclusion

The seven factors presented in this chapter offer a framework for creating a successful television programme in a small media market like Jamaica. Considering these seven factors – people, funding, technology, production, content, relevance and routine – can help producers create better shows. Television programmes can be successful if they utilize available technology and funding in creative ways to produce televisual material that is relevant and routinely accessible by viewers.

---

### Checklist of Questions for the Television Producer

*People*
- Who will be working on the production and what will they bring to the process?
- How will the show resonate with the audience?

*Funding*
- Do you have a funding model to meet the resource demands of the programme?
- Have you ensured that there are no hidden costs not accounted for in your budget?

*Technology*
- How will technology support your production?
- How will technology influence the access to and the viewing of your show?

*Production*
- Have you created a system for each phase of production?
- Is there a mechanism in place for regular review of the production?

*Content*
- What is the story you hope to show in your programme?
- Is your content created in a visually appealing way that follows the language of television?

*Relevance*
- Do you have a plan for the feasible and efficient use of available resources?
- Is the show suited to your audience and its cultural background?

*Routine*
- Is there a defined format and structure for the programme?
- Will the programme be aired at a regularly scheduled time when there is an audience for it?

# 8

# Coming Up
## Shows Watched and Ones to Watch

Some indigenous television shows have been more successfully produced and sustained on air than others. Now we reflect on some of these in different genres and consider the relationship between genre and sustainability in Jamaica. There is no guarantee that producing a show in a particular genre will lead to success but, arguably, some have been attempted more often than others here.

A search of programme schedules in Jamaican print media yielded a list of 314 local television shows produced and aired at various times between 1963 and 2015. Based on information discovered through interviews and desk reviews, these shows were sorted and categorized using established genres found in the literature on television studies. They fell within the following fourteen genres: animation (one), children's (twenty-one), current and public affairs (forty-nine), drama (twenty-five), entertainment (forty-eight), factual (fifty-two), magazine (thirteen), quiz and game show (twenty-one), reality (twenty-two), religion (fourteen), social advocacy (three), sports (twelve), talk show (twenty-nine) and other (four). A complete listing can be seen in appendix 4.

The history of Jamaican television programmes reveals movement from a single public broadcaster to a commercial model. The four long-running shows in our study started under the public broadcasting model and continued under a commercial model. There are various factors that allowed for their longevity, including an attention to the people involved, funding, technology, production, content, relevance and routine. While these four exemplify requirements for producing television in small media markets, it would be remiss not to mention the many others that are present in the local sector. These other shows may not have run as long, but they arguably can demonstrate what has been achieved in Jamaican television. The intent here is to provide information on a range of local television shows in the fourteen genres identified that have been or are still being aired. For each genre, we highlight one or two shows of note, and discuss how aspects of the seven factors – people, funding, technology, production, content, relevance and routine – have helped in their production.

## Animation

Local animated television content in Jamaica first appeared in advertisements and music videos. Some examples of animated advertising between the mid-1980s and the early-1990s are commercials for food products such as Quench Aid and Grace Vienna Sausages, and the insect spray Shelltox. It is not surprising that animation started appearing in the mid-1980s, because shortly before that, African American producers Floyd Norman and Leo Sullivan travelled to Jamaica with a business plan focused on establishing an animation studio in Kingston. Though the studio never came to life, Norman and Sullivan taught animation classes at the University of the West Indies while producing commercials for the growing Caribbean animation market.[1] In addition to animation for advertisement and entertainment, it was also introduced to Jamaica for development purposes.

In 1991, a collaboration involving the United Nations Children's Fund, Walt Disney Studios, JIS and the Caribbean School of Media and Communication at the University of the West Indies established the project "Film Animation for Development Jamaica". This effort aimed to promote cartoons as a tool for addressing social issues by training individuals from the English-speaking Caribbean in the basics of film animation. The workshops held at the university resulted in the creation of "Johnny Sad Boy", a forty-eight-second cartoon released in 1993 which addressed child abuse.[2]

Adrian Lopez of Digital Liquid Light Studio has been credited with being the first Jamaican to introduce 3D animation in commercials and music videos to local television after beginning his animation work professionally in 1994 and winning a first prize award in the 2002 Animae Caribe Animation Festival in Trinidad.³ Since 2011, other contributions to the development of animation in Jamaica involved a Toon Boom/World Bank/Jamaica Promotions Corporation initiative to train cartoonists who could be employed by studios outsourcing animation jobs. The staging of various animation festivals, the establishment of animation studios such as Alcyone in 2010, SkyRes in 2011 and Reel Rock GSW Animation in 2012, and the incorporation of the Jamaica Animation Nation Network by July 2013, augur well for the future of animation content in Jamaica. Alongside these formations, independent and mostly self-trained animators have generated short-form content for music videos, and for depicting social commentary, satire and comedy which is shared on social-media platforms such as YouTube.

Perhaps the most committed effort to an animated television show in Jamaica was by Alcyone Animations Productions. In 2010, that studio, with writer Alison Latchman, her husband and business partner, animator Aneiph Latchman and illustrator Marlo Scott, created *Cabbie Chronicles*. This animated comedy features a cab driver, Delphos "Delly" McDuffus, who traverses the intricacies of modern Jamaican life. Viewers first saw three- to five-minute versions on the show's website cabbiechronicles.com, and also on a YouTube channel called *Cabbie Chronicles*.

The first episode "Drive thru Drama" won the D.E.W. (Dunstan E. Williams) Best Caribbean Animation Award at the Animae Caribe Animation and New Media Festival Show in Port of Spain, Trinidad in November 2010. Since then the series has received other awards and was made available on Flow's VOD service between February and August 2011. Flow is a telecommunications and subscription television provider in Jamaica. In 2012, it aired on TVJ and then on CIN TV – free-to-air and cable television. It is also available on the website and YouTube channel as well as on the social-media platforms Facebook and Instagram.

The initial realization of *Cabbie Chronicles* exemplifies aspects of the seven factors that help to determine successful television in small markets. A committed team of individuals produces the show with expertise in their respective areas. In addition to Alison, Aneiph and Marlo, Noel Reid, Alison's cousin, voices 'Delly', the main character. Many of the other voices were created by Anya Gloudon-Nelson, and Cleo Walker, Mario Hackett and Valton Craigie also performed several characters. Richard Sven Patterson worked on music and sound recordings. Dianne Wan was the lead animator. Herman Webley was the executive producer. In terms of technology, *Cabbie Chronicles* has applied the available technology appropriately to the cartoon's distribution. Not only have they used VOD on cable, they have also broadcast the cartoon on a terrestrial channel while also maintaining a presence on a range of online platforms, thus ensuring audiences can easily access their content. The show maintains its relevance by creating episodes around events of national interest, such as Jamaica's fiftieth year of independence, the increase in the mosquito population and the Christmas holiday season. Despite these positive developments, limited funding support and the time consuming nature of animation continue to affect the sustenance of the production and the routine of releasing content at regular intervals.

For now, short-form content and episodic series seem to be the most feasible local output option for Jamaica's animation studios. Though animation may be the genre with the lowest number of productions when compared to others we have listed, it is probably the one with the potential for the greatest growth. Given the events which have occurred since the start of the twenty-first century in Jamaica, this genre seems poised for continued development. With the various training programmes available, digital technology and platforms for distribution, it is likely that animators will create more content here for local and international audiences.

## Children's

Children's programming has appeared consistently on local television since its beginning in 1963. There have been twenty-one such shows spanning all the decades. Of these shows, *Ring Ding* was the most popular among Jamaican children. The fact that CPTC later in 2006 revived the format of the original show with a production called *Ring Ding Again* hosted by Marjorie Whylie and Amina Blackwood Meeks underscores its popularity.

Jamaica's television audiences will remember *Ring Ding*, which aired on JBC on Saturdays for twelve years beginning on Saturday, 19 September 1970. Bari Johnson, one of the show's producers, had initially approached

Leonie Forbes to host the show. Forbes suggested Jamaican folklorist Louise Bennett, also known as Miss Lou, to be the host. During the first meeting with Bennett at her Gordon Town residence to discuss the concept, Forbes and Johnson recalled that it was Bennett's passionate reaction to the idea that led to the show's name. Having heard the idea, using her way with words, Miss Lou said, "Oh, you mean like a Ring Ding."[4] And appropriately so, because the show would incorporate ring games for children.

The show's first airing was quite by chance. According to the producers, the usual foreign cartoons aired during weekday evenings were somehow misplaced and at the last minute, the *Ring Ding* pilot programme was used as a filler.[5] Notes from the Louise Bennett collection at Jamaica's National Library indicate that the first two showings were on Friday 28 August and Monday 31 August 1970. Forbes remembers an overwhelming reaction from viewers as JBC's switchboard was jammed with calls.[6] When television expanded its weekend broadcast to include morning transmission beginning at 9:00, the station's general manager eventually allowed *Ring Ding* to be presented on Saturday mornings as an introduction to *Sesame Street* which also began airing in September 1970. The schedule for 19 September 1970 included *Ring Ding* from 9:00 a.m. to 9:10 a.m., followed by *Sesame Street* from 9:10 a.m. to 10:10 a.m.; more *Ring Ding* from 10:10 a.m. to 11:00 a.m. and then another *Sesame Street* until 12 noon. Later in the 1970s it aired at 3:20 p.m. and then moved up to the 4:00 p.m. slot, the 5:00 p.m. slot and sometimes the 1:00 p.m. slot on Saturdays. The format evolved from its beginnings as enhanced continuity for *Sesame Street* and became a concert featuring children performing. A typical *Ring Ding* started thus:

> **Miss Lou**: Ring Ding!
> **Children**: Ring Ding!
> **Miss Lou**: Concert time!
> *Miss Lou and children sing as Marjorie Whylie accompanies them on piano:*
>
> There's a concert here for you and me, there's a concert here today
> There's a concert here for all o' we, there's a concert here today
> Get you ready, there's a concert here today
> Come along, there's a concert here today
> So take your seat and pose your best
> There's a concert here today. Pom! Pom!

## COMING UP: SHOWS WATCHED AND ONES TO WATCH

The children would settle as Miss Lou began telling stories and posing riddles. Miss Lou asks, "Riddle me this, riddle me that. Guess me this riddle and perhaps not. Sweet water stand up . . ." The children looking puzzled, mumble "Sweet water stand up? Sweet water stand up?" A child jumps up and answers, "Sugar cane!"

*Ring Ding* showcased young Jamaicans performing and participating in activities led by host Louise Bennett before a studio audience of children. Its success was due in part to the widespread appeal of its content to Jamaican children, their family members, friends and teachers. It survived for twelve years because of the dedication of host Louise Bennett and musician Marjorie Whylie supported by willing children who showed up on a Saturday morning eager to perform.

Funding was limited and the host complained about JBC's lack of support. The show made it on air through creativity, and the dedicated team of producers and host would use personal connections to secure sponsors such as those who provided refreshments for the children. Producers recalled Miss Lou's determination which kept the show alive, recounting how at times, in the early years, she would personally bring children from her community in Gordon Town to help make up audience numbers.

Utilizing available technology, *Ring Ding* was pre-recorded and sometimes went out live from studio with the occasional pre-recorded insert. Video recording technology enhanced the show's production but, unfortunately, most of the content was erased as tapes were recycled. This content was truly Jamaican and aimed to entertain and educate viewers using folk songs and ring games. Viewers were also exposed to non-Jamaican content when the culture of other countries was featured. The relevance of the production for a Jamaican audience was evidenced by the many letters from viewers requesting the chance to appear as a performer or member of the studio audience. At one point in 1975, there was even a *Ring Ding* club. The show's routine was simple: it involved children performing for children, aired consistently on Saturdays during a time slot convenient to them, thus helping to maintain a loyal viewership.

Despite the show's popularity, it came to an end when one Saturday morning Miss Lou along with Miss Whylie and children showed up to the studio, only to be told there would be no show that day.[7] *Ring Ding* appeared for the last time on the television programme schedule of JBC TV on 21 August 1982. Shortly thereafter, Miss Lou migrated with her husband to North America. Typically, the end of the programme featured the Jamaican farewell song:

> Walk good on your way
> And good duppy walk with you ... walk good
> Walk good everyday
> And good duppy walk with you ... walk good
> Every day ... walk good ... on your way
> Walk good, good follow you, if you just walk good.

Since the show's end, there have been other shows, such as *It's a Smart World* and *Vibrations*, that continued the *Ring Ding*-like tradition of children's programming – cultural performances and educational activities involving youngsters. In 2011, *Kids Say ...* began airing and has the potential to be a long-running local children's show given its talk format and seasonal broadcast schedule. Seasonal children's programming with magazine and talk show formats seems to be the type of television that could survive in a small market like Jamaica.

## Current and Public Affairs

Forty-nine shows have been produced in the current and public affairs genre in Jamaica. Some have been produced out of the newsrooms of television stations where current affairs content is created daily. Additionally, this genre offers the opportunity for producing programmes that are appealing yet affordable. In the early years of television in Jamaica some of these were *Focus, Firing Line, Press Conference* and *The Verdict Is Yours*. Since then, there has been a steady stream, including *Round Table Talk, Thwaites and Company, Perspective, Tuesday Forum, Your Issues Live, Probe* and *Impact with Cliff Hughes*. Some have focused on specific areas of current and public affairs, such as in-depth exploration of news topics, politics, development and government issues, business and finance, social and popular cultural themes, and lifestyle and entertainment.

Shows such as *Live @ Seven* and the Zahra Burton–hosted *18 Degrees*

*North* have had a sustained presence. The latter has been promoted on TVJ as a show whose main purpose is to uncover stories related to the Caribbean that have gone unreported or under-reported for too long.[8] CVM TV's *Live @ Seven* first aired 26 July 2010, and featured a host with one, two or three guests at most, in studio.[9] On weekends, *The Best of Live @ Seven* summarized the most interesting topics discussed during the weeknight version of the programme.

Before *Live @ Seven* and *18 Degrees North* made it to the screen, *All Angles* aired in 2006 as a pre-recorded current affairs show featuring a studio panel discussion of topical issues supported by location footage, reports or vox pops. The show's concept evolved out of discussions by the station's management. The idea was for the series to move beyond a simple news story and provide an in-depth look at current issues in the news from all angles, hence the name. Moya Thomas, group head of news at the RJR Communications Group at the time, was charged with the responsibility of making it happen. Lawyer and journalist Dionne Jackson-Miller, who also hosts a weekday evening news radio programme *Beyond the Headlines* on RJR 94 FM, became the show's main host with journalists Milton Walker or Earl Moxam appearing as alternate host on occasion. Jodi Brown-Lindo was the show's first producer.

Early reaction to *All Angles* was positive, and it was not long before it started airing live to accommodate audience interaction through phone calls and text messages. The main host recalled receiving a huge response, over four thousand text messages, to a show that dealt with praedial larceny.[10] With the advent of social media, viewers could also participate by posting questions and comments on social-media platforms such as Twitter and Facebook using the hashtag #TVJAllAngles.

While the programme's typical format involves mainly a moderated studio panel discussion, there have also been special shows – one-on-one interviews such as that with the country's opposition leader in 2013, Andrew Holness; discussions involving youth featuring either young achievers or issues affecting Jamaican adolescents; and investigative specials featuring on-location re-enactments. One notable investigative special was "What Really Happened the Night Dwayne Jones Was Killed". It aired in July 2014, on the first anniversary of the murder of transgender teen Dwayne "Gully

Queen" Jones. This show included a re-creation of the story and interviews with Jones's friends.

*All Angles* is perhaps best known for its episode on "The Bleaching Phenomenon" in Jamaica that aired on 19 June 2013 and for which the show won the Jamaica Broiler's Fair Play Award in September 2013. The focus was on the practice of using a concoction including a mix of skin creams, chemicals, toothpaste or curry powder to lighten one's complexion. This episode worked because it was television in its purest form. The cameras focused on Jamaicans who 'bleach' their skin and the footage of their experiences made for not only current content but revealing visual storytelling. The effort that went into that particular show could easily be estimated as two months of full-time production work. Keeping in mind that *All Angles* is a product of the newsroom, staff who must produce daily newscasts are not always able to devote the time required to produce an episode like this on a regular basis. For the show to produce award winning and appealing episodes like "The Bleaching Phenomenon" more frequently, a dedicated team of full-time producers, reporters and technical crew would be needed to exploit the visual potential in all the various current affairs topics.

*All Angles* continues to benefit from the commitment of people who have worked on it since it began such as broadcast journalists Archibald Gordon, Vashan Brown, Andre Jebbinson and Kaneal Gayle. In terms of technology, the show has utilized various mechanisms for involving viewers ranging from texting to social media. The production has moved from being pre-recorded to being mainly live with the occasional recorded piece supporting the studio discussion. The one-hour show has aired at different times on Wednesdays, starting as early as 8:30 p.m. or as late as 9:30 p.m. Despite the changing times, audiences have grown used to the routine of *All Angles* being on Wednesdays. Preparation for the live show includes generating ideas on the previous Friday; shooting segments, if required, during the weekend; and then starting editing, if necessary on Monday – all to get the show ready for its live mid-week airing. Though its weekly live broadcast routine has been well established, viewers can also access past episodes on the RJR Communications Group's 1Spotmedia live-stream and VOD service.

Another long-standing entrant in the current affairs genre worthy of mention is *On Stage* that is aired on CVM TV and hosted by Winford

Williams. The show features location reports focusing on entertainment and is characterized by a key in-studio interview or interview segments conducted by Williams. It has been on air since 1997 and, apart from its weekly airing on CVM TV, reruns are broadcast on Flow, which distributes what it calls *On Stage Encore* on its Flow 100 channel.[11]

What is interesting about these current affairs shows is that a number of them are products of the newsrooms of a broadcast entity. This suggests that programming can be developed in the newsroom and make the transition to the programmes department. Anthony Miller's *Entertainment Report* started in the newsroom. The current and public affairs genre presents producers with a chance for creating television shows that address content that is not only recent, relevant and attractive to audiences, but also relatively affordable in terms of financing. With appropriate funding models, consistent technical support, and committed media professionals, current and public affairs shows are likely to do well in small television markets.

## Drama

The drama genre has some memorable television shows in Jamaica with twenty-five having been produced here in this category. *Life with the Littles*, *Dear Mama* and *Great Junction* were mini-series produced by JIS TV in the 1970s and early 1980s. Hall Anthony Ellis's thirteen-episode mini-series *Pullet Hall*, which featured rural life in Jamaica, was aired in 1998.[12] Perhaps one of the more memorable local drama productions was the series *Oliver at Large*, featuring Jamaican comedian Oliver Samuels, and the spin-offs *Oliver* and *Sarge in Charge*. Of a similar format were shows such as *Titus*, starring actor Glen Campbell, and *Claffy*, with comedian Volier Johnson. Both men are well known on the local theatre scene and programmes revolved around their characters' mishaps and antics. Following in that tradition but decades later, in 2014, CVM TV aired *Shebada in Charge*, a half-hour sitcom set in a shop managed by a character played by local comedy theatre personality Keith "Shebada" Ramsey.

In more recent times, plays that have appeared on stage have been produced for television in a strategy aimed at meeting the demand for local programming. Some of these productions are one-off and others have been developed into short mini-series. Munair Zacca's *Play It* was produced by CPTC for television as *The Play's the Thing*. Dahlia Harris's stage productions *Thicker than Water* and *God's Way* have appeared on TVJ – each as a mini-series with six thirty-minute episodes. Sabrena McDonald-Radcliffe's *Run di Track* has been aired on TVJ on Sunday nights in the station's "Home Grown Series". It should be noted that Jamaican theatre productions have been recorded on video and offered for sale or shown on cable as on-demand content. Some memorable titles include *Maama Man*, *Bashment Granny* and *Passa Passa*.

Among the most successful and long-running series was *Royal Palm Estate* that began airing on CVM TV in 1994 as a drama about the life and loves of those associated with the titular estate.[13] Its multiple characters and storylines were a slice of Jamaican life. The show's pilot was created in 1991 and it was not until after CVM TV began broadcasting in 1993 that it made it to the air. At first it aired on a weeknight before settling into a regular Sunday evening slot for twenty-seven seasons. There were about fifteen episodes per season and each occupied a one-hour slot on the programme schedule. In 2009, *The Blackburns*, which lasted for eight seasons, was created as a spin-off that continued the stories of characters from the original *Royal Palm Estate*.

The series featured over fifty Jamaican actors who remained committed to the production. Reggie Carter, Carol Campbell-Williams, Karen Harriott, Beth Hyde, Paul Issa, John Jones, Michael Nicholson, Bobby Smith, Cyrene Tomlinson and Munair Zacca played memorable characters and made appearances in most – if not all – seasons. On the production side, it was produced and directed by Lennie Little-White, who also was in charge of the story and concept as well as a team of writers. He was supported by Trevor Johnson as the main cinematographer for about eighteen seasons. Radcliffe McBean served as editor, Tebel Largie worked as sound and lighting technician and Carole Reid did make-up. Both crew and cast were supportive over the years, and the show's success was in part due to people's willingness to help in any way that they could, using their professional and personal connections to source costumes, encourage advertisers to support the show and to negotiate contra-deals with hotels.

*Royal Palm Estate* was a costly undertaking and the producer relied on creative ways of funding to maintain the programme for its duration. After initial support from CVM TV and major sponsors such as Red Stripe beer and Sherwin Williams paints for the first five seasons, additional funding models were conceptualized. One strategy was product placement. Some advertisers felt that a short twenty- or thirty-second advertisement did not promote their products as much as having those very same products appear for longer periods during the show with the characters making commentary on them. Advertisers included Wray and Nephew, GraceKennedy and Digicel. Little-White notes that maintaining relationships with marketers was important especially when they were willing to lend support regardless of the brand they managed. The show also benefited from the fact that Mediamix Limited that created the show owned its production equipment and did not need to incur rental costs in this area. Producing advertisements for various clients was also a source of income to help cover the huge expenses associated with multiple location shooting and a large cast and crew.

Starting with two seasons per year, after five years this was reduced to one. To successfully complete twenty-seven seasons over twenty-one years meant that the show had to observe a strict production routine. All rural scenes for a season were shot at one time and the urban scenes were done on an ad hoc basis. Post-production then took place to get the entire season ready for the airwaves. An episode was broadcast on Sundays at 9:00 p.m. and repeated on a weeknight. Reminiscing on the show's relevance for its Jamaican audiences, Little-White noted that even though there were characters that portrayed "poor people", the series never depicted them in a negative manner as the aim was always to convey positive and dignified images of Jamaicans.

*Royal Palm Estate* had loyal fans who have called the station asking about their favourite drama series. The show's popularity extended beyond Jamaica as it was also shown in other Caribbean countries such as Trinidad and Tobago on TV6 and Barbados on CBC. The final episode aired on CVM TV in May 2015 after producer Little-White announced that the series would come to an end, citing a change in the CVM TV landscape as part of the reason. "Even though I am still a shareholder," he said, "there was no benevolence and I was paying the station more than I was earning. It was just not feasible anymore."[14] Later on while being interviewed for this book, he said that his work on that series had been inspired by *Lime Tree Lane*, another drama series that began airing in late 1988 on JBC TV.

School principal Melita Samuels was approached by Don Bucknor, then head of television at JBC, to write scripts for a show that would involve about four actors and make Jamaicans laugh.[15] Samuels had completed a diploma in Drama in Education at the Jamaica School of Drama where her exceptional skills at playwriting had led her tutor Michael Reckord to recommended her to Bucknor. Early in 1988, producer and director Pablo Hoilett was also asked by Bucknor to do a series of comedy sketches to use as five-minute fillers. Samuels and Hoilett worked as part of the team that created *Lime Tree Lane*, and remained on board until its end.

By the summer of 1988, about ten episodes of the show had been created for initial airing but Hurricane Gilbert in September of that year delayed its transmission. Its later debut was timely as it was now seen as a way to help Jamaicans cope with the aftermath of the hurricane. As the show developed, it moved from being a short comedy to a series with recurring characters and a continuing storyline addressing topical social issues. There were also the occasional one-hour specials. The show appeared on air daily during weekdays with two showings per day, one during JBC TV's morning programme and the other just before the station's nightly newscast. This was a well-established scheduling routine that helped to maintain interest among viewers.

Audiences appreciated the show so much that they were willing to see past the basic sets, props and potted plants that created the backdrop. The content revolved around Jamaican morals and values and portrayed characters that were relevant to local viewers. It was about the people living in a fictional community called Lime Tree Lane – a name that had no relation to the Lime Tree Lane off Negril's West End Road or to the one to be found off Olympic Way in St Andrew. It has been rumoured that the names of these places were inspired by the television series.

The show's longevity was possible because of sacrifices made by the many people associated with the show. Mas' Gussie, Miss Zella, Sammy, Bubbles, Miss Upton and Johnny were some of the memorable characters portrayed respectively by actors Silton Townsend, Dorothy Cunningham, Patrick Prendergast, Erica Brown, Judith Thompson and Christopher Daley.

Melita Samuels, the show's main scriptwriter, was eventually supported by Michael Reckord, Althea Smikle, some of the actors and producer Hoilett, who all helped to pen scripts.

*Lime Tree Lane* was an effort in producing "something out of nothing", to use the expression of producer Hoilett.[16] By applying creative solutions in a limited resource environment, the show was able to sustain its airing for about ten years. Initially, the production was done mainly in-studio using three cameras. After the station's late night newscast, the studio space and other production facilities – that would normally not be in use at that time of night – were now utilized to create the show. It meant actors and crew worked during the nights and editing would follow in the early hours of the morning, to ensure it was ready for airtime. In an attempt to improve the show in its later years, it was shot on location using a single camera set-up.

During its time on JBC TV, *Lime Tree Lane* attracted sponsors such as Ramson, Eve Foods, Jamaica Biscuit Company and Butterkist. After the sale of JBC TV in 1997, producing *Lime Tree Lane* on location and airing it in its usual prime-time slot were no longer financially viable. The programme no longer runs on free-to-air television but old episodes can be seen on PBCJ's cable channel. A spin-off programme, *Mas' Gussie's Views*, featuring the character played by Silton Townsend is also shown on PBCJ.

After ten years of *Lime Tree Lane* and twenty-one years of *Royal Palm Estate*, Jamaican audiences have not seen many local drama series sustained on television. In 2009, the first season of thirteen half-hour episodes of *Me and Mi Kru* aired with its third season advertised in late 2013. Challenges associated with creating appropriate funding models to support local television dramas and retain good scriptwriters have been offered as some of the reasons that this particular format is not seen more. Producers of the drama genre in small television markets may achieve more by creating series that are seasonal and have fewer episodes that are relatively short in length. Established series formats using the typical thirteen episodes that may each be one hour or thirty minutes in length does not have to be the standard for drama series shown in small markets.

## Entertainment

The entertainment genre has been another popular format appearing on Jamaican television. There have been forty-eight shows produced in this category, from shows that report on happenings in the entertainment industry to shows that aim to provide entertainment to viewers. *D'Wrap* and *Intense* use a magazine format with links and interviews. *Fi We Choice Top Ten* is a chart show featuring music videos of local artistes linked in studio or on location. *Video Alley* and *V'Mix* are two other magazine shows with a focus on music and the party scene.

There are some shows that do not merely report on entertainment, but instead aim to entertain its viewers. *The Ity and Fancy Cat Show* is a comedy show that started in 2008 and includes a combination of pre-recorded skits, vox pop, on the street gags with various people and the stars doing stand-up in front of an audience. Ian "Ity" Ellis and Alton "Fancy Cat" Hardware are the comedic duo after whom the show is named. They began performing in 1992 after appearing in a Courts Jamaica Limited furniture promotional campaign that allowed them to connect with and become known among Jamaicans. Since then they have done shows at various clubs and theatres in Jamaica and overseas.

It is produced by Ellis International Jamaica Limited, which was formed in 2004 by brothers Aston, Ian and Owen Ellis. In addition to this television show the company also does work in theatre, comedy, music, poetry and the martial arts. Ellis International Limited negotiates airtime for the show with TVJ and also takes charge of the sale of advertising slots. Sponsors such as Courts Jamaica Limited, KFC and Jamaica's major telecommunications service providers Digicel and Flow have given advertising support at various points throughout its broadcast history.

The comedy sketches are mostly scripted by Owen "Blakka" Ellis, a comedian in his own right. The various items are recorded weekly to keep them topical and links are recorded before an audience. There are ongoing skits with recurring characters as well as one-off sketches featuring the comedy duo as well as guest comedians. The show is probably best known for its on-location hidden camera sequences that allow for public participation. Diaspora audiences have also enjoyed it as it can be viewed on channels in Canada and England as well as on CIN TV that serves New York, Connecticut and New Jersey.

In October 2015, *The Ity and Fancy Cat Show* began its eighth season that included the show's one hundredth episode. During a typical season, the thirty-minute show airs on TVJ on Sunday nights at 9:00 with a repeat on a weeknight (such as Tuesday) at 11:00. Initially the season lasted for thirteen weeks starting in March, April or June. Over time, the producers recognized that the show works better in the last quarter of the calendar year, starting around October or November with a season lasting about ten weeks. Given its sustained presence on air since it started in 2008, this show has the potential to be a long-running show on Jamaican television.

*Where It's At*, hosted mainly by Alphonso Walker, began in 1971 and was an entertainment show that aired for much longer. The idea had been conceptualized as part of a final project by Walker when, as a young videographer, he attended a training course at the British Broadcasting Corporation in the United Kingdom. In the early years, the show had various presenters, including Elaine Wint. Walker, who produced and directed the show, eventually became its main host.

Described as the hit TV teenage dance show, *Where It's At* was designed as an outlet for the views and creative energy of young people as well as to provide its audience with an authentic picture of where *it* was *at* on the Jamaican music scene. The show therefore featured Jamaican music for its youth demographic with performances in studio that showcased local talent. Another segment of the show was called "Say It Loud" which involved discussion on youth issues. Well received by Jamaican viewers, many artistes credited the show with giving them early career exposure. Eventually it was revamped. The discussion segment was replaced with a segment featuring new dance moves that helped to boost the show's popularity.

*Where It's At* occupied a regular Friday evening slot on the programme schedule of JBC TV airing at 7:00. At some points during its time on air, it was seen as early as 6:02 p.m. on Fridays. The thirty-minute show was pre-recorded with each show containing a mix of several recorded sessions that would occur when artistes and studio were available. This often happened late at night. Walker's commitment to the show led him to take on several production roles, including editing. The established routine for the production and scheduling of *Where It's At* helped to sustain the show on air until 1986. Jamaica's reggae music industry and theatre scene continue to provide a basis upon which programming in the entertainment genre can be produced. Pre-recorded shows not exceeding a relatively short length of about thirty minutes with entertainment content such as comedy sketches, music and dancing seem to be a format that can be sustained in small television markets like Jamaica.

## Factual

The factual genre includes television programmes that document and present information and facts about a range of topics or subjects such as the arts, sciences, history, culture, commerce, health and education, and lifestyle (travel, cooking, home and living, and consumer affairs). Programmes in this category have been broadcast in Jamaica with at least fifty-two having appeared since the start of television in 1963. Within the factual genre, one subgenre could be the documentary, which in itself covers a wide range of topics. In Jamaica, television documentaries have been presented as one-off productions rather than as ongoing series. Some examples include the work of Cynthia Wilmot and Hilary Nicholson of Video for Change: *The Drums Keep Sounding*, on the life of Jamaica's cultural icon Louise Bennett; and *Son of Jamaica, Father of the Nation*, on the life of Jamaica's national hero Norman Manley.

Carey Robinson, former general manager of JBC, produced Jamaica's first full-length docu-drama in 1965 called *Time of Fury* that documented the Morant Bay Rebellion, an uprising against colonial oppression. Robinson has also produced several other documentaries about Jamaica's history. There is little evidence of sustained effort to create documentary series in Jamaica, whether it is a documentary series on various topics or a single topic. During special periods of the year in Jamaica, such as Independence time in August and Heritage Week in October, television stations often air local and foreign documentaries for interested audiences.

On Sunday night, 17 July 1983 at 8:00, *Trails* premiered on JBC TV. Produced and hosted by Roy Brown, the thirty-minute show comprised three features, each about seven to eight minutes long, telling stories of Jamaicans connecting with each other. Brown had returned from overseas in 1981 to work in the newsroom of JBC TV and, after being fired in 1982, went about the business of independently producing a show to be called *Country Trails Jamaican Style* that Gloria Lannaman, then JBC general manager, changed to *Trails*.[17]

Advertising agency Moo Young Butler and Associates brokered the relationship between JBC TV, independent producer Brown and the show's sponsor, NCB. The pilot had taken a year to produce but it was just in time for funding as the bank was looking for something local to support.

Community Television Systems, which would later become the C in CVM TV, provided production assistance for the pilot and Phase Three Productions worked on subsequent episodes. It was produced weekly and the routine involved travelling across Jamaica to find and shoot stories between Monday and Wednesday. Editing, writing links, recording narration and other post-production work started Thursday to ensure the show was ready for its broadcast on Sunday night.

Brown compiled features that would guarantee a Sunday night audience. The first item would be one that connected immediately with viewers and the last or third item would be something that viewers really wanted to watch. *Trails* won a national award for the best human-interest show. Television critic, Harry Milner, lauded it as the best documentary series on local television and it was described as "very popular" by *Gleaner* columnist Marguerite Gauron, writing in 1985. Donald Miller, in a letter to the editor also in 1985, congratulated JBC on the programme and commended the scripting, videography and the high standards, suggesting that Roy Brown was supported by a dependable team.

The show had entered its second season when a change in the bank's advertising strategy reduced the agreed sponsorship from twenty-six weeks to thirteen, and on 10 December 1987, the *Gleaner* reported that *Trails* had been removed from JBC TV.[18] Despite its apparent popularity, it never returned to Jamaican television after 1987.

*Creative Cooking*, that aired for over twenty-five years, was a factual show that ran for much longer. In 1985, Heather Little-White, then manager of Grace Kitchens and Consumer Centre, a subsidiary of GraceKennedy Limited, conceptualized and presented the programme to promote the company's food products used in the many recipes developed by the facility. As the first local television cooking show, it was recorded at the studios of JBC TV, directed by Don Bucknor with videography by Louis Burke.[19] After some time, Little-White was replaced by Mazie Miller, who became the main host. In its early years, it appeared on JBC TV from Mondays to Fridays, all year round, just before *Lime Tree Lane*, in the half-hour slot leading up to the station's newscast at 7:00 p.m.

*Creative Cooking* moved between Jamaica's two main terrestrial television broadcasters. It initially appeared on the public station JBC TV, and continued on the privately owned TVJ. The five-minute show that was scheduled at 6:55 p.m. would sometimes run overtime and delay the start of the live newscast. CVM TV offered a ten-minute slot before their newscast at 8:00, so for a while it was seen on that station on Tuesdays and Fridays at 7:50 p.m. It returned to TVJ eventually, appearing during its morning programme *Smile Jamaica* on Mondays at 7:35 a.m. with a repeat on Sundays at 2:20 p.m. Selected episodes of the show could also be seen on CIN TV.

The Marketing Counselors Limited, a Jamaican advertising agency, helped to produce the show using studio facilities such as those at the CPTC. Over the years the pre-recorded show adjusted its routine from its year-round daily weekday broadcasts to three days per week with a "Best of" episode on Sundays and eventually it aired two days per week.

*Creative Cooking* sometimes included special episodes when Mazie Miller would host guest chefs or well-known Jamaicans as guest cooks on the show. At one point, the show would go on the road to feature chefs associated with hotels across Jamaica as well as cuisine associated with different parishes. There have been specials such as the "Chef Series", "Chef Challenge", "Cooking Kids", "Recession Busters" and the "Traditional Jamaican Dishes" series, among others. When GraceKennedy sponsored Jamaican athletes in the 2012 Olympics, *Creative Cooking* featured meals prepared for the athletes. In 2012, the show also commemorated the ninetieth anniversary of GraceKennedy as well as the fiftieth anniversary of Jamaica's independence. Though broadcasts ended in 2013, past episodes of the show can be seen online on the Grace Foods YouTube channel, created in April 2009. The most popular of these has been viewed over 250,000 times and features a recipe for Jamaican Christmas cake.

COMING UP: SHOWS WATCHED AND ONES TO WATCH

Another noteworthy television programme in the factual genre is *Walk n' Talk*, which first aired in 1987 on JBC TV, nightly Mondays to Fridays at 8:00, after the evening news. Doreen Brown, then head of JIS TV, approached Carmeta Tate about producing and presenting a five-minute show that would feature Jamaicans talking about their experiences. Although produced by JIS, the government's information agency, the show presented its content in a fun and appealing manner. Production involved travelling across Jamaica and even to overseas locations to find human-interest stories that would offer a balance to the more serious government news. One trip could yield several stories that would be edited and canned as a week's worth of shows. Producer Tate was supported by a small, committed crew including editor Kirk Buchanan. Though audience reaction was positive, the show did not last on JBC TV.[20]

Despite the fact that *Trails*, *Creative Cooking*, and *Walk n' Talk* are no longer broadcast, the factual genre continues to yield new shows. *Island Dreams* is aired on CVM TV with host Kimberley Mais-Issa on Sunday evenings at 6:30. The half-hour home design programme series explores island living, and started its eighth season in November 2014. *Hidden Treasures* and *Nyammings*, focus on Jamaican locations and cuisine respectively. *Two Sisters and a Meal* is also food related and mixes interviews and travelling. Generating television shows in the factual genre may seem feasible because it allows for dealing with situations that can be captured on location, avoiding production costs associated with renting studio time. Maintaining these factual shows will require creative ways to sustain support from both sponsors and viewers.

### Magazine

At least thirteen shows have exemplified this genre on Jamaican television. Some prominent morning magazine shows include *CVM at Sunrise* and TVJ's *Smile Jamaica* which evolved from *Morning Time* on JBC TV. CPTC produced *Rappin'* from 1990 to 2001, which focused on high schools across Jamaica. It featured interviews with members of the school community, a discussion segment with students and entertainment. *Teen Seen* was sponsored by the National Family Planning Board and addressed adolescent reproductive health issues.

*Smile Jamaica – It's Morning Time* began in 1998 with hosts Nicole Haughton and Neville Graham. The initial shows were seen as a transition from the *Morning Time* show that aired on JBC TV up to 1997. It was felt that keeping *Morning Time* in the title of the new programme would help to keep loyal viewers. Eventually the subtitle was dropped and the show became known as *Smile Jamaica*. Produced by Sandra Rose, formerly of JBC TV news, the show included various mini segments linked by the hosts and produced or reported by various individuals, including Sheena Johnson, Michelle Geister, Richard Moss, Karl Williams, Jackie Haughton, Gail Sommerville and Romke Eluwemi-Ennis. The company User Friendly TV co-produced the show with TVJ. Eventually it was sold to TVJ which continued its production.

Later, sportscasters Neville Bell and Simon Crosskill joined the show as presenters on Fridays to do a lighter programme with a sports focus. They ended up becoming two of the main hosts, joined by other regulars such as Simone Clarke-Cooper, Dahlia Harris and Emprezz Golding. Sakina Deer joined later as host for the *Weekend Smile* that appeared on Saturdays from 8:00 a.m. to 9:30 a.m. The weekday version of the show airs live from 6:00 a.m. to 8:30 a.m. with various pre-recorded features and segments. It is supported by advertisers who either pay for sponsored segments or commercials. The programme maintains a presence on various social-media platforms and past episodes are available for purchase on RJR Communications Group 1Spotmedia platform. Content that is relevant for its Jamaican audience includes news, weather, interviews, entertainment and lifestyle features.

Magazine shows covering various topics and comprising different types of content are a feasible format for small television markets. This allows for variety that has the potential to appeal to a wider cross section of an already relatively small market. The literature on television genres does not always acknowledge the "magazine" format. Jeremy Tunstall, in writing about the British Broadcasting Corporation and its television genres in 2015, does not use the term "magazine" to describe any of the television shows that he documents.[21] Others, such as Glen Creeber, in writing about television genres, have.²² Despite the inconsistency in its use, magazine, when used in reference to television programmes, suggests a focus on a variety of subjects within a single episode. Arguably, small television markets can exploit the opportunities offered by such a format when creating content to address the varying interests of a diverse yet small audience.

## Quiz and Game Shows

Twenty-one quiz and game shows have been produced on Jamaican television. In 2006, for a short period, a quiz programme sponsored by Digicel aired on TVJ; viewers were asked to call in to answer questions and win prizes. The callers were charged a premium rate.²³ In the United Kingdom such shows were investigated and, in many cases, were taken off the air.²⁴ Similar premium-rate call-in game shows appeared locally and then mysteriously disappeared. Other game shows emerged such as *Deal or No Deal*, hosted by Simon Crosskill, on TVJ from 2009 to 2010,²⁵ and *Family Bonanza*, hosted by Karl Binger and produced by CPTC, from 1991 to 1992.²⁶ *Deuces Wild* was a dating game show hosted by Lisa Hanna in 1998.²⁷ *Claro Cash Cab* was on for a short time, having started in 2010.²⁸

In terms of quiz game shows, there was the *KFC Junior Quiz*, a half-hour schools quiz show for ten- to thirteen-year-olds that ran on CVM TV from 2002 to 2010, hosted by Scripps Spelling Bee champion Jody-Ann Maxwell.²⁹ The Gleaner Company's Spelling Bee Competition has offered television content which has been aired on local television, as has Burger King's National Secondary Schools' Debating Competition.³⁰ Reading competitions have also been broadcast.

*Junior Schools' Challenge Quiz* is a spin-off of the long-established *Schools' Challenge Quiz*. It first aired on TVJ in 2003 with a pilot season that involved sixteen schools at the pre-secondary level. Wolmer's Preparatory School won the first season. Since then, the show has grown to accommodate ninety-six schools in one season that typically lasts from September to December. The thirty-minute quiz matches are pre-recorded in studio on Mondays and then aired on TVJ from Mondays to Fridays at 6:30 p.m. with a repeat the following day at 8:30 a.m. The final quiz is broadcast live.

Michael Gonzales, producer of the senior *Schools' Challenge Quiz*, also produces this. The junior show's format is fairly similar to the senior show with two teams of four members each answering questions posed in three segments. The first segment contains alternate questions for each team and the last segment requires pressing a buzzer before being allowed to answer a question. The second segment is different for the junior quiz show. It involves a face-off where one member of each team gets at least five seconds to answer five questions in specific subject areas.

Questions are posed in mathematics, science, social studies and language arts. Primary-level educators Dr Margaret Bailey and Doreth McFarlane have served as judges on the show since its inception and St Andrew High School sixth former Kathryn Lewis was quizmaster for the first two seasons. Archibald Gordon served briefly as quizmaster before becoming TVJ's main evening newscast anchor. Since then, Toni-Kay Dawkins, Khadene Foote and Sheldon Reid have been quizmasters.

With its increasing popularity and a long waiting list of schools wanting to participate, the producers introduced *Quest for Quiz* in 2015 as a preliminary qualifying round occurring in the summer months before the actual show starts in September. NCB's Omni Educator, an education savings plan, has been sponsor since 2003; others have included Grace Vienna Sausage and the Jamaica Biscuit Company. The show helps to groom candidates for the senior event. Windward Road Primary has won for four consecutive years and Mona Preparatory has also dominated. One year, the Campion College high school team in the senior show comprised members who had all participated at the junior level, mostly from Mona Preparatory. There are attractive prizes including scholarships, trophies, electronic gadgets such as tablets, computers and laptops; weekends at resorts; trips to theme parks; books, cash and other incentives for schools. Media audience surveys suggest that the *Junior Schools' Challenge Quiz* remains the number one programme in the 6:30 p.m. to 7:00 p.m. slot on Jamaican television.[31]

Though the quiz and game shows have proved to be popular, not all shows in this genre created for local television have stood the test of time. However, short-term seasonal formats, linked to an annual supply of contestants such as schoolchildren, with a guaranteed audience of family, friends and teachers, do provide an option for sustainable programme development in small television markets like Jamaica.

COMING UP: SHOWS WATCHED AND ONES TO WATCH

## Reality

This genre has grown in popularity on Jamaican television with twenty-two reality shows identified. Examples of this genre include the *Tastee Talent Search Competition* which came to television in 2010 after thirty years in venues across the island. *Mission Catwalk* on TVJ sees designers vie for the top prize after undergoing a number of design challenges. In a *Gleaner* interview at the end of the fourth season in 2014, executive producer and host Keneea Linton-George noted that "we were literally on the brink of cancelling the season. We found a way to do it and we can see ourselves getting to season 10."[32] Recent years have seen the emergence of branded programming; hence, shows such as *KFC on the Verge, Magnum Kings and Queens of Dancehall*, and *NCB Capital Quest* have emerged.

*Digicel Rising Stars* began in June 2004 as a reality competition show in which Jamaicans performed songs for judges and a live audience as well as viewers who could vote for contestants by texting using cellular phones. It was created by former Irish magazine-publisher Michael Hogan, who, through his company New Reality Television, produced the show with its title sponsor Digicel, one of Jamaica's telecommunications service providers. The show has benefited from a committed production team led by Irishman Mark Kenny, who joined as consultant producer, Sharon Schroeter as series producer, and Tahnida Nunes, Digicel's senior sponsorship manager, who is an executive producer. The competition's judges have included Nadine Sutherland, Anthony Miller, A.J. Brown, Clyde Mckenzie, Conroy Wilson and Alaine Laughton. Hosts have included Denise Hunt, Lady Renae, Yendi Phillips and Terri-Karelle Reid along with Sanjay Ramanand, who interviews contestants back stage during the show. Ian Guthrie has worked as videographer for several seasons.

The competition is funded mainly by Digicel and associate sponsors have included NCB, Sony Ericsson, The Knutsford Court Hotel, RJR Communications Group, the *Star*, Pepsi and KFC. It has aired annually on TVJ since its inception and now occupies a one-hour slot on Sundays, starting as early as 8:00 p.m. Auditions air starting in June, then the competition begins in July and ends in September or October. Pre-recording, scripting and editing of audition shows is done in April or May. The twenty to twenty-five person production team works on the three-camera, two-audio production, on location across Jamaica. After the contestants are selected, postcard features – mini-vignettes – are done on each competitor. The show then goes live with weekly performances in studio until a winner is selected. To accommodate the crowd of supporters, the live season finale has been done on location at venues such as the Courtleigh Auditorium, Hilton Hotel poolside and the Knutsford Court Hotel carpark.

The producers recognized that they had underestimated its popularity when in the second season, the live finale set for Emancipation Park in New Kingston had to be moved to studio as the crowd of overenthusiastic fans got out of control rooting for finalists Chris Martin and Noddy Virtue.[33] The show has been described as one of the most popular on local television, a family favourite which has started the careers of various reggae artistes such as Chris Martin (2005), Romain Virgo (2007), Cameal Davis (2008), Shuga (2009) and saxophonist Verlando Small (2013). Other Caribbean territories where Digicel also offers telecommunications services including Trinidad and Tobago, Barbados and Haiti, produce their own versions of *Rising Stars*. With the backing of a major corporate sponsor, a sound income-generating model and an interactive contest that allows for audience participation, the reality competition genre can yield content to fill airtime in small television markets.

## Religion

Religious programmes run the gamut from televised church services either live or recorded to religious themed talk shows, documentaries, dramas and gospel music videos or performances. In Jamaica, a number of these types of programmes have been and are on air. Our research found fourteen shows in the religious genre. Some of these programmes are ones where the producers pay for airtime for the broadcast of a church service, such as *Faith Deliverance*. There have also been programmes that combine the spoken word with gospel music. Pastor David Keane was the host of what has been described as the one of the earliest gospel shows on television on JBC in 1978; later, in 2001, he hosted *Catch the Fire* on CVM TV.[34] Though Love TV, established in 1998, carries religious content, other terrestrial stations also continue to air some local religious-themed programmes such as *Faith Deliverance*, *Reformation Now* and *CVM Gospel Report*.

*Something More* with Bishop Herro Blair is an example of a long-standing religious programme on Jamaican television.[35] The show appeared as early as 1 January 1984, listed in the TV guide of the *Gleaner* as occupying a one-hour slot starting at 8:00 a.m. Then the one-hour programme involved the praise, worship and preaching that would make up the church service at the Faith Cathedral Deliverance Centre at 104 Waltham Park Road, Kingston. In its early years, a video production company recorded the service and JBC TV aired it. Over time, the Faith Cathedral established a media centre that manages the production and distribution of its audio-visual programme content. *Something More* has kept pace with media distribution technology and has aired on not only terrestrial broadcast entities in Jamaica but also on cable television, online and mobile platforms.

The church service that makes up *Something More* streams live on Sundays on Mercy and Truth Ministries Television, a Christian television network accessible via the Internet at www.livetsream.com/fcdc on any device. In addition to the live-streaming online, the service is also recorded and edited for airing on Sundays a week later on CVM TV at 6:30 a.m. as a pre-recorded thirty-minute show, on PBCJ's cable channel at 9:30 a.m. with a repeat at 9:00 p.m., as well as on other cable channels across Jamaica.

Given the church's involvement in the production of media content in Jamaica, the religious genre has the potential to sustain its presence in the programme schedules of various media entities. With churches actively producing television content, this genre could be sustained in small media markets.

## Social Advocacy

The social advocacy genre – also known as social action television – is based on human-interest content. Programmes in this category attempt to highlight challenges to the human condition with clear calls to action or recommend ways of addressing particular situations. Factual information is used to emphasize the need for social and civic responsibility, and examples are presented depicting ways in which various entities have responded to need through acts of kindness. In Jamaica, this genre has evolved to be associated with a television station's news product whether it is a short feature within the newscast or a feature appearing right after. Given Jamaica's development challenges, the social advocacy genre allows producers to make a contribution towards solving the society's ills.

*Inspire Jamaica* and *A Ray of Hope* are both short features appearing within the newscasts of Jamaica's two main terrestrial broadcasters. CVM TV's *Inspire Jamaica* focuses on children with health issues and *A Ray of Hope* on TVJ features stories on various social problems.

*The Teller* allows beneficiaries of the corporate social responsibility and philanthropic programmes of the Scotiabank Foundation to tell stories of life improvement. It began in 2007 as a seasonal show starting in September. Typically it takes a break in December, returns in January and runs until June, then breaks again for July and August.

It started when Scotiabank Foundation executive director Joylene Griffiths-Irving, a former member of the news staff at JBC TV, brought a team together and brainstormed the concept. This process involved getting permission to employ a producer as this was not something a bank would normally do. With approval, she brought in Zoe Welsh from the BBC and recruited an assistant, Rochelle Dixon, who eventually became the producer. A camera crew and editor, involved from the show's conceptualization, were retained, but were allowed to do other jobs outside of the season. Carlington Silburn and Ian Guthrie have served as part of the production team.

Reactions to *The Teller* have been positive. So well received was the show that when it went off air for an extended period, viewers would call the station asking about it. The five-minute short format leaves the viewer wanting more. Production is ongoing throughout the season, with a typical episode taking about three days to produce. The promo for the Sunday night showing is usually out by the previous Wednesday. It airs consistently at 8:00 right after the night's newscast on TVJ, presenting what can be considered a positive balance to a newscast of mostly negative content – a breath of fresh air after the bad news.

As a corporate entity, the Scotiabank Jamaica Foundation funds the production of *The Teller* and then negotiates rates for airtime with TVJ. An episode would normally start with an opening montage, followed by shots of various activities. When the story starts, the specific name of the feature, such as "Nutrition for Learning", comes across the screen. There are no breaks and the show stays away from voice-over narration. Instead, the focus is on beneficiaries telling their stories about differences made in their lives by the outreach activities of the foundation. It is also available on the Scotiabank Jamaica YouTube channel and has been promoted on social-media platforms such as Facebook.

Though only three examples of social advocacy television shows have been detailed, this genre has potential for growth. The relatively short formats and the ease with which such productions can be completed on a regular basis make them appropriate for small television markets. These short formats may also offer appropriate sponsorship opportunities as small markets are likely to be beset by social problems that, along with their related solutions, would provide content for an ongoing social advocacy television series.

## Sports

International and local sporting activities are regular elements in the schedules of both CVM and TVJ. These include horse racing, football, athletics and cricket. In addition, stations will present major sporting events such as World Cup Football and the Olympics, coverage of which often leads to a change in schedules to accommodate them. In recent years, the stations have presented exclusive coverage of the proceedings and at other times this has been shared. In 2004, CVM TV's exclusive deal for coverage of World Cup Football led their competitor TVJ to seek a deal to tie up exclusive rights in upcoming years.[36] Though not the focus of this book, Sportsmax, a subscription television cable channel, illustrates how important this genre is in Jamaica, warranting a dedicated channel.[37] Annual high school sporting events, such as the Inter-Secondary Schools Association Boys and Girls Champs, continue to provide prime content for broadcast on the free-to-air stations.[38] There are at least twelve shows in the sports genre in Jamaica.

*Thursday Night at the Fights* is an example of a long-running television programme in the sports genre. Based on its earliest appearance in the *Gleaner*'s TV guide, it started in 1984 and appeared on JBC TV on Thursday nights at 11:00, just before the station signed off. It provided a roundup of current boxing matches and a look at archived fights that had been aired on JBC TV. Presenters who would provide commentary for the featured boxing matches included Patrick Anderson, Keith Brown, Hugh Crosskill and Ali McNab.

The show was popular and, according to Patrick Anderson, wives were happy that it was on on Thursday nights because it meant that husbands would arrive home early to watch. There were a number of local gyms that trained boxers such as Trevor Berbick and Richard "Shrimpy" Clarke to participate in local or international matches. The show was therefore relevant as it helped to promote boxing. It was done in association with Dragon Stout, which provided sponsorship, and the presenters all worked in the sports department of JBC TV. The production routine involved acquiring footage of boxing matches and writing and recording local commentary. Though for a while on Thursday nights it was replaced by wrestling, more recently the schedule on TVJ has included the boxing-related reality show *Wray and Nephew Contender*. Given its appeal to audiences, the sports genre is another one that has the potential to yield content that could be sustained in small television markets.

### Talk Shows: General and Special Interest

The talk show is perhaps the most ubiquitous type of programming on Jamaican television. Talk shows can be delivered more economically, as there is less pressure to cover the costs of production and facilities. There have been twenty-nine shows in this category in Jamaica, some of which have been done well for a period. Others have not got off the ground and some have begun to establish themselves in recent years.

*The Diana Wright Show* was produced at the CPTC between 1991 and 1992. During this time it aired on JBC TV and later moved its production to those facilities, but soon went off air.[39] *Our Voices*, with Lisa Hanna and Carlene "The Dancehall Queen" Smith, ran in 2003 on CVM TV.[40] *The Naked Truth* aired on CVM TV for two seasons from October 2012. This featured four women sharing their perspectives on such topics as business, finance, entertainment, lifestyle, parenting and everyday issues.[41] In

October 2013, a third season was promised but this had not materialized as at December 2015.

*Wealth Magazine Business Access* comprising mostly interviews featuring prominent business personalities, as well as coverage of corporate events, appeared first on TVJ in 2011.[42] The parent company Creative Media and Events Limited, became more serious about business, and began operating a channel called "Business Access TV"on Flow's cable network on 12 July 2015.[43]

*The Susan Show*, produced by Simber Productions Limited, has been on air since 28 April 2005. It aired originally on CVM TV and in its fifth year, moved to TVJ.[44] The show is seasonal and appears on Tuesdays between 8:30 p.m. and 9:30 p.m. with a repeat on Thursdays from 1:05 p.m. to 2:00 p.m. A season typically comprises seven one-hour episodes, each of which is pre-recorded in studio with an audience or on location with guest interviews. The host, Susan Simes, had prior production experience having been at other media houses such as Mediamix, then at TVJ as an editor and supervising editor, then later hosting and producing her own programme *Hype Zone*.

The show follows a strict business plan. Simber Productions Limited negotiates airtime rates with TVJ and manages the sale of advertising. Simes also formed a foundation to be able to manage giveaways which are a feature on the show; in some cases the giveaways are written into the sponsorship deal.

The tagline "Doing good in your neighbourhood" suggests that it aims to be positive and to build a better Jamaica by showing Jamaicans at their best. Specially themed shows have included Christmastime giveaways, back-to-school and Caribbean connection, which reunites people across the region.

In 2005, when a gentleman travelled from Canada and sought her help in reuniting with his family in Jamaica, Simes conceptualized the idea and introduced a segment on family reunions. She focuses on the plight of people in Jamaica who have lost contact with their families.[45] They tell their stories and disclose information on the relatives being sought. The programme conducts investigations including DNA testing and the results lead to reunions mediated by the host. She has resisted the idea of devoting the entire programme to this issue as investigation requires a lot of resources. She also fears that it may be too emotional for viewers. However, it is such a popular feature that there is a waiting list of over two hundred people who have made requests to be reunited with relatives or partners.[46]

Audiences express deep attachment to the show and to its host, who is affectionately called Aunty Susan. She also has a programme targeting children called *Kids Say . . .*, which started in February 2011. *The Susan Show* has received many accolades, including the United Nations Population Fund 2008 Gold Award. The programme maintains a presence on social-media platforms Twitter and Facebook.

This show has taken different types of elements from various television categories and integrated them with the talk show genre resulting in a hybrid that includes reuniting family members, social issues, personality profiles, makeovers, reality show type competitions, charity and so on. The number of different features and segments is perhaps a reflection of the need to provide a range of content that can broaden the base of viewership in the small market.

The talk show presents opportunities for producers to create programming which allows viewers and guests to tell their stories. Based on the number of these produced since the start of terrestrial broadcasting in Jamaica, this genre continues to be a feasible one for creating content in small television markets.

## Others

Vox pop and other short packages – usually lasting five minutes or less – as well as infomercials of varying lengths, typically used to fill airtime, are among the other formats found in Jamaica's television market. In this category, there was *Weh Yuh Seh* on TVJ that was hosted by Basil "Bagga" Brown and ended with his death in 2011.[47] *Wat a Gwaan*, also a vox pop, appeared on CVM TV.

For a short while, the *Mega Shopping Show*, a trade show with Colombian businessmen marketing goods via infomercials, aired during the daytime. The antics of the outgoing salesmen speaking Jamaican creole with a Spanish accent added an entertainment edge.[48] This was oftentimes confused with the *Bashco* and *Megamart Shopping Shows* which began airing about the same time. Bashco is the name of a Jamaican chain of department stores promoting low prices and a wide range of goods. Megamart is another Jamaican department store chain that also carries food items. Members and non-members can shop but the members get discounted prices.

The *Bashco Shopping Show* started in 2009 with media personalities Denise Hunt and Elva "Queenie" Ruddock. Hunt left the show and Omar Azan, marketing and public relations officer at Bascho Trading Co. Limited began hosting with Queenie. This thirty-minute infomercial was aired twice daily from Mondays to Fridays, but since 2014 it has been aired once daily from Mondays to Saturdays on CVM TV.

The *Megamart Shopping Show* started in 2010 on TVJ and featured broadcaster Doraine Samuels. It then moved to CVM TV and was hosted by actor Christopher "Johnny" Daley. These thirty-minute infomercials were designed to promote the goods and services of the outlets Bashco and Megamart. They filled airtime in a way that would make a programme manager's job easy as it became a way to avoid repeated content. These formats can be produced in small media markets as content to fill airtime and earn income.

## Discussion

From the foregoing description of television shows by genre, we recognize that some of these have had their run, and others are still on air and have the potential to become long-running. For those that did not continue on air, why did that happen? For those that ran and were not renewed, why were they not renewed? For those that have the potential to stay on air, what can they do to ensure that this happens? These questions could form the basis for future research and analysis of select television shows in Jamaica, and contribute to the body of literature on television studies.

In some cases the programmes did not attract an audience, while others that did could not maintain their viewership and they folded because of financial problems. Some ended because they were not supported by strong marketing research – producers having little access to reliable quantitative data that could yield estimates of ratings or viewership. At best, qualitative reactions offer some insight into performance.

Lack of sponsorship can be given as a major reason for why most television shows go off air but there are others worth considering. The ability to attract sponsorship through advertising is a mark of success. This of course can be affected by the time slot as a show can be aired when no one is likely to be watching. As possibilities for access to media content change, viewers are no longer making appointments to watch their favourite shows when they can choose to watch instead whenever they can, on a variety of platforms.

Then there are problems related to programme quality or production values. These could arise from issues with the talent or host associated with a show. In some cases, those which identify strongly with a particular personality have terminated when that person's involvement ends. There is also the matter of scripting. Many producers may have an idea but have challenges translating that into something that is televisual or suitable for television. In trying to achieve a televisual product, there are often ambitious attempts at staging which are not always feasible to maintain.

Programmes also go off air because of weak and uncommitted producers or other personnel. Some productions have no dedicated person who will fight for the show's survival. With one person working across several programmes, it is often difficult to devote the necessary time to a single production in order to make it a success. The production facilities, where the show is physically produced, also affect the outcome. In whose studio or editing suite is the work done? Who owns the production? There are cost-cutting benefits to the association with some established production companies. The four programmes under our lens were inadvertently subsidized during the JBC years. Others did not benefit from this sort of grooming, or what could be described as the "incubator effect". They were developed under a public service broadcasting model before moving to a television entity operating under a commercial model.

In concluding this chapter, we assert that television programmes experience different levels of success depending on the show's genre. There are programmes that were short lived and did not go beyond a first series or first season even though they had the potential to do so, such as *Deuces Wild* and *Claro Cash Cab*. *Teacha's Pet* on CVM TV and online ended prematurely due to the legal troubles of the star, dancehall artiste Vybz Kartel.[49]

## COMING UP: SHOWS WATCHED AND ONES TO WATCH

There are programmes that did their run, completing several series but being discontinued after a while. One such example is *Our Voices* with Carlene Smith and Lisa Hanna.[50] *Round Table Talk* evolved into other talk shows. *Rappin'* did its time on air and since then, other youth television talk shows have been evolving in Jamaica. *Jamaica DWL* (dead with laugh or dying with laughter) did one season with the potential to return for future seasons.[51] In fact, any of these could return to air, assuming that there is audience and advertising interest. Worthy of mention as examples of shows that had sustained runs of between ten to twenty-nine years but eventually ended are *Lime Tree Lane* (ten years), *Ring Ding* (twelve years), *Where It's At* (fifteen years), *Royal Palm Estate* (twenty-one years) and *Creative Cooking* (twenty-nine years).

Those programmes that are still on air – but not for as long as the four which form the main focus of this book – and have the potential to continue include *Religious Hardtalk*, *All Together Sing*, *Junior Schools' Challenge Quiz*, *The Susan Show* and *On Stage*. These have all passed the ten-year on air mark. There are some current and public affairs shows such as *All Angles* that also have the potential to be long-running. Note that these shows are from particular genres: entertainment, current and public affairs, quiz and game show, and talk show. This suggests that genre should be considered when producing a television show for a small market. This is supported by the television studies literature. Joseph Straubhaar in describing genres in national and local television production noted from as early as 1995 that "television genres have developed remarkably over the last twenty to thirty years. . . . More importantly, in some ways, is that a number of very low cost genres have evolved which can be produced almost anywhere with the simplest and cheapest of equipment: news, talk, variety, live music, and games."[52] Indeed, the genre of the show has implications for its success and time on air in small television markets like Jamaica.

# 9

# Sneak Preview
## Future Trends in Jamaican Television

Ever since early experimental forms of television appeared in the late 1920s, television has grown into a ubiquitous piece of technology that continues to evolve and appeal to viewers worldwide.[1] There are trends which suggest that though elements are changing, there are indications that television will still serve a purpose in the future. Some notable trends which have emerged relate to television audiences, content production and distribution, as well as media convergence.

Television audiences are changing their consumption habits. With access to technology that allows for mobility and Internet connectivity, VOD and streaming services, digital video recording and the availability of archived content, audiences are changing the way they view television content. In addition to what they watch, how they watch has changed. While the television set is the main means of accessing content, people can watch content on cell phones and smart devices such as game consoles and tablets. The new technology allows viewing on demand and has eroded one of the mainstays of free-to-air television, the idea of appointment television – the notion that viewers will make an arrangement to watch a show at the time it appears on the station. There is a move away from this habit of watching a programme according to the schedule determined by the programme distributor or broadcaster. Viewers can watch their favourite programmes when and where they feel like it. With the rise of social media and smart devices, viewers enhance their experience with second screening, the tendency to use two or more screens at the same time, to watch television programmes and participate in online discussions over social-media platforms such as Twitter or Facebook. Viewers feel as if they are part of an audience that extends beyond their viewing space. Live events which have international appeal such as beauty pageants and sports have attracted second screening behaviour globally. For example, Ellen DeGeneres's selfie at the 2014 Oscar Awards in the United States was retweeted over 3.3 million times.[2]

Some television shows also utilize social media during their programming. This helps to increase the engagement of viewers and create a buzz about the show. Binge watching is closely related to the idea of setting your own agenda. As archived content becomes more accessible, audiences can view many episodes of a show at their own pace, rather than wait for the station's scheduled programming. Unlike during the early years, audiences now have other means of accessing televisual content. In addition to free-to-air channels, there are now cable channels, satellite channels and Internet streaming services such as YouTube and Netflix. Audiences have a wider choice and can choose what they want to watch. What they watch is not determined by a programme manager. They are now also producers of content as distribution allows for uploading either user-generated content or content copied, albeit illegally, from elsewhere, such as regular television programming. Some users have become YouTube celebrities and have expanded to other platforms such as cable channels.

The audience consumption habits being practised now are partly a result of trends in distribution. Traditionally, television content was broadcast through terrestrial transmission. Now, programmes are shared using a range of platforms. Programmes can be viewed on not only cable channels or satellite channels but also on either free or paid streaming services. These distribution trends have posed challenges to producers and broadcasters who worry that their potential earnings are compromised because of the threat of piracy, where programmes are uploaded and shared illegally with no compensation for the creators. In limited resource markets, some producers and broadcasters cannot control the illegal distribution allowed by the technology.

One response to this is to make it easier for viewers to see the content through the television station's or producer's own online platforms. Some content is offered through third-party websites with or without permission from the copyright holder. Format exporting and franchising are other ways to share programmes, but in these cases, it is the idea or format of an already proven concept that is shared or sold. Local producers can do local versions following the format "bible" or established rules for creating the show. In this situation, there is no fear of being accused of stealing ideas or of criticisms of penetration of foreign programming, as the locally produced version of the internationally traded format is made relevant for local audiences. Some popular TV show formats exported around the world include *The Voice*, *Who Wants to Be a Millionaire*, *Survivor* and *Big Brother*. Within the Caribbean, *Digicel Rising Stars*, which came out of an Irish franchise, started in Jamaica and has been successfully exported to Haiti, Barbados, Trinidad and Tobago, and other parts of the Eastern Caribbean.[3]

Globally, digital television transmission uses available bandwidth more effectively, which allows it to be integrated with other digital services. Digital television has better resolution and sound than analogue broadcasting and can offer more channels. However, most free-to-air broadcasters do not have the financial resources to operate a number of channels with the same quality of content. The digital switchover has begun in many countries and has been completed in some.[4] Other countries are still making plans to complete their digital transition. What is clear is that the future of television in Jamaica will be affected by this phenomenon.

As distribution patterns change so will production patterns. With more outlets available for showing content, there is greater need for a constant supply and so producers now search for ways to provide this in a cost efficient manner. For example, *Schools' Challenge Quiz*, which airs each weekday in Jamaica during its season, is pre-recorded on the first day of the week. In other words, five or six shows are created in one day for airing over the five-day week. This makes sense if there are limited studio facilities available. It is more efficient than shooting one episode per day. Television stations instead of doing all productions in-house may consider commissioning other production entities to create shows. There is a range of arrangements, from co-production deals to contra-deals to split-revenue models, which requires the usual negotiations. One interesting development which has appeal to audiences in different cultural contexts is the cross-border production where the content relates to two or more cultural contexts. This is essentially a co-production that can be distributed in both of the markets of the participating entities such as the television shows *The Bridge* or *Mr Selfridge*. The production companies in each location jointly create and finance the product and distribute to both markets.[5] This is one way to spread the cost of a production and to broaden the potential audience.

Some local television stations will buy foreign shows, which is nothing new in television, but the reason for doing so now is different. In the past, popular foreign shows were affordable and filled airtime. With competition from cable channels, popular foreign shows are not only more affordable for local stations but also bring viewers from cable channels to the local stations and make them stay.

With exclusivity deals, local stations can become the only authorized channel to transmit a foreign show to local audiences with that show being blocked from its originating foreign channel on cable which was previously accessible to those audiences. This idea had mostly been associated with sporting events such as World Cup Football and the Olympics. However, in recent years, this has expanded to include programme series, as was the case when TVJ bought the rights to NBC's *The Voice* on which Jamaican singer Tessanne Chin was a competitor, and again when TVJ acquired the rights to *Empire*, a top-rated show from the Fox network.[6] Other shows popular on cable that have been acquired by free-to-air stations in Jamaica include *Scandal*, *Suits* and *The Good Wife*. Again, deals are negotiated between content owners and programme distributors to meet the need for productions to fill the increasing space available for showing content.

Such developments could be seen as a negative for free-to-air stations, but there is evidence that stations are moving to use the new platforms and viewing habits to their advantage. This can be seen in the fact that the two major stations have a significant web and social-media presence, with websites for programmes – some live-streaming and archived content – available online. The RJR Communications Group launched its 1Spotmedia Internet media service in March 2015 that allows viewers to access content online for free, with some archived content attracting a fee.[7]

Some programme producers who initially created shows for airing on free-to-air channels have extended their programme offerings to cable channels. The *Wealth Magazine Business Access* television show, which was a programme aired on TVJ, eventually moved to the cable channel "Business Access TV". With the increasing outlets for showing content, producers are able to move programmes to outlets where they feel they can get the best return on their investment.

With this development, everyone is now more concerned with ownership rights. Producers have tried to move what they thought was their programme from one station to another, only to find out they did not own the programme nor had they any rights to the content, even though at the time of producing they created everything associated with the show. The usual explanation is that the show was created while the producer was a full-time employee and so the station owns the show. Now, more producers are ensuring that they pay attention not only to the production details, but also to rights and ownership issues. More sophisticated approaches to negotiation are helping to shape creative arrangements to facilitate an increase in television productions.

Other producers create content for online platforms and have been able to transfer the content to free-to-air. For example, *Listen Mi News*, a commentary on current affairs sung to a dancehall beat originated by Bay C of Jamaican dancehall group TOK, began on YouTube in October 2013.[8] This has been seen on CVM TV. Increasingly, YouTube is the birthplace of varied video content that eventually makes it to mainstream television. In Jamaica, Toni "Bella" Blair has expanded from YouTube to Reggae Entertainment Television on cable. Russhaine Jonoy Berry has parlayed his fast-talking, high-pitched "DuttyBerry" into a character that has made appearances on television.

In the fifty and more years since the introduction of television in Jamaica, technology associated with production, distribution and viewing has developed dramatically. In the area of programmes, production technology and changes to the way audiences can view content have and will continue to have an impact. A positive development is the introduction of digital technology that has led to higher quality recording and a decrease in the price of equipment. On the viewing side, the biggest change the technology effected is the increase in options for viewing. From one television station for almost thirty years, Jamaica has moved to three free-to-air stations and a network of cable providers. These offer customers a multitude of local and international channels, and on-demand programming either free or at a premium, which means that free-to-air stations are competing with a myriad of subscriber channels. By law, cable companies have to provide access to the free-to-air stations via cable through the "must carry" rule.9 Computer technology and the rise of the Internet have given viewers further options for viewing television programming, including the introduction of subscription streaming services from Netflix that can be paid for in Jamaican currency. This service not only distributes, but also produces content – films and television programmes – that it commissions. Those savvy enough on the Internet can use simple clicks and searches to uncover programming from North America and Europe for free.

In competing with this range of content, free-to-air stations have tried to attract viewers by broadcasting a mix of local and international programmes and have invested in top-rated shows, in some cases, as earlier noted, by signing exclusive deals. Arguably, the Jamaican television sector is not really creating many local shows. It continues to purchase foreign content to attract local audiences.

While content providers outside the region have created popular shows that are seen and enjoyed the world over including in Jamaica, it could be said that they do not understand the Caribbean audience and are not in a position to create relevant programme packages. Those within Jamaica may be best suited for this task. However, other issues, such as lack of sponsorship and lack of means to make and continue to make programmes, have affected the amount of local content on television. One attempt to create content for the Caribbean was evident with the introduction of the Tempo channel from MTV, which is seen on cable in Jamaica and is also available in the Caribbean and North America.10

Apart from audience, distribution and production trends, media convergence is also revolutionizing the television industry in Jamaica. This phenomenon occurs at different levels. At the technology level, traditionally separate media forms are now being merged as a result of digitization and computer networking. At the organizational level, media entities that created traditionally distinct products are now merging. Again, digitization and government deregulation have helped to facilitate this. Print media houses have acquired radio stations. Radio stations have acquired television stations. These mergers have implications for shows. Should *Entertainment Report*, a television show, be produced for radio? *Religious Hardtalk* and *Talk Up Yout* are now television shows but they started in radio. Telecommunication service providers are now acquiring media outlets. In December 2010, Lime launched mobile TV or television accessible on a mobile device – a short-lived experience suspended in March 2013.[11] In 2014, Digicel launched a news service branded as Loop and acquired cable service provider Telstar.[12] Cable and Wireless Communications, which provided fixed and mobile telephone services through its Lime brand, is now merged with Columbus Communications, which provides cable television, broadband and telephony services as Flow Jamaica. In August 2015, the RJR Communications Group and the Gleaner Company announced their merger.[13] Will we see more mergers in the future? Will traditional media have to get into telecommunications as telecommunication entities are getting into media content creation and distribution?

With these trends, the role of various organizations is being challenged and redefined. The BCJ, Jamaica's media regulatory body that traditionally regulated electronic media, is now forced to reconsider its role as all media are electronic, including the traditional print media which can now be accessed electronically online. Should the Commission regulate media content shared online or only content shared over the free-to-air airwaves which has been its usual regulatory role?[14] Other associations in the industry will also need to consider how they will function in a future media environment. How will an organization like the Jamaica Promotions Corporation, which has tried to promote filmmaking in Jamaica, function in the future? The Media Association of Jamaica which historically fostered better relationships with advertising agencies, must now consider how it will measure media audiences and ratings in the new environment and align these with advertising rates. CIN, which has traditionally distributed content to Jamaican and Caribbean diaspora markets, must now grapple with how to maintain those markets. The Jamaica Film Producers Association now renamed and constituted as the Jamaica Film and Television Association must now consider how it will support producers of film and televisual content in a converged media market.[15] How will Jamaica participate in the global television (and film) trade? How can what is produced locally fit into world trends? Will piracy and informal distribution networks continue to pose challenges to the local industry? Do the answers lie in more franchising and format exporting where the focus should be on exporting formats conceptualized here rather than importing formats created elsewhere? Or should it be a fair trade where, for every format we export, we also import? Producing imported formats locally might be a big challenge, but developing and exporting formats may be something worth considering.[16] Or does the answer lie in cross-border productions aimed at regional markets? The practice of producing a local version of a franchised television show is not new to Jamaica. *Romper Room* was a franchised show produced and aired on JBC TV in the 1960s and 1970s. Local producers were able to add their own local hosts but most content and scripts were provided.[17] The franchise company for *Romper Room* was the Fremantle Corporation headed by Paul Talbot.[18]

What will become of the four long-running shows in Jamaica featured in this book? Because *Schools' Challenge Quiz* showcases teams of schoolchildren, it will have a steady supply of teams and in the same way a built-in renewal of potential viewers. There have been a number of other Jamaican quiz shows but *Schools' Challenge Quiz* has outlasted them all and led to a spin-off series *Junior Schools' Challenge Quiz*, which itself is doing well in terms of staging an annual season. The senior quiz show has also led to *Schools' Challenge Quiz Access* and *Schools' Challenge Quiz* preview programmes, which are on air because of the appeal of the original programme. Another show *All Together Sing* comes from the same production stable as *Schools' Challenge Quiz* and is over ten years old. This time the teams from schools sing in a knockout competition to find the best choir.

*Entertainment Report* spawned an occasional programme series called *ER2*. This programme repurposed original *Entertainment Report* content into themed programmes and aired on a Saturday evening when sponsored. Miller, who produces *Entertainment Report*, also judges on *Digicel Rising Stars*. Ian Boyne, the originator of *Profile*, was also behind another successful programme, *Religious Hardtalk*. This is, yet again, a simple studio show with minimal set and the host and guest sitting at a table to discuss religious issues. *Hill an' Gully Ride* may not have obvious spin-offs but other shows have had elements of the concept, such as *Trails* and *Hidden Treasures*. These programmes travel the length and breadth of the country and bring Jamaica to the viewer. Other programmes such as *Weh Yuh Seh* and *Wat a Gwaan* have an essence of the *Hill an' Gully Ride* show in that they let the audience see and hear Jamaicans as they are.

The four longest-running shows still on air in 2015 in Jamaica are essentially JBC TV's legacy. The onus now is on TVJ, a commercial entity, to manage these programmes which came out of a public broadcasting ethos. Will the shows become too commercialized and lose their essence? Can audiences still enjoy programmes which originally aimed at national development and now also aim to please the corporate sponsors with the promise and delivery of high viewership?

Still on air? Will the shows remain as they are? This calls into question succession planning. As much as these shows experience some amount of success when compared to others, what about their succession planning? Who is being groomed to continue the production of these shows? Do the shows go off air once long-standing producers are no longer associated with them? Who will manage social media for these shows? *Entertainment Report* has a Twitter account. *Schools' Challenge Quiz* has a Facebook page. Comments appear on Twitter and other social-media platforms about *Profile* and its host Ian Boyne, but are these social-media comments acknowledged with viewers being engaged and encouraged to remain loyal fans?

What do the current trends discussed so far imply for the future of these shows? We cannot predict exactly what they and other television shows will be in the future, but we can focus more on possibilities. Some relate to media convergence, franchising and format exporting, feasible genres, distribution and audience trends. These are discussed in the next chapter.

# 10
# Still Ahead
Possibilities and Recommendations

Jamaica's experience in television production has been characterized by successes and failures. Since its introduction in 1963, the broadcast television sector has yielded over three hundred shows in varying genres and lasting for different periods on air. Shows such as *Schools' Challenge Quiz, Profile, Hill an' Gully Ride* and *Entertainment Report* demonstrate that it is possible to sustain television programmes on air in small television markets. These have survived in an under-resourced environment where the attempt was made to provide television content using a public broadcasting model. They continue to air under a privatized broadcaster. With the evolution of the media landscape, opportunities are now available to further sustain these and other potentially long-running shows for Jamaican audiences. Possibilities worth considering relate to media convergence, franchising and format exporting, feasible genres, distribution and audience trends.

## Media Convergence

Media convergence offers the opportunity for cross-promotion of the televised product. The same content can be repurposed and creatively shared and promoted on different platforms. This has implications for the structure and format of the shows. Marketing departments can offer package deals across platforms. A television show could now have an accompanying print magazine and a blog with a photo gallery of images from the content shared initially during the show. The blog could feature more details about the show's content, shared before as preview material or after as review material. There could be extended versions of interviews which were edited for the television version of the show. There could be audio clips or dedicated podcasts of the content as well. All these could be formatted so that they could be shared online over social media or on the website associated with the show. There could be behind the scenes and themed clips packaged as additional content. This could help to build the brand and increase loyalty among audiences, creating a community of engaged followers. These followers could do more than just watch – they could be allowed to comment on content, vote for story plots and be involved in a range of other ways. Targeted online advertising could be used to increase the earning of the brand associated with the television show. Critics of this development argue that it can be costly for newcomers to enter a converged media market because of the high cost of producing content suitable for the various platforms.[1] However, the newcomer could be given a probationary period to establish the viability of the new show before investment is made to expand it across converged platforms. Also, producers would have to explore new formats for the converged media environment. A sitcom may not need to be thirty minutes long per episode. It could be segmented into smaller units – such as six shorter five-minute parts – which may be easier for viewing and sharing on online and mobile platforms.

### Franchising and Format Exporting

Trends in franchising and format exporting present possibilities for Jamaican television producers. Format exporting does not involve the sale of completed productions; instead it is the sale of a programme idea or concept that can be adapted to be used in different countries, cultures and language markets.[2] The beginnings of format exporting can be traced to radio when many programmes were remade for television. For example, the game show *What's My Line* originated in the United States but was adapted by the British Broadcasting Corporation where it became a success first on radio and then on television.[3] Albert Moran, in his work *Copycat TV: Globalisation*

## STILL AHEAD: POSSIBILITIES AND RECOMMENDATIONS

*Program Formats and Cultural Identity*, noted a number of things needed for format exporting to happen. The most important of these is the programme "bible", containing information about the target audience demographics, scheduling and a consultancy service provided by the company that owns the format.[4]

A possible approach for Jamaican television producers is to consider not only importing formats from elsewhere and producing them locally or engaging in format adaptation, but also developing formats which can be exported or franchised to markets outside of Jamaica. This means that producers should not focus so much on creating final programmes for export but should aim to sell the idea or format of the show to other producers who can localize the template for their markets. One issue that has beset Jamaican producers is the concern that a good television show concept or idea could be stolen, but if managed properly, these fears can be allayed by adhering to copyright legislation. The expression of the concept or idea as a successful finished television programme can give potential buyers an example of what the show could be. Establishing production guidelines in a format bible which helps to promote the creation of consistent episodes to support the brand in a series is something worth considering. A television show that has been created in Jamaica and is deemed successful with local audiences could be developed and exported as a format for production in other geo-linguistic markets. A franchise could be developed eventually, requiring holders to pay the originator. The main challenge of this possibility is that television shows deemed successful among Jamaican audiences – a relatively small market, may not guarantee success for producers hoping to create the show elsewhere in similar small markets.

### Feasible Genres

There are opportunities regarding the particular genres of television shows produced locally. While genres are established worldwide, Jamaican producers do not need to adhere to all the elements of the genre. Typically, some suggest a certain length – there is the thirty-minute sitcom, the one-hour documentary or the one-hour drama series. Producers should be willing to adjust these formats by doing shorter versions to begin with and then expanding as the work gains traction. If one cannot afford a product that is the typical length of a particular genre, then consider doing a shorter version and allowing it to grow as resources become available as it gains in popularity. Another possibility is cross-genre or hybrid productions which have the potential to appeal to a wider audience because of the combined elements. However, care should be taken to ensure that fans of a particular category are not alienated. Some genres are likely to be more successful than others depending on the cultural and financial context of a market. If dramas have not been sustained on air successfully in a television market for whatever reason, such as poor scripting or no financing, contemplate using a different approach to production. This strategy may involve experimenting with the genre and finding feasible ways of creating a product – a strategy that could be applied to a range of genres.

## Distribution

Developments in distribution of television content also provide opportunities for Jamaican producers. There is an increase in distribution platforms. A show may be created for viewing on television, traditionally a device located in the home. Programmes may now be viewed on a mobile phone, computer screen, tablet or game console and even on video display outdoor billboards, assuming the programme provider is making the show available for access on these various platforms. As audiences are becoming familiar with these new points of access, there is an expectation that the content must be available in a timely manner. Audiences become frustrated when they expect to see a programme online but the provider has not made it available there until weeks later. This has implications for how shows are created. In creating subsequent episodes of shows, producers may want to take stock of and respond to commentary appearing online on social-media platforms so that audiences feel that they are playing a part in the show's development. A television show that attracts feedback via online platforms cannot ignore these comments forever. Audiences may eventually leave if they feel ignored. Producers must find ways to react to or acknowledge online interactions. With the opportunities for distribution on various platforms, producers must be aware of a major associated downside. Content shared widely across

## STILL AHEAD: POSSIBILITIES AND RECOMMENDATIONS

platforms can be downloaded illegally and repurposed to profit others not involved in the origination. If a producer is unable to manage distribution across multiple platforms, there is the possibility of not reaping the associated benefits. Strong branding of television shows that clearly establishes the copyright owner can address this.

### Audience Trends

Audiences have always played an important part in the life of a television show because without an audience, there is no show. With the current trends in media consumption habits – second screening, binge watching, viewing VOD – producers need to ensure that they are keeping up with the ways that audiences want to view their programmes. Producers may need to find ways to engage audiences outside of the show's airtime. Researching audiences is going to be even more important if they are expected to keep coming back. This cannot only focus on ratings, but must aim to understand how, when and why viewers consume the show and how they can be better served. The research must also help to measure and understand how audience behaviour across multiple platforms affects ratings and ultimately determines online advertising and on-channel promotion.[5] Producers must recognize that audiences exist in a space with a lot of content competing for attention. How do you ensure that they watch content and keep viewing it? A show's survival can be affected if audiences are not wooed into watching and won over as faithful viewers. Research into audiences will give more insight. Some genres naturally guarantee a sustained audience. A high school quiz show will always have the interest of students, parents and teachers who go through the school system. An entertainment news magazine show will always be able to find entertainment related events and issues on which to report. Producing genres with the potential for a guaranteed audience will contribute to a show's time on air.

In addition to the foregoing possibilities, we make two recommendations relating to how a show's time on air is measured and how information about a show should be documented.

## Assessing Time on Air

Individuals have assessed a show's success by considering its length in terms of the number of years on air or the number of seasons or episodes produced. This means that the more years a show is on air or the more seasons and episodes produced, the greater the longevity. However, such measures of length ignore context and affect comparisons of long-running shows across different markets. Measuring a television show's time on air could also benefit from a consideration of the particular market in which it is produced.

Different markets have different broadcasting histories. A show on air for thirty-five years in one market should not be seen in the same light as one which has lasted the same amount of time in a different and smaller market. When thinking of longevity, one might be tempted to compare shows produced in the same genre in different markets. One might argue, for example, that the US-produced *It's Academic*, which has been on air for fifty-five years, since 1961, is a longer-running show than the Jamaican produced *Schools' Challenge Quiz*, which began airing in 1970 and has been running for forty-six years up to 2015. This is a factual statement.

However, if we consider when television was introduced in each country, and calculate the years on air as a proportion of the television broadcast years of the country, then we get a different picture. In the United States, television was introduced in 1946 while in Jamaica, television began in 1963. This means that the United States has had sixty-nine television broadcast years while Jamaica has had fifty-two. A show on for fifty-five years in a country with television for sixty-nine years has aired for only 78 per cent of the possible broadcasting life there, while a show on for forty-six years in a country with fifty-two years of television has been on air for 87 per cent of its television years. In this context, the data presents an additional way of assessment. Appendix 2 compares some of the longest-running shows against broadcast life in various countries.

## Documenting Television Shows

In order to assess a show's length of time on air, one would need information about the show's start date. Also, as audiences make decisions about which

## STILL AHEAD: POSSIBILITIES AND RECOMMENDATIONS

shows to watch, it is likely that they will expect information about these shows to be easily available. Television studies research will also benefit from any background information that enhances scholarly analysis. Therefore, producers of video content shared on traditional terrestrial television and on more modern platforms online must document the history of their shows and provide that information alongside any archived content. A blog post or Wikipedia entry about the show's development would help viewers learn more. In completing this work, most of the documented information about Jamaican television shows came from Jamaican newspapers. We recommend that producers provide the following information about their shows in an accessible format:

- Title
- Genre
- Created by
- Presented by (if applicable)
- Country of origin
- Original language
- Number of seasons
- Number of episodes
- Location
- Running time
- Camera set-up
- Production company
- Distributor
- Original TV channel or online platform
- Other channels (if applicable)
- Original release date

See examples of the information presented in the "At a Glance" figures presented at the end of chapters 3, 4, 5 and 6.

Long-running and successful television shows are possible in media environments with limited resources. That four of the longest-running shows still on the air in 2015 on Jamaican television were created and nurtured under a public service broadcast ethos and have been able to cross over and continue to be commercially viable in privately owned media operating in a competitive environment suggests that there must be a compromise between the business imperative and the public good. Television shows that reflect a people's cultural interests and have found feasible ways to achieve acceptable production values are likely to sustain the interest of sponsors and audiences in small media markets.

## APPENDIX 1

# Definitions of Some Typical Genres for Free-to-Air Television

The concept of genre has come to television from other types of media, most notably literature and film. It relates to the idea that certain formats and elements are present or recognizable in programme categories. The elements may include such areas as setting, content, treatment, acting, style and subject matter. For producers, a genre can guide production and help identify audience, scheduling, channels and networks. Genre is complex and there is not one definitive interpretation of a particular genre. There are groups and subgroups, hybrid genres or mixed genres. Some programmes can be categorized as falling into one or more, depending on the categorization or the naming of a genre. A genre might be considered a category of its own, a subgenre of another or linked to another, or not considered in one genre list as a genre at all.

The line between genre and format is sometimes blurred, with elements considered as identifying a genre appearing to be issues of format. In some circumstances, various elements take precedence in defining a genre so that there are some cases of genre that can be identified as mainly driven by content or subject matter, such as religious or sports programming. An interview programme about a sports issue could be defined as belonging to the sports genre if content is considered, or to the talk show genre if format is considered. A drama about a religious topic might be considered religious programming or drama; a music programme featuring gospel music might find itself categorized as music, entertainment or religious. Some genres are combined in categorization – for instance, science fiction as a genre would encompass programmes with themes of the future and scientific settings, but sometimes science fiction is included in a genre called fantasy or sci-fi and fantasy. This would encompass science fiction and programmes set in the past, present or future with themes of the supernatural.

Defining genres may sometimes be driven mainly by the purpose of the definition, in terms of production, or funding. Certain channels and networks may have broad genre categorizations to help the audience navigate its channel offerings, while those who study the area may opt for broader, or more refined definitions. As such, the list of genres on a television network website may be different from that of a streaming subscription site or an academic work.

Genre is not static. They may rise and wane and new ones develop over time. Other factors affecting genre include market, culture and geography. Some may be common in one market and non-existent in another. The importance of a genre may also change over time and location – in the United States, the prime-time Western staple of network schedules in the 1960s gave way to the ascendance of the police procedural in the 1970s. Telenovelas are ubiquitous and popular in Latin America whereas in Europe and North America the soap opera is favoured.

As in filmmaking, television productions are often underpinned by the aesthetics employed within the audio and visual communication and are not isolated from contemporary, cultural, technological and historical contexts. Effective television production should entail an awareness of how genre characteristics can influence production and reception.

| Main Categories | Subgenres | Mainly Driven by: |
|---|---|---|
| **Animation** | | |
| Moving images created by animating the inanimate; drawings, objects, computer images, puppetry and animatronics. | Adult animation<br>Anime<br>Cell animation<br>Children's<br>Puppetry<br>Stop motion | Technique |
| **Charity** | | |
| Designed to appeal to the audience for funds or support for a charitable organization or social issue. | Appeals<br>Features<br>Telethons | Content<br>Purpose |
| **Children's** | | |
| Made for and about children and their issues and interests. | Comedy<br>Drama<br>Entertainment<br>Factual<br>Music<br>News<br>Sport | Content |
| **Comedy** | | |
| Focus on humour and amusement with humorous situations, events or jokes and storytelling. | Gag<br>Impressionist<br>Mockumentary<br>Satire<br>Sitcom<br>Sketch<br>Slapstick<br>Spoof<br>Stand-up comedy | Content<br>Purpose |

*Appendix 1 table continues*

| Main Categories | Subgenres | Mainly Driven by: |
|---|---|---|
| **Current and public affairs** | | |
| Matters of public interest involving policy and sociopolitical issues, presented either in time-sensitive short formats or in-depth investigative, contextual long formats. | Bulletins<br>Commentary<br>Discussion<br>Events coverage<br>Interview<br>News discussion<br>News programme | Content |
| **Drama** | | |
| Scripted fictional programming telling a story often on serious subjects with actors portraying characters. | Action<br>Adventure<br>Biographical<br>Courtroom and legal<br>Crime<br>Docudrama<br>Horror<br>Medical<br>Musical<br>Period<br>Police<br>Political<br>Psychological<br>Romance and relationships<br>Science fiction<br>Soap opera<br>Supernatural and fantasy<br>Teen<br>Telenovela<br>Thriller<br>Western | Presentation |

*Appendix 1 table continues*

| Main Categories | Subgenres | Mainly Driven by: |
|---|---|---|
| **Educational** | | |
| Designed to show viewers "how to"; to instruct or educate on subjects. | Adult<br>Distance<br>Instructional<br>Languages<br>School<br>Tertiary | Content<br>Purpose |
| **Entertainment** | | |
| Entertainment content, variety or specific types. | Dance<br>Magic illusion<br>Music<br>Music hall<br>Variety<br>Ventriloquism | Purpose |
| **Factual** | | |
| Non-fiction, events, special subjects or topics. | Animals<br>Antiques<br>Art and culture<br>Beauty and style<br>Consumer<br>Crime and justice<br>DIY and repairs<br>Documentary<br>Food and drink<br>Health<br>Home and garden<br>Lifestyle<br>Media<br>Nature<br>Politics<br>Science<br>Travel | Content |

*Appendix 1 table continues*

| Main Categories | Subgenres | Mainly Driven by: |
|---|---|---|
| **Infomercials** | | |
| A type of television advertisement; long or short form utilizing a variety of techniques to present a product or products. | Brand equity<br>Call-in<br>Demonstration<br>Documentary<br>Hosted | Purpose |
| **Magazine** | | |
| Programmes containing multiple features, clips, segments or reports. The programme may be a potpourri or related to a theme. | Lifestyle<br>Public affairs | Presentation |
| **Music** | | |
| Programmes that have music as their theme and content. | Charts<br>Concerts<br>Live events<br>Music videos<br>Performances | Content |
| **Quiz and game shows** | | |
| Featuring celebrities and or members of the public as individuals or in teams, in competition in areas such as knowledge, physicality, skills and games. | Celebrity<br>Challenge<br>Entertainment<br>Knowledge<br>Panel<br>Skills | Content<br>Purpose |
| **Reality** | | |
| Featuring celebrities and or others in real or created situations. The reality situations may be based around challenges, talent, observation and skills. | Challenge<br>Competition<br>Court shows<br>Dramality<br>Lifestyle<br>Romance<br>Survival<br>Talent | Presentation |

*Appendix 1 table continues*

| Main Categories | Subgenres | Mainly Driven by: |
|---|---|---|
| **Religious or inspirational** | | |
| Sometimes produced by religious organizations. Events, services, sermons, documentary, religious topics, interview, discussion. | Church services<br>Discussion<br>Drama<br>Music | Content |
| **Sports** | | |
| News, events commentary and discussion on sports issues. | Commentary and discussion<br>Events coverage<br>Sports news | Content |
| **Social advocacy** | | |
| Programmes that aim to highlight or encourage action on social and community issues. | Feature<br>Interview<br>Talk | Purpose |
| **Talk shows** | | |
| Featuring a host and or guests and studio audience. | Daytime<br>Late night<br>Personality<br>Special interest<br>Tabloid | Presentation |
| **Weather** | | |
| Covering weather and climate topics. | Events<br>Coverage<br>Forecasts<br>News | Content |

APPENDIX 2

**Some of the Longest-Running Shows in Various Countries (Along with the Broadcast Life of Those Countries)**

| Category | TV Show Name | Country | Channel and Duration | Start Year of Show | Length of Show in Years | Frequency | Number of Episodes* | Number of Seasons | Start of Regular TV Broadcasting in Country | Length of TV Broadcasting Years (BY) | Proportion |
|---|---|---|---|---|---|---|---|---|---|---|---|
| Animated | *Sazae-san* | Japan | Fuji Television: 1969–present | 1969 | 46 | Weekly on Sunday nights; three vignettes per episode | 7,400 | N/A | 1953 | 62 | 74% |
| Children's show | *Blue Peter* | United Kingdom | BBC: 1958–2012, CBBC: 2012–present | 1958 | 57 | Weekly | 4,900 | N/A | 1946 | 69 | 83% |
| Comedy | *Sábados Felices* | Colombia | Caracol: 1972–present | 1972 | 43 | Weekly | 2,300 | N/A | 1954 | 61 | 70% |
| Current affairs | *Meet the Press* | United States | NBC: 1947–present | 1947 | 68 | Weekly on Sunday mornings | 17,630 | 68 | 1946 | 69 | 99% |
| Current affairs | *Panorama* | United Kingdom | BBC One: 1953–present | 1953 | 62 | Weekly | N/A | 63 | 1946 | 69 | 90% |
| Current affairs | *Four Corners* | Australia | ABC: 1961–present | 1961 | 54 | Weekly | N/A | 54 | 1956 | 59 | 92% |
| Drama | *Maalaala Mo Kaya* | Philippines | ABS-CBN: 1991–present | 1991 | 24 | Weekly | N/A | 24 | 1953 | 62 | 39% |
| Drama | *Casualty* | United Kingdom | BBC One: 1986–present | 1986 | 29 | Weekly & seasonal | 950 | N/A | 1946 | 69 | 42% |
| Drama | *Tatort* | Germany | Das Erste: 1970–present | 1970 | 45 | Weekly & seasonal | 940 | N/A | 1954 | 61 | 74% |
| Drama | *Coronation Street* | United Kingdom | ITV: 1960–present | 1960 | 55 | Between 1 and 4 episodes broadcast weekly at different times | 8,930 | N/A | 1946 | 69 | 80% |

*Appendix 2 table continues*

| Category | TV Show Name | Country | Channel and Duration | Start Year of Show | Length of Show in Years | Frequency | Number of Episodes* | Number of Seasons | Start of Regular TV Broadcasting in Country | Length of TV Broadcasting Years (BY) | Proportion |
|---|---|---|---|---|---|---|---|---|---|---|---|
| Entertainment | *Entertainment Report* | Jamaica | JBC TV: 1991–1997; TVJ 1998–present | 1991 | 24 | Weekly | 1,200 | N/A | 1963 | 52 | 46% |
| Entertainment | *Programa Silvio Santos* | Brazil | SBT: 1963–present | 1963 | 52 | Weekly on Saturday nights | N/A | 52 | 1950 | 65 | 80% |
| Entertainment | *NHK Nodo Jiman* | Japan | NHK: 1953–present | 1953 | 62 | Weekly | 3,030 | N/A | 1953 | 62 | 100% |
| Entertainment | *Rage* | Australia | ABC1: 1987–present, ABC2: 2005–2009, Fly TV: 2001–2003 | 1987 | 28 | Weekly on Fridays & Saturdays | N/A | 28 | 1956 | 59 | 47% |
| Entertainment | *Eat Bulaga!* | Philippines | RPN: 1979–1989; ABS–CBN: 1989–1995; GMA Network: 1995–present | 1979 | 36 | Weekdays & Saturdays | 10,960 | N/A | 1953 | 62 | 58% |
| Entertainment | *Allsång på Skansen* | Sweden | SVT1: 1979–present | 1979 | 36 | Seasonal | N/A | N/A | 1956 | 59 | 61% |
| Magazine | *Teleclub* | Costa Rica | Teletica ExperTV: 1963–present | 1963 | 52 | Weekdays | N/A | N/A | 1960 | 55 | 95% |
| Magazine | *Country Calendar* | New Zealand | TV One: 1966–present | 1966 | 49 | Weekly & seasonal | 1,470 | 30 | 1960 | 55 | 89% |

*Appendix 2 table continues*

| Category | TV Show Name | Country | Channel and Duration | Start Year of Show | Length of Show in Years | Frequency | Number of Episodes* | Number of Seasons | Start of Regular TV Broadcasting in Country | Length of TV Broadcasting Years (BY) | Proportion |
|---|---|---|---|---|---|---|---|---|---|---|---|
| Quiz show | Schools' Challenge Quiz | Jamaica | JBC TV: 1969–1997; TVJ: 1998–present | 1969 | 46 | Weekly & seasonal | Between 21 and 78 episodes per year | 46 | 1963 | 52 | 88% |
| Quiz show | It's Academic | United States | NBC-owned WRC TV; NBC affiliate WVIR; CBS affiliate WJZ TV: 1961–present | 1961 | 54 | Weekly & seasonal | N/A | 55 | 1946 | 69 | 78% |
| Reality | COPS | United States | Fox: 1989–2013; Spike: 2013–present | 1989 | 26 | Weekly | 970 | 29 | 1946 | 69 | 38% |
| Reality | Hill an' Gully Ride | Jamaica | JBC TV: 1989–1997; TVJ 1998–present | 1989 | 26 | Weekly | 1,222 | N/A | 1963 | 52 | 50% |
| Religious | Le Jour du Seigneur | France | RTF, ORTF, TF1, Antennae 2, France TV: 1949–present | 1949 | 66 | Weekly on Sundays | 3,432 | N/A | 1944 | 71 | 93% |
| Talk show | The Tonight Show | United States | NBC: 1954–present | 1954 | 61 | Weeknights | 11,462 | 61 | 1946 | 69 | 88% |
| Talk show | Profile | Jamaica | JBC TV: 1987–1997; TVJ: 1998–present | 1987 | 28 | Weekly | 1,400 | N/A | 1963 | 52 | 54% |
| Variety show | Súper Sábado Sensacional | Venezuela | RCTV: 1968–1972; Venevisión: 1972–present | 1968 | 47 | Weekly | 2,444 | N/A | 1952 | 55 | 75% |

*These are approximate figures as at December 2015.

Note: There were countries where television services began before World War II in 1939 and continued during the conflict; in other cases, operations were suspended. This table takes the post-war operations as its starting point.

APPENDIX 3

# Market Research Figures for Four Jamaican Television Shows (*Schools' Challenge Quiz, Profile, Hill an' Gully Ride, Entertainment Report*)

*Note*: The figures in these tables were sourced from the *All Media Surveys* conducted by Market Research Services Limited. Thanks to Don Anderson and Nadine Shaw of Market Research Services Limited for their assistance.

## Schools' Challenge Quiz

| Year | Day Aired | Time Aired | Media Audience Watching | Total Possible Audience | Date of Fieldwork | Report Published | Notes |
|---|---|---|---|---|---|---|---|
| 1970 | Thursday | 6:00 p.m. | | | | | |
| 1971 | Tuesday | 7:00 p.m. | | | | | |
| 1972 | Tuesday | 7:00 p.m. | | | | | |
| 1973 | Tuesday | 7:00 p.m. | | | | | Radio only |
| 1974 | Tuesday | 7:00 p.m. | | | | | Radio only |
| 1975 | Tuesday | 7:00 p.m. | | | | | |
| | Thursday | 7:00 p.m. | | | | | |
| 1976 | Tuesday | 7:00 p.m. | | | | | |
| | Thursday | 7:00 p.m. | | | | | |
| 1977 | Tuesday | 7:00 p.m. | 92,000 | 306,000(?) | September 1977 | November 1977 | 30% (avg. 89,000) |
| | Thursday | 7:00 p.m. | 76,000 | 306,000(?) | September 1977 | November 1977 | 25% (avg. 89,000) |
| 1978 | Tuesday | 7:00 p.m. | | | | | |
| | Thursday | 7:00 p.m. | | | | | |
| 1979 | Tuesday | 7:00 p.m. | | | August 1979 | February 1980 | Only radio figures seen |
| | Thursday | 7:00 p.m. | | | | | |
| 1980 | Tuesday | 7:00 p.m. | | | | | |
| | Thursday | 7:00 p.m. | | | | | |
| 1981 | Tuesday | 7:00 p.m. | 143,000 | 482,000 | October 1981 | April 1982 | |
| | Thursday | 7:00 p.m. | 198,000 | 482,000 | October 1981 | April 1982 | (Avg. 180,000) |
| 1982 | Tuesday | 7:00 p.m. | | | | | |
| | Thursday | 7:00 p.m. | | | | | |

*Appendix 3 table continues*

*Schools' Challenge Quiz (cont'd)*

| Year | Day Aired | Time Aired | Media Audience Watching | Total Possible Audience | Date of Fieldwork | Report Published | Notes |
|---|---|---|---|---|---|---|---|
| 1983 | Tuesday | 7:00 p.m. | | | | | |
| | Thursday | 7:00 p.m. | | | | | |
| 1984 | Tuesday | 7:00 p.m. | 199,000 | 628,000 | 10–30 November 1983 | 1984 | |
| | Thursday | 7:00 p.m. | 199,000 | 628,000 | 10–30 November 1983 | 1984 | |
| 1985 | Tuesday | 6:30 p.m. | | | | | |
| | Thursday | 6:30 p.m. | | | | | |
| 1986 | Monday | 6:30 p.m. | 191,000 | Not reported | November 1986 | February 1987 | |
| | Wednesday | 6:30 p.m. | 223,000 | Not reported | November 1986 | February 1987 | |
| | Friday | 6:30 p.m. | 209,000 | Not reported | November 1986 | February 1987 | |
| 1987 | Tuesday | 6:30 p.m. | | | | | No survey |
| | Thursday | 6:30 p.m. | | | | | |
| 1988 | Tuesday | 6:30 p.m. | 190,000 | 878,000* | 30 April–21 May 1988 | 7 September 1988 | *Potential audience estimated overall (viewing audience average over Monday to Saturday = 214,000 for 6:00 p.m. to 10:30 p.m. slot) |
| | Thursday | 6:30 p.m. | 130,000 | 878,000† | 30 April–21 May 1988 | 7 September 1988 | †Potential audience estimated overall (viewing audience average over Monday to Saturday = 214,000 for 6:00 p.m. to 10:30 p.m. slot) |

*Appendix 3 table continues*

Schools' Challenge Quiz (cont'd)

| Year | Day Aired | Time Aired | Media Audience Watching | Total Possible Audience | Date of Fieldwork | Report Published | Notes |
|---|---|---|---|---|---|---|---|
| 1989 | Tuesday | 6:30 p.m. | 120,000 | 894,000 | 6–21 May 1989 | 28 June 1989 | Potential audience estimated overall (viewing audience average over Monday to Saturday = 194,000 for 6:00 p.m. to 10:30 p.m. slot) |
| | Thursday | 6:30 p.m. | 130,000 | 894,000 | 6–21 May 1989 | 28 June 1989 | Potential audience estimated overall (viewing audience average over Monday to Saturday = 194,000 for 6:00 p.m. to 10:30 p.m. slot) |
| 1990 | Monday | 6:15 p.m. | 192,000 | 240,000 | 6–19 May 1990 | 17 July 1990 | |
| | | | 235,000 | 240,000 | | | This for 6:30 to 7:00 p.m. |
| | Tuesday | 6:15 p.m. | 156,000 | 240,000 | | | |
| | | | 242,000 | 240,000 | | | This for 6:30 to 7:00 p.m. |
| | Thursday | 6:15 p.m. | 156,000 | 240,000 | | | |
| | | | 235,000 | 240,000 | | | This for 6:30 to 7:00 p.m. |
| 1991 | Tuesday | 5:20 p.m. | 130,000 | 292,000 | 18 May–1 June 1991 | 29 July 1991 | |
| | Thursday | 5:20 p.m. | 148,000 | 292,000 | | | |
| | Friday | 5:20 p.m. | 185,000 | 292,000 | | | |
| 1992 | Tuesday | 5:30 p.m. | 154,000 | 314,000 | 23 February–14 March 1992 | May 1992 | 314,000 – average viewing |
| | Thursday | 5:30 p.m. | 179,000 | 314,000 | | | |
| | Frwiday | 5:30 p.m. | 179,000 | 314,000 | | | |

*Appendix 3 table continues*

## Schools' Challenge Quiz (cont'd)

| Year | Day Aired | Time Aired | Media Audience Watching | Total Possible Audience | Date of Fieldwork | Report Published | Notes |
|---|---|---|---|---|---|---|---|
| 1994 | Tuesday | 5:30 p.m. | 102,000 | 176,000 | 16–22 October 1994 | 16 January 1995 | |
| | Wednesday | 5:30 p.m. | 120,000 | 177,000 | | | |
| | Thursday | 5:30 p.m. | 64,000 | 125,000 | | | |
| 1995 | Monday | 5:30 p.m. | 31,000 | 218,000* | 14–28 May 1995 | July 1995 | *Average audience for TV Monday to Friday |
| | Wednesday | 5:30 p.m. | 107,000 | 218,000 | | | |
| | Thursday | 5:30 p.m. | 120,000 | 218,000 | | | |
| 1996 | Monday | 8:30 p.m. | 326,000 | 547,000 | 13–25 March 1996 | June 1996 | |
| | Wednesday | 8:30 p.m. | 256,000 | 521,000 | | | |
| 1997 | Tuesday | 8:30 p.m. | 264,000 | 512,000 | March–April 1997 | June 1997 | |
| | Thursday | 8:30 p.m. | 200,000 | 392,000 | | | |
| 1998 | Tuesday | 8:30 p.m. | 291,000 | 733,000 | 19 April–9 May | July 1998 | |
| | Thursday | 8:30 p.m. | 269,000 | 732,000 | | | |
| 1999 | Tuesday | 8:30 p.m. | 303,000 | 714,000 | 3–17 March 1999 | May 1999 | |
| | Thursday | 8:30 p.m. | 339,000 | 871,000 | | | |
| 2000 | Tuesday | 8:30 p.m. | 77,000 | 877,000 | 27 August–7 Sept | December 2000 | |
| | Thursday | 8:30 p.m. | 128,000 | 791,000 | | | |
| 2001 | Monday | 6:00 p.m. | | | | | |
| | Tuesday | 8:30 p.m. | | | | | |
| | Thursday | 8:30 p.m. | | | | | |

*Appendix 3 table continues*

## Schools' Challenge Quiz (cont'd)

| Year | Day Aired | Time Aired | Media Audience Watching | Total Possible Audience | Date of Fieldwork | Report Published | Notes |
|---|---|---|---|---|---|---|---|
| 2002 | Monday | 6:00 p.m. | 242,000 | 338,000 | November 2002 | | FTA unfinished |
| | Tuesdays | 8:30 p.m. | 231,000 | 344,000 | | | |
| | Thursdays | 8:30 p.m. | 242,000 | 343,000 | | | |
| 2003 | Monday | 6:00 p.m. | | | | | No survey |
| | Tuesday | 8:30 p.m. | | | | | |
| | Wednesday | 6:00 p.m. | | | | | |
| | Thursday | 8:30 p.m. | | | | | |
| 2004 | Monday | 8:30 p.m. | | | | | No survey |
| | Tuesday | 8:30 p.m. | | | | | |
| | Wednesday | 8:30 p.m. | | | | | |
| | Thursday | 8:30 p.m. | | | | | |
| 2005 | Monday | 8:30 p.m. | 471,000 | 1,223,000* | March 2005 | May 2005 | *Both FTA and cable |
| | Tuesday | 8:30 p.m. | 446,000 | 1,323,000 | | | |
| | Wednesday | 8:30 p.m. | 431,000 | 1,207,000 | | | |
| | Thursday | 8:30 p.m. | 361,000 | 1,302,000 | | | |
| 2006 | Monday | 6:30 p.m. | 62,000 | 1,564,000 | 6 September–19 October 2006 | November 2006 | |
| | Tuesday | 6:30 p.m. | 67,000 | 1,564,000* | | | *Both FTA and cable |
| | Wednesday | 6:30 p.m. | 176,000 | 1,564,000 | | | |
| | Thursday | 6:30 p.m. | 77,000 | 1,564,000 | | | |
| | Friday | 6:30 p.m. | 116,000 | 1,564,000 | | | |
| | Saturday | 11:30 a.m. | 91,000 | 1,564,000 | | | |

*Appendix 3 table continues*

## Schools' Challenge Quiz (cont'd)

| Year | Day Aired | Time Aired | Media Audience Watching | Total Possible Audience | Date of Fieldwork | Report Published | Notes |
|---|---|---|---|---|---|---|---|
| 2007 | Monday | 6:30 p.m. | 279,000 | 351,000* | November 2007 | April 2008 | Both FTA and cable |
| | Tuesday | 6:30 p.m. | 242,000 | 350,000 | | | 24th survey |
| | Wednesday | 6:30 p.m. | 301,000 | 346,000 | | | |
| | Thursday | 6:30 p.m. | 366,000 | 448,000 | | | |
| | Friday | 6:30 p.m. | 357,000 | 435,000 | | | |
| 2008 | Monday | 6:30 p.m. | 250,000 | 357,000 | November–December 2008 | March 2009 | |
| | Tuesday | 6:30 p.m. | 343,000 | 370,000 | | | |
| | Wednesday | 6:30 p.m. | 148,000 | 205,000 | | | |
| | Thursday | 6:30 p.m. | 145,000 | 308,000 | | | |
| | Friday | 6:30 p.m. | 240,000 | 305,000 | | | |
| 2009 | Monday | 6:30 p.m. | 270,000 | 358,000 | October–November 2009 | February 2010 | 26th survey |
| | Tuesday | 6:30 p.m. | 242,000 | 344,000 | | | |
| | Wednesday | 6:30 p.m. | 361,000 | 472,000 | | | |
| | Thursday | 6:30 p.m. | 347,000 | 441,000 | | | |
| | Friday | 6:30 p.m. | 338,000 | 422,000 | | | |
| 2010 | Monday | 6:30 p.m. | | | | | No survey |
| | Tuesday | 6:30 p.m. | | | | | |
| | Wednesday | 6:30 p.m. | | | | | |
| | Thursday | 6:30 p.m. | | | | | |
| | Friday | 6:30 p.m. | | | | | |

*Appendix 3 table continues*

*Schools' Challenge Quiz (cont'd)*

| Year | Day Aired | Time Aired | Media Audience Watching | Total Possible Audience | Date of Fieldwork | Report Published | Notes |
|---|---|---|---|---|---|---|---|
| 2011 | Monday | 6:30 p.m. | | | | | No survey |
| | Tuesday | 6:30 p.m. | | | | | |
| | Wednesday | 6:30 p.m. | | | | | |
| | Thursday | 6:30 p.m. | | | | | |
| | Friday | 6:30 p.m. | | | | | |
| 2012 | Monday | 6:30 p.m. | 212,000 | 262,000 | 27 April–6 June | July 2012 | |
| | Tuesday | 6:30 p.m. | 199,000 | 248,000 | | | |
| | Wednesday | 6:30 p.m. | 158,000 | 201,000 | | | |
| | Thursday | 6:30 p.m. | 320,000 | 348,000 | | | |
| | Friday | 6:30 p.m. | 196,000 | 222,000 | | | |
| 2013 | Monday | 6:30 p.m. | | | | | No survey |
| | Tuesday | 6:30 p.m. | | | | | |
| | Wednesday | 6:30 p.m. | | | | | |
| | Thursday | 6:30 p.m. | | | | | |
| | Friday | 6:30 p.m. | | | | | |
| 2014 | Monday | 6:30 p.m. | 585,000 | 700,000 | November 2014–January 2015 | March 2015 | |
| | Tuesday | 6:30 p.m. | 463,000 | 535,000 | | | |
| | Wednesday | 6:30 p.m. | 413,000 | 463,000 | | | |
| | Thursday | 6:30 p.m. | 475,000 | 525,000 | | | |
| | Friday | 6:30 p.m. | 562,000 | 612,000 | | | |
| 2015 | Monday | 6:30 p.m. | | | | | No survey |
| | Tuesday | 6:30 p.m. | | | | | |
| | Wednesday | 6:30 p.m. | | | | | |
| | Thursday | 6:30 p.m. | | | | | |
| | Friday | 6:30 p.m. | | | | | |

*Appendix 3 table continues*

## Profile

| Year | Day Aired | Time Aired | Media Audience Watching | Total Possible Audience | Date of Fieldwork | Report Published | Note |
|---|---|---|---|---|---|---|---|
| 1987 | Sunday | 4:30 p.m.* | | | | | No survey |
| 1988 | Sunday | 4:30 p.m.† | 168,000 | 196,000 | 30 April–21 May 1988 | 7 September 1988 | Total possible audience is an average |
| 1989 | Sunday | 4:30 p.m.‡ | 212,000 | 196,000 | 6–21 May 1989 | 28 June 1989 | Average |
| 1990 | Sunday | 4:30 p.m.§ | 220,000 | 200,000 | 6–19 May, 1990 | 17 July 1990 | Average |
| 1991 | Sunday | 3:20 p.m. | 170,000 | 270,000 | 18 May–1 June 1991 | 29 July 1991 | 3:00–3:30 |
| | | | 200,000 | 270,000 | | | 3:30–4:00 |
| 1992 | Sunday | 3:00 p.m. | 195,000 | 232,000 | 23 February– 14 March 1992 | May 1992 | Average of people watching between 3:00 p.m. and 11:00 p.m. |
| 1993 | Sunday | 3:00 p.m. | 270,000 | 280,000 | 13–27 March 1993 | 18 May 1993 | |
| 1994 | Sunday | 3:00 p.m. | 241,000 | 280,000 | 16–22 October 1994 | 16 January 1995 | |
| 1995 | Sunday | 3:00 p.m. | 220,000 | 332,000 | 14–28 May 1995 | July 1995 | |
| 1996 | Sunday | 3:00 p.m. | 150,000 | 270,000 | 13–25 March 1996 | June 1996 | |
| 1997 | Sunday | 3:00 p.m. | 80,000 | 200,000 | March–April 1997 | June 1997 | |
| 1998 | Sunday | 3:00 p.m. | 151,000 | 313,000 | 19 April–9 May 1998 | July 1998 | |
| 1999 | Sunday | 3:30 p.m. | 133,000 | 318,000 | 3–17 March 1999 | May 1999 | |
| 2000 | Sunday | 6:30 p.m. | 168,000 | 288,000 | 27 August–7 September | December 2000 | |
| 2001 | Sunday | 6:30 p.m. | — | | | | No survey |
| 2002 | Sunday | 6:30 p.m. | 253,000 | 371,000 | November 2002 | | FTA unfinished |
| 2003 | Sunday | 6:30 p.m. | — | | | | No survey |

*Appendix 3 table continues*

Profile (cont'd)

| Year | Day Aired | Time Aired | Media Audience Watching | Total Possible Audience | Date of Fieldwork | Report Published | Note |
|---|---|---|---|---|---|---|---|
| 2004 | Sunday | 6:30 p.m. | — | | | | No survey |
| 2005 | Sunday | 6:30 p.m. | 223,000 | 353,000 | March 2005 | May 2005 | *Both FTA and cable |
| 2006 | Sunday | 6:30 p.m. | 142,000 | 1,564,000 | 6 September–19 October 2006 | November 2006 | Both FTA and cable |
| 2007 | Sunday | 6:30 p.m. | 265,000 | 353,000 | November 2007 | April 2008 | |
| 2008 | Sunday | 6:30 p.m. | 339,000 | 479,000 | November–December 2008 | March 2009 | |
| 2009 | Sunday | 6:30 p.m. | 264,000 | 403,000 | October–November 2009 | February 2010 | 26th survey |
| 2010 | Sunday | 6:30 p.m. | | | | | No survey |
| 2011 | Sunday | 6:30 p.m. | | | | | No survey |
| 2012 | Sunday | 6:30 p.m. | 125,000 | 160,000 | 27 April–6 June 2012 | July 2012 | |
| 2013 | Sunday | 6:30 p.m. | | | | | No survey |
| 2014 | Sunday | 6:30 p.m. | 377,000 | 418,000 | November 2014–January 2015 | March 2015 | |
| 2015 | Sunday | 6:30 p.m. | | | | | No survey |

\* Also seen at 5:00 p.m. in 1987 on some Sundays.
† Also seen at 4:00 p.m.; 5:00 p.m.; 5:30 p.m. on some Sundays.
‡ Also seen at 4:00 p.m. on some Sundays.
§ Also seen at 3:05 p.m.; 3:45 p.m.; 3:50 p.m. on some Sundays.

*Hill an' Gully Ride*

| Year | Date Aired | Time Aired | Media Audience Watching | Total Possible Audience | Date of Fieldwork | Report Published | Note |
|---|---|---|---|---|---|---|---|
| 1989 | Sunday | 11:30 a.m. | — | | 6–21 May 1989 | 28 June 1989 | |
| 1990 | Sunday | 11:30 a.m. | 86,000 | 116,000 | 6–19 May 1990 | 17 July 1990 | Potential TV audience 821,043 |
| 1991 | Sunday | 11:30 a.m. | 90,000 | 120,000 | 18 May–1 June 1991 | 29 July 1991 | Average from 5:30 a.m to 11:59 a.m. |
| 1992 | Sunday | 11:30 a.m. | 24,000 | 56,000 | 23 February–14 March 1992 | May 1992 | Average from 5:30 a.m. to 11:59 a.m. |
| 1993 | Sunday | 11:30 a.m. | 11,000 | Not reported | 13–27 March 1993 | 18 May 1993 | Show not on when survey was done |
| 1994 | Sunday | 11:30 a.m. | 84,000 | 101,000 | 16–22 October 1994 | 16 January 1995 | |
| 1995 | Sunday | 6:00 p.m. | 165,000 | 332,000 | 14–28 May 1995 | July 1995 | |
| 1996 | Sunday | 6:00 p.m. | 161,000 | 273,000 | 13–25 March 1996 | June 1996 | |
| 1997 | Sunday | 6:00 p.m. | 112,000 | 216,000 | March–April 1997 | June 1997 | |
| 1998 | Sunday | 6:00 p.m. | 172,000 | 323,000 | 19 April–9 May 1998 | July 1998 | |
| 1999 | Sunday | 6:00 p.m. | 145,000 | 351,000 | 3–17 March 1999 | May 1999 | |
| 2000 | Sunday | 6:00 p.m. | 157,000 | 340,000 | 27 August–7 September | December 2000 | |
| 2001 | Sunday | 6:00 p.m. | — | | | | No survey |
| 2002 | Sunday | 6:00 p.m. | 186,000 | 304,000 | November 2002 | | |
| 2003 | Sunday | 6:00 p.m. | — | | | | No survey |
| 2004 | Sunday | 6:00 p.m. | — | | | | No survey |
| 2005 | Sunday | 6:00 p.m. | 198,000 | 325,000 | March 2005 | May 2005 | |

*Appendix 3 table continues*

*Hill an' Gully Ride (cont'd)*

| Year | Date Aired | Time Aired | Media Audience Watching | Total Possible Audience | Date of Fieldwork | Report Published | Note |
|---|---|---|---|---|---|---|---|
| 2006 | Sunday | 6:00 p.m. | 142,000 | 1,564,000 | 6 September–19 October 2006 | November 2006 | Both FTA and cable |
| 2007 | Sunday | 6:00 p.m. | 250,000 | 338,000 | November 2007 | April 2008 | |
| 2008 | Sunday | 6:00 p.m. | 272,000 | 412,000 | November–December 2008 | March 2009 | |
| 2009 | Sunday | 6:00 p.m. | 242,000 | 366,000 | October–November 2009 | February 2010 | |
| 2010 | Sunday | 6:00 p.m. | — | | | | No survey |
| 2011 | Sunday | 6:00 p.m. | — | | | | No survey |
| 2012 | Sunday | 6:00 p.m. | 115,000 | 141,000 | 27 April–6 June 2012 | July 2012 | |
| 2013 | Sunday | 6:00 p.m. | — | | | | No survey |
| 2014 | Sunday | 6:00 p.m. | 293,000 | 335,000 | November 2014–January 2015 | March 2015 | |
| 2015 | Sunday | 6:00 p.m. | — | | | | No survey |

*Appendix 3 table continues*

*Entertainment Report*

| Year | Day Aired | Time Aired | Media Audience Watching | Total Possible Audience | Date of Fieldwork | Report Published | Note |
|---|---|---|---|---|---|---|---|
| 1991 | Friday | 7:30 p.m. | 382,000 | 274,000 | 18 May–1 June 1991 | 29 July 1991 | Done during the news time slot; average |
| 1992 | Friday | 7:30 p.m. | 354,000 | 314,000 | 23 February–14 March 1992 | May 1992 | Average viewers |
| 1993 | Friday | 8:00 p.m./8:30 p.m. | 450,000 | 500,000 | 13–27 March 1993 | 18 May 1993 | |
| 1994 | Friday | 8:30 p.m. | 229,000 | 447,000 | 16–22 October 1994 | 16 January 1995 | |
| 1995 | Friday | 8:00 p.m. | 261,000 | 532,000 | 14–28 May 1995 | July 1995 | |
| 1996 | Friday | 8:00 p.m. | 317,000 | 675,000 | 13–25 March 1996 | June 1996 | |
| | Friday | 8:30 p.m. | 192,000 | 472,000 | | | |
| 1997 | Friday | 8:30 p.m. | 224,000 | 464,000 | March–April 1997 | June 1997 | |
| 1998 | Friday | 8:30 p.m. | 323,000 | 765,000 | 19 April–9 May 1998 | July 1998 | |
| 1999 | Friday | 9:00 p.m. | 315,000 | 763,000 | 3–17 March 1999 | May 1999 | |
| 2000 | Friday | 8:30 p.m. | 282,000 | 589,000 | 27 August–7 September 2000 | December 2000 | |
| 2001 | Friday | 8:30 p.m. (?) | — | | | | No survey |
| 2002 | Friday | 8:30 p.m. | 467,000 | 1,209,000 | November 2002 | | FTA unfinished |
| 2003 | Friday | 8:30 p.m. | — | | | | No survey |
| 2004 | Friday | 8:30 p.m.* | — | | | | No survey |
| 2005 | Friday | 8:00 p.m. | 377,000 | 1,346,000 | March 2005 | May 2005 | Both FTA and cable |
| | | 8:30 p.m. | 295,000 | 1,209,000 | | | |

*Appendix 3 table continues*

*Entertainment Report (cont'd)*

| Year | Day Aired | Time Aired | Media Audience Watching | Total Possible Audience | Date of Fieldwork | Report Published | Note |
|---|---|---|---|---|---|---|---|
| 2006 | Friday | 8:00 p.m. | 186,000 | 1,564,000 | 6 September–19 October 2006 | November 2006 | Overall potential audience for TV; total audience includes local TV and cable |
| 2007 | Friday | 8:00 p.m. (?) | 279,000 | 1,000,000 | November 2007 | April 2008 | |
| | | 8:30 p.m. (?) | 240,000 | 803,000 | | | |
| 2008 | Friday | 8:30 p.m. (?) | 208,000 | 741,000 | November–December 2008 | March 2009 | |
| 2009 | Friday | 8:30 p.m. (?) | 316,000 | 882,000 | October–November 2009 | February 2010 | |
| 2010 | Friday | 8:30 p.m. | – | | | | No survey |
| 2011 | Friday | 9:00 p.m. | – | | | | No survey |
| 2012 | Friday | 9:00 p.m. | 247,000 | 1,647,000 | 27 April–6 June 2012 | July 2012 | Overall potential audience for TV; total audience includes local TV and cable |
| 2013 | Friday | 8:30 p.m./9:00 p.m. | – | | | | No survey |
| 2014 | Friday | 8:30 p.m. | 361,000 | 923,000 | November 2014–January 2015 | March 2015 | |
| 2015 | Friday | 8:30 p.m. | – | | | | No survey |

*Also seen on Saturdays at 8:30 p.m. in some programme schedules.

Notes: *ER2* appeared on Saturdays at 8:30 p.m. in 2006.

In 1998, the top shows were: *Young and Restless*, *Newswatch* and *Prime Time News*, *Malcolm and Eddy*, *Bold and Beautiful*, *Parenthood*, *Sybil*, *News Radio*, and *Murphy Brown* – of note is that, among these, only the news was locally produced.

# APPENDIX 4

# Television Programmes Produced and Aired in Jamaica

Jamaican audiences have seen many television shows on national free-to-air stations. In this list, we present examples of the wide range of shows seen according to their genre. Some of these have been aired for various lengths of time before going off air, while others show clear signs of continuing. Both seasonal series as well as daily and weekly shows scheduled year-round are included. Different genres are represented as well as government-related programmes. While the list refers to regularly scheduled programmes, it does not include a station's major newscast, special events, sporting events or one-off television events or productions. For each, the title is given along with a description and its broadcast status. This list is not exhaustive. We welcome any updates for future researchers.

## Animation

Title: *Cabbie Chronicles*

Description: *Cabbie Chronicles* is a Jamaican animated series about a taxi driver navigating the absurd complexities of modern Jamaican life. It was first shown on the cable channel FLOW and then appeared on the free-to-air channel, TVJ.

Status: Aired 2012.

## Children's Programmes

Title: *A Graders*

Description: A thirty-minute educational docu-drama that seeks to help students and their families prepare for the Grade Six Achievement Test by providing real-life, culturally specific situations. The executive producer was Deborah Hickling and the producer was Kathy Gayle.

Status: Aired for one season from January to March 2009 on CVM TV and rebroadcast on TVJ.

Title: *Anansi Stories from an Island*

Description: A children's programme in six episodes hosted by Joan Andrea Hutchinson and Steve Higgins. Produced by Phase Three Productions, the programme sought to tell young Jamaican children about their heritage through "duppy" stories and Anancy tales.

Status: Aired in 1997 on JBC TV and CVM TV.

Title: *Bandana Boat*

Description: Kathy Gayle produced this show for children at CPTC.

Status: Pilot aired in 1995 on JBC TV.

Title: *Children's Corner*

Description: A children's show hosted by Barry Davies and Erica Allen and usually aired Mondays and Wednesdays mostly at 5:30 p.m. and sometimes at 6:00 p.m.

Status: Aired on JBC TV from 1963 to 1966.

Title: *Children's Special*

Description: Aired on Fridays at 5:30 p.m., this show included drama, dance, games and fun holiday features for young children.

Status: Aired 1971.

Title: *Hello World Jamaica*

Description: This show was created by children's television producer Mary Collins to educate viewers about Jamaica's history and the natural beauty of its environment and people. The show featured several puppets with the main character being "Ragga Boo Boo". It included songs, music and video and ran twice weekly for twenty-six minutes on CVM TV. There was merchandising of the show's images on clothing. There were books associated with the production and a comic strip based on the show appeared in the *Jamaica Observer*.

Status: Aired 2004 to 2006.

## APPENDIX 4

Title: *It's a Smart World*

Description: A show for children that aired on Saturdays at 9:30 a.m. It lasted for one hour and included features such as "First Aid Corner", "Spanish Corner" and "Smart Art", along with information and entertainment.

Status: Aired on JBC TV from 1982 to 1983.

Title: *Kids Say . . .*

Description: A programme hosted by Susan Simes and aired on TVJ highlighting things children say.

Status: First aired February 2011.

Title: *Mini Matters*

Description: A thirty-minute show made for and by children and aired on Saturdays at 11:30 a.m. Children host and prepare their own scripts and questions for interviews. They present features including science activities, tips for parents, a music corner and a segment called "The Explorer".

Status: Began airing in 2013 on TVJ as a seasonal show and became a regular Saturday morning programme.

Title: *Music and Youth*

Description: Presented in association with the Ministry of Education, this show examined Jamaican music by presenting young Jamaicans as they experienced music as an expression of human feelings and values. About twenty thousand young Jamaicans participated during its time on air.

Status: Began airing in 1978.

Title: *National Schools' Debating Competition*

Description: Burger King is the main sponsor of this debating competition involving over 110 secondary schools. The competition usually begins in November with the fourth round, semi-finals and finals televised in the first quarter of the year.

Status: Began 1987 with a likely annual broadcast season from March to April on JBC TV and then on TVJ.

Title: *Play Pen*

Description: A children's programme hosted by Margery McGregor and aired on Wednesdays at 6:02 p.m.

Status: Aired on JBC TV from 1975 to 1977.

## TELEVISION PROGRAMMES PRODUCED AND AIRED IN JAMAICA

Title: *Ring Ding*

Description: A weekly programme for children hosted by Louise Bennett with Jamaican songs, poems and games with a cast of children in the studio. The show, aired on Saturdays, included performances by children.

Status: Aired on JBC TV from 1970 to 1982.

Title: *Ring Ding Again*

Description: Based on the original *Ring Ding*, it was recreated with musicologist Marjorie Whylie and storyteller Amina Blackwood Meeks. The show was produced by CPTC.

Status: A season of thirteen episodes began airing on TVJ in April 2004.

Title: *Romper Room*

Description: A franchised show originating in the United States with local hosts guiding children in various activities in studio. Dubbed the "TV Kindergarten", it was first hosted by Sonia Anderson, and then by Sheila Hill, Margery McGregor and Pat Lazarus. The show usually aired Mondays to Fridays at 5:00 p.m. but was also scheduled as early as 4:30 p.m. or as late as 5:30 p.m., depending on sign-on times.

Status: Aired on JBC TV from 1967 to 1974.

Title: *Schools' Challenge Quiz Access*

Description: The programme follows the action in the quiz show with comments, highlights of matches played and a look forward to coming matches.

Status: Seasonal and started airing in 2012.

Title: *Schools' Challenge Quiz Preview*

Description: A preview programme aired on TVJ, looking forward to the matches coming up in the quiz season.

Status: Seasonal; aired from 2007 until 2011.

Title: *SCQ Beat*

Description: This usually appeared on Saturdays at 5:30 p.m. and was the first behind-the-scenes look at the *Schools' Challenge Quiz*. It later became *Schools' Challenge Quiz Preview*.

Status: Seasonal; started airing in 2004.

## APPENDIX 4

Title: *Sing n' Learn*

Description: This show was based on cassette albums with original children's songs by recording artiste J.C. Lodge, who was invited by TVJ to produce a local children's educational television series. It aired on Saturdays at 12 noon.

Status: Aired starting in 2000.

Title: *Vibrations*

Description: A children's programme that aired mostly on Saturdays at 5:00 p.m. The thirty-minute show included features and performances by youngsters. This was a programme done for children by children, looking at interesting subjects through the eyes of the programme's participants.

Status: Aired on JBC TV from 1988 to 1992.

Title: *Watch n' Win*

Description: A three-hour collection of children's programmes including animation, features, series and movies hosted by children and aired during the summer months between 2:00 p.m. and 5:00 p.m. A question-and-answer feature gave children watching a chance to call in and win prizes.

Status: Started in 1998 and still on air.

### Current and Public Affairs

Title: *18 Degrees North*

Description: An investigative news magazine featuring stories about the Caribbean that have global impact. Produced and hosted by Zahra Burton, the programme relies on a network of journalists committed to improving in-depth storytelling and investigative reporting about the Caribbean.

Status: First aired in 2013.

Title: *All Angles*

Description: Mainly hosted by Dionne Jackson-Miller, this show features a panel of guests discussing topical issues in the studio with occasional stories from reporters.

Status: A weekly show that first aired in 2006.

Title: *Business Day*

Description: This is a daily programme looking at the top business news of the day and is shown Mondays to Thursdays on TVJ during its nightly news package.

## TELEVISION PROGRAMMES PRODUCED AND AIRED IN JAMAICA

This three- to five-minute package has been presented by Keri-Ann Lee, Dwayne Berbick and Milton Walker, among others.

Status: Began airing 1998.

Title: *Business Review*

Description: This is a weekly look at entrepreneurship in Jamaica focusing on business issues or a single, usually new, small company. This four-minute feature is aired on Sundays during TVJ's nightly news programme.

Status: Began airing 1998.

Title: *Business Watch*

Description: This was a short financial feature aired during CVM TV's nightly newscast.

Status: Unknown.

Title: *Commentary*

Description: This show aired at 6:30 p.m. on Tuesdays and Thursdays with Rex Nettleford and John Hearne commenting on topical issues.

Status: Aired 1972.

Title: *Controversy*

Description: This discussion programme began on Mondays at 10:40 p.m. and eventually aired on Wednesdays at 9:30 p.m.

Status: Aired 1967.

Title: *Cover Stories*

Description: CVM TV's weekly news review programme that aired on Sundays at 10:30 a.m. It examined the major stories of the week, giving viewers a chance to watch those that they may have missed.

Status: On air since 2002.

Title: *D'Wrap*

Description: Entertainment news magazine programme on CVM TV produced and presented initially by Saudicka Diaram, who left the show in March 2015.

Status: First aired in 2010 and continued with a new host, Vanessa Carby, in 2015.

## APPENDIX 4

Title: *Dialogue*

Description: This discussion show appeared on Monday at 9:00 p.m. on JBC TV.

Status: Aired in 1977.

Title: *Direct*

Description: Hosted by Garfield Burford Wednesday at 9:00 p.m. on CVM, the show featured discussion of current affairs topics with news-makers and experts.

Status: Started in 2006.

Title: *Double Take*

Description: A five-minute news analysis on TVJ shown during the station's Sunday newscast with producers/presenters Anthony Miller and Yvette Rowe.

Status: Aired for one season 2000–2001.

Title: *Entertainment Prime (E-Prime)*

Description: Entertainment news aired within *Prime Time News* on weekdays on TVJ. The show was hosted initially by Deborah "Debbie" Bissoon, who was followed by Kerry-Ann "Kiki" Lewis in 2015.

Status: Began in December 2010.

Title: *Entertainment Report*

Description: A show featuring aspects of Jamaican popular culture. Produced and hosted mainly by Anthony Miller, it appears on Fridays on TVJ.

Status: First aired in 1991 and still on air.

Title: *ER2*

Description: This was a spin-off of *Entertainment Report* that aired occasionally on Saturday evenings. The show repackaged content that was previously aired on *Entertainment Report*.

Status: Aired in the early 2000s.

Title: *Exposure*

Description: This show aired on Sunday afternoons on TVJ.

Status: Aired 2002 to 2003.

Title: *Financial Week*

Description: This four-minute weekly feature examined business news including stock markets, foreign exchange rates and other aspects of the Jamaican economy. Initially aired on Fridays during the nightly news package on JBC TV in October 1992, the feature continued as part of TVJ's news programming on Fridays in 1998.

Status: First aired in 1992.

Title: *Financially Focused*

Description: This is a thirty-minute business and investing programme shown on CVM TV on Sundays at 6:00 p.m. and also seen on CIN in New York on Sundays at 12:00 noon. The executive producer and host is Dennise Williams, with Al Edwards and Erica Crawford Bryan as co-hosts.

Status: First aired in 2014.

Title: *Firing Line*

Description. This was aired at 9:15 p.m. on Tuesdays and included a panel of journalists interviewing a guest.

Status: On air 1974 to 1976.

Title: *Focus*

Description: Ronnie Thwaites chaired this stimulating discussion programme on Mondays at 9:15 p.m., which was also heard on Sundays on JBC Radio. It included comments by Jamaican citizens, an in-depth exploration of social issues of the day as well as an incisive, constructive, analytical panel discussion. Aggrey Brown also moderated the show at times.

Status: Started airing in January 1972 up until about 1978.

Title: *Here and Now*

Description: This was JBC TV's Sunday night news magazine programme, produced by Bobby Ghisays. It was aired after 8:00 p.m. on Sundays after the news and sports.

Status: Aired starting in 1970.

Title: *Impact with Cliff Hughes*

Description: This is a news and current affairs talk show, including video reports and hosted mainly by Cliff Hughes. Emily Crooks and Khadine "Miss Kitty" Hylton have also hosted on occasion. The programme started on TVJ before moving to CVM TV.

Status: Premiered in 2002.

## APPENDIX 4

Title: *Intense*

Description: Entertainment news, happenings and interviews linked by two studio hosts aired weekly on TVJ on Saturday at 8:00 p.m.

Status: First aired in 2007.

Title: *Issues and Answers*

Description: A government-sponsored show addressing matters of public affairs hosted by Ian Boyne starting in 1998 and produced by the Jamaica Information Service; sometimes aired as part of their programme *Jamaica Magazine*.

Status: Started in 1998.

Title: *Jamaica Magazine*

Description: This is a government information programme that is delivered free of charge to free-to-air television stations. It covers news, current affairs and government information. The show includes a number of features on different topics.

Status: Start date unknown but still on air.

Title: *Listen Mi News*

Description: A commentary on news sung to a dancehall beat by Bay C and other members of TOK, a popular Jamaican music group. The show started on YouTube and then on CVM TV in 2014.

Status: Started in 2014.

Title: *Live @ Seven*

Description: Topical discussion programme in studio with Simon Crosskill that airs on CVM TV at 7:00 p.m from Mondays to Fridays opposite the main newscast on TVJ. Elon Parkinson hosted the show before Crosskill took over. Yaneek Page and Jodi Brown-Lindo also hosted the show at times in its early years.

Status: First aired in July 2010.

Title: *Nightview*

Description: The show produced by JIS TV initially aired five times weekly before settling on Mondays, Wednesdays and Fridays. It was seen mostly at 10:00 p.m. and at times as early as 7:00 p.m.

Status: Aired 1985 to 1992.

## TELEVISION PROGRAMMES PRODUCED AND AIRED IN JAMAICA

Title: *On a Personal Note*

Description: A half-hour personal finance programme with host Owen James. The show won the Press Association's top award for financial journalism in its first year. It was first aired on TVJ from 2003 to 2011 and then on CVM TV at 3:00 p.m. on Sundays.

Status: Started in 2003.

Title: *On Assignment*

Description: This was a current affairs investigative news programme that appeared on Sundays after the evening news at about 8:00.

Status: Aired since 2003.

Title: *On Stage*

Description: A weekly look at the world of entertainment through reports and in-studio interviews with artistes, conducted by Winford Williams on CVM TV since 1997.

Status: First aired in 1997 and still on air.

Title: *Perspective*

Description: An informative programme, scripted and produced by Wenty Bowen, that looked at pertinent social issues, aspects of national life and interviews with people in and behind the news headlines. It aired on Sundays starting between 7:45 and 7:50 p.m. as a forty-five-minute news programme.

Status: Aired 1972 to 1974.

Title: *Perspective*

Description: A Sunday afternoon television talk show focusing on news and current affairs aired on JBC TV and then on TVJ. It featured a panel of guests along with a host taking a probing look at pertinent social issues in the news. It typically aired on Sundays at around 1:00 or 1:30 p.m.

Status: Aired 1992 to 2001.

Title: *Point Counterpoint*

Description: This thirty-minute discussion show aired on Tuesday and Thursday nights at 9:30 p.m. on JBC TV and had hosts such as Wilmot Perkins.

Status: Aired 1983 to 1984.

## APPENDIX 4

Title: *Portfolio*

Description: Wilmot Perkins hosted this show on Mondays at 9:00 p.m. It examined national issues with ministers of government, experts from the public sector and an audience comprising members of the press and representatives of private sector organizations.

Status: Aired 1983 to 1984.

Title: *Press Conference*

Description: One-hour in-depth interview show with ministers and news-makers with a panel of journalists. Later in the series, viewers could submit questions. The show aired on Tuesdays at 9:15 p.m.

Status: First aired in 1972.

Title: *Probe*

Description: A weekly current affairs show that was aired on Thursdays at 9:30 p.m. with host Hu Gentles on JBC TV.

Status: Started in 1967.

Title: *Probe*

Description: An investigative journalism programme aired on CVM TV on Sundays at 8:00 p.m.

Status: Aired around 1994 to 1999.

Title: *Question Time*

Description: A discussion show moderated by Dennis Hall, who answered questions on business, better living and consumer problems.

Status: Aired 1973.

Title: *Round Table Talk*

Description: A JBC studio talk show about current affairs with host Ronnie Thwaites on Tuesdays on JBC TV that usually aired as early as 8:30 p.m.

Status: Aired 1987 to 1990.

Title: *Scan*

Description: This was a current events programme dealing in depth with politics, sociology, and economics, which was in part on film and in part live from the studio.

Status: Aired 1967.

TELEVISION PROGRAMMES PRODUCED AND AIRED IN JAMAICA

Title: *Sunday Report*

Description: A weekly programme looking at personalities, events, and developments of interest to viewers in Jamaica. It aired on Sundays at 7:50 p.m. on JBC TV.

Status: Aired 1974 to 1975.

Title: *The Best of Live @ Seven*

Description: A compilation of clips from the weekday show *Live @ Seven* appeared on Sundays at 10:00 a.m.

Status: Weekly show that first aired in July 2010.

Title: *The Owen James Report*

Description: This daily financial news programme began airing on CVM TV during its nightly news package in August 2011 with host Owen James.

Status: Started in 2011.

Title: *The Verdict Is Yours*

Description: This was the television version of the programme that ran on JBC radio. The studio discussion was moderated by a host and featured a panel focused on topical issues.

Status: Aired in the 1960s and 1970s on JBC TV.

Title: *Topic for Today*

Description: A Friday programme that highlighted topics of current interest.

Status: Aired starting in 1965.

Title: *Tuesday Forum*

Description: Studio discussion programme hosted initially by Claude Robinson and then later by Elaine Wint-Leslie. Usually featured a panel of guests and a studio audience.

Status: Aired 1990 to 1997.

Title: *Wadup*

Description: This was an entertainment magazine show aired on CVM TV with host Tyrone Thompson. It initially aired on Tuesdays and Thursdays at 5:30 p.m. and then moved to Thursdays only with a repeat on Saturdays at 6:00 p.m.

Status: Aired December 2006 to August 2007.

## APPENDIX 4

Title: *Your Issues Live*

Description: A news and current affairs outside broadcast programme shot on location and transmitted live with an audience from the community, a panel and hosts. It was hosted mainly by Michael Sharpe on TVJ.

Status: Started airing in 2005.

### Drama

Title: *Claffy*

Description: Volier Johnson starred as Claffy in this comedy produced by Phase Three Productions.

Status: Aired in the 1990s.

Title: *Dear Mama*

Description: This drama presentation, shown on Sundays at 6:50 p.m., was written by Daphne Innerarity and performed by JIS staffers. The plot focused on a Kingston secretary who became pregnant after an affair with her boss.

Status: Aired late 1970s.

Title: *God's Way*

Description: Dahlia Harris wrote and directed this stage play about faith, deception and relationships that was eventually recorded and produced for television in a series of six thirty-minute episodes. It aired on TVJ.

Status: Aired 2013/2014.

Title: *Great Junction*

Description: This series was shot on location in St Elizabeth, produced by JIS TV and aired on Sundays at 6:00 p.m. on JBC TV. Written by Hall Anthony Ellis, the cast included Aston Cooke, Stan Irons, Sharon McGlashan, Erica Brown and Ann-Marie Fuller. The thirty-minute episodes dealt with the experiences of Mr Monk, a young teacher from an urban area who ended up working in a rural village.

Status: Aired 1982 to 1983.

Title: *Joint Tenants*

Description: This Jamaican comedy focused on a group of tenants living with a strict landlord. It aired on Sundays at 9:00 p.m.

Status: Aired starting in 2011.

## TELEVISION PROGRAMMES PRODUCED AND AIRED IN JAMAICA

Title: *Life with the Littles*

Description: An entertaining drama centred on the life of a Jamaican family headed by Lorna and Horace Little. Its educational content included information about decimal currency conversion, literacy and health. This was produced by JIS TV and aired on JBC TV at 6:30 p.m. on Sundays with radio adaptations on RJR at 6:15 p.m. and JBC Radio at 7:00 p.m.

Status: Began airing in 1969 and ended in 1974.

Title: *Lime Tree Lane*

Description: A Jamaican drama which started on JBC TV in 1988 and focused on various characters living in the fictional lane.

Status: Aired 1988 to 1997.

Title: *Me and Mi Kru*

Description: This soap opera is based on the life of Jamaican entertainer Benzly Hype and his involvement in the music business. It began on CVM TV in 2009 before moving to TVJ.

Status: Started in 2009.

Title: *Miranda Hill*

Description: A television drama series shown on JBC starring Tony Hendricks, Leonie Forbes, and Peter Lloyd alongside a cast of other Jamaican actors. The show focused on a Jamaican middle class family whose members found themselves involved in mystery and adventure.

Status: Aired in 1995 on JBC TV.

Title: *Oliver at Large*

Description: This series was created and owned by Calvin Butler. Oliver Samuels played the lead in this comedy about the schemes and situations in which his namesake character found himself. Each episode occurred at different locations depicted in a studio set-up. A number of five-minute vignettes aired starting in October 1985 and served as the pilot for the series.

Status: Aired in 1987 to 1988.

**STILL ON AIR APPENDIX 4**

Title: *Oliver*

Description: The series called *Oliver* was produced by JBC TV and aired later in the early 1990s. The thirty-minute episodes aired on Fridays at 8:05 p.m.

Status: Aired in the early 1990s.

Title: *Onstage*

Description: This programme was produced by JIS TV and featured dramatic presentations, including a re-run of the popular JIS series *Great Junction*.

Status: Aired in the mid-1980s.

Title: *Pullet Hall*

Description: This mini-series was named after a remote community in northern St Elizabeth that was also the location for filming the thirteen episodes about rural life. The pilot for this series was called *Country Time*, which was shown as part of "Jamaican Showcase" on JBC TV.

Status: Aired from 1995 to 1996 on JBC TV.

Title: *Real Friends*

Description: This is a thirty-minute teen drama looking at the lives of six high schoolers in Jamaica. It aired on Saturday nights at 8:30 on TVJ.

Status: Aired starting in 2015.

Title: *Royal Palm Estate*

Description: A Jamaican soap opera which followed the lives and loves of characters associated with the estate. It began on CVM in 1994 and ran for over twenty years.

Status: Aired 1994 to 2015.

Title: *Run di Track*

Description: This show included a cast of characters in a plot revolving around a fictional reality show.

Status: On air in 2015.

Title: *Sarge in Charge*

Description: Produced by Ed Wallace at the CPTC and featured Oliver Samuels.

Status: Unknown.

## TELEVISION PROGRAMMES PRODUCED AND AIRED IN JAMAICA

Title: *Shebada in Charge*

Description: Theatre star of comedies such as *Bashment Granny*, Keith "Shebada" Ramsey plays the title character in this CVM TV comedy set in a shop.

Status: Debuted October 2013.

Title: *The Blackburns*

Description: A spin-off from *Royal Palm Estate* following the lives of some of the characters established in that programme on CVM TV.

Status: Aired 2009 to 2015.

Title: *The Chameleon Series*

Description: A mini-series of one-off dramas produced by Paul Campbell at the CPTC and directed by Chris Browne. It had three episodes, "Country of the One-Eyed God" in 1994, "Final Verdict" and "Happily Ever After", produced in 1995. The series was presented on JBC TV as part of "Jamaican Showcase", quality Jamaican drama from the JBC, CPTC, JIS and independent producers.

Status: Aired during 1994 to 1995.

Title: *Thicker Than Water*

Descriptions: Dahlia Harris wrote and directed this stage play that was produced and aired on TVJ in six thirty-minute episodes. It featured an all-female cast and explored the bond between siblings set against a backdrop of workplace conflict.

Status: Aired 2013/2014.

Title: *Titus*

Description: Glen Campbell played the title character in this half-hour comedy series which followed the antics and mishaps of the Titus of the title.

Status: Aired in 1990s.

Title: *Traxx*

Description: This was a twenty-four-minute programme that delivered a mix of comedy and musical entertainment. It was a spin-off from the television series *Royal Palm Estate* prompted by the million-dollar winnings of the caretaker character "Mackie".

Status: Started airing in 1997.

# APPENDIX 4

Title: *Uppers and Downers*

Description: A thirty-minute comedy about the interplay of a lady of means and her helper. The show was written by Alma Mock Yen and produced by Wycliffe Bennett at CPTC.

Status: Pilot produced. Aired in 1991.

Title: *Win Some, Lose Some*

Description: A drama on life in a typical Jamaican household.

Status: On air 1992–1993.

## Entertainment

Title: *Ah ZuzuWah*

Description: A dance and song show produced by Leonie Forbes aired monthly every third Sunday initially at 6:02 p.m. and then at 8:30 p.m. The show featured entertainers such as the Jamaica Folk Singers, the Eddy Thomas Dancers and the Alpha Omega Band, among others.

Status: Aired 1972 to 1973.

Title: *Bandstand*

Description: This show was aired on Mondays and sometimes Wednesdays between 9:00 p.m. and 9:30 p.m. At times, Roy Hall hosted the show, which featured a Jamaican band.

Status: Aired 1967.

Title: *Buzz*

Description: An entertainment showcase highlighting Caribbean fashion, drama and other arts. This programme aired on CVM TV on Thursdays at 8:00 p.m. and was hosted by Kathy Owen and narrated by Ernie Smith.

Status: Started in June 1993.

Title: *Close Up*

Description: This show provided a glimpse of Jamaica's top entertainers and personalities as they were interviewed during performances before studio cameras of JBC TV.

Status: Aired 1963.

TELEVISION PROGRAMMES PRODUCED AND AIRED IN JAMAICA

Title: *Countdown*

Description: This was weekly show highlighting the top ten popular songs of the week on Saturdays at 9:00 p.m.

Status: Aired 1975.

Title: *Disco Jam*

Description: This was an entertainment show that aired briefly but was not sustained.

Status: Aired 1984.

Title: *Duckunoo*

Description: This was JBC TV's nightclub show that aired on Mondays at 10:00 p.m. with host Desmond Elliott.

Status: Aired 1966 to 1967.

Title: *Fi Wi Choice Top Ten*

Description: A countdown chart show featuring popular music videos and interviews with artistes that was originally aired on TVJ on Saturdays at 6:30 p.m. starting in 2009. It aired on CVM TV on Fridays at 9:30 p.m. from 2011 to 2013 before returning to TVJ in April 2014. Viewers are invited to vote for their favourites.

Status: Aired starting in 2009.

Title: *Groove Music*

Description: A show which looked at the local and overseas music and party scene featuring music videos chosen by viewers. It was aired on TVJ.

Status: Aired early to mid-2000s.

Title: *Hit List*

Description: Broadcast every Monday and Friday on CVM TV and designed for teenagers and young adults who vote for numerous music videos produced each week. A host and resident DJ requests text voting to establish the hits. Viewers also get a chance to win prizes on *The E-Strip*.

Status: Unknown.

Title: *In the Dance*

Description: This programme aired at 9:30 p.m. on Fridays on CVM TV as a thirty-minute show exposing new dance talent before a studio audience, along with the

## APPENDIX 4

top ten dance picks and interviews with established acts. The second season was aired on TVJ in 2011 and could also be seen in other Caribbean territories.

Status: Aired 2009 to 2011.

Title: *Jack Mandora*

Description: Storyteller Vernon Lopez told Jamaican tales on this show produced by JIS TV and aired on Mondays at 6:30 p.m.

Status: Aired 1963.

Title: *Jamaica DWL*

Description: A programme highlighting comedic talent focusing on local and international Internet-based content and vloggers. Created and produced by Emprezz Golding and hosted by the vlogger Kevin "Kevin2wokrayzee" Swaby, Jamaica DWL capitalizes on the spirit of laughter that pervades Jamaican society.

Status: First season aired on TVJ during September to November 2014 with plans for future seasons.

Title: *Layers of Soul*

Description: This was a one-hour programme featuring a concert by Jamaican musical artistes presented with a studio audience. It airs monthly on Sundays at 9:00 p.m. on TVJ.

Status: Started airing in 2011.

Title: *Music My Hobby*

Description: Barry Davies presented the series on second Sundays and then on third Sundays he hosted another show called *Youth and Music*.

Status: Aired 1973.

Title: *JBC's National Song Competition*

Description: Original songs were performed in a special three-part series where competitors vied for cash prizes.

Status: Aired in 1971 and 1972.

Title: *Nommo*

Description: *Nommo* was a weekly half-hour programme produced by Dermot Hussey that featured music and cultural topics. Richard Ace and the Youth Band, the Jose Marti School, Bob Marley and Tuff Gong, Feya Daughter of Zion, and the

Ethiopian Zion Coptic Church were some of the subjects covered by the show. It aired on Fridays at 7:00 p.m.

Status: Aired 1979 to 1982.

Title: *Paleface Point of View*

Description: A programme of stand-up comedy and monologue from comedian Tony Hendricks. The show ran for five seasons of thirteen episodes (first and second season comprising five-minute episodes, thereafter ten minutes) plus a special episode on the gas riots of 1999.

Status: Aired 1995 to 1999.

Title: *Peradventure*

Description: This programme was a cross between a review and a variety show with Leonie Forbes and Ken Maxwell. It aired at 9:00 p.m. on Saturdays.

Status: Aired 1967.

Title: *Pulsation*

Description: *Pulsation* was a new musical programme for JBC TV which was hosted by Phillip St J. Hill. The show placed emphasis on black music, its roots and exponents. The format of show included entertainment on stage and looks behind the scenes. It was produced by Julius McCalla.

Status: Aired 1973.

Title: *Reggae Trail TV*

Description: This was a show that took the audience backstage at concerts and festivals and looks at current happenings in the music industry. It aired on CVM TV before airing on TVJ in 2001.

Status: Aired on TVJ from 2001.

Title: *Saturday Night Sit-In*

Description: Bobby Ghisays was the host, comic, entertainer and interviewer in this half-hour variety programme with special guests and a studio audience. It aired on Saturdays at 9:20 p.m. Gloria Lannaman was the executive producer and Donat Bucknor was the director.

Status: Aired 1971.

## APPENDIX 4

Title: *See Tyah*

Description: The show aired Saturdays at 9:30 p.m. and was produced and hosted by Neville Willoughby and directed by Noel Gayle. It involved a blend of the amusing and informative with host Neville talking to interesting guests. Every week there was a show business personality on hand to demonstrate his or her talents.

Status: Aired 1968.

Title: *Showcase*

Description: This appeared on JBC TV on Sundays at 8:30 p.m. and was hosted by Tony DaCosta and produced by Eric Douglas.

Status: Aired 1972.

Title: *Sing Along with Sweet and Lovely*

Description: This monthly half-hour show was produced by Leonie Forbes in keeping with the trend towards "Jamaicanizing" television content.

Status: Aired 1971.

Title: *Six O'Two (6:02 p.m.) Wrap*

Description: A reggae pop half-hour programme based on an idea from Julius McCalla and presented by Radcliffe Butler. It appeared after the two-minute news headlines at 6:00 p.m. Later the show changed to the *Seven O'Clock Wrap* when the time slot was changed from 7:00 p.m. on Thursdays

Status: Aired 1972.

Title: *Sounds of the Seventies*

Description: This half-hour swing session was produced and presented by Julius McCalla. This disco-type programme featured some the island's leading artistes and aired at 6:02 p.m. on Thursdays. It aimed at promoting Jamaican talent, providing "with it" entertainment and introducing foreign talent.

Status: Aired 1971 and 1972.

Title: *Spectrum*

Description: This was a cultural interest programme aired on Sundays at 8:00 p.m. on JBC TV. It was hosted at times by Neville Willoughby.

Status: Aired 1971 to 1972.

## TELEVISION PROGRAMMES PRODUCED AND AIRED IN JAMAICA

Title: *Sunday Theatre*

Description: This was produced by JIS TV and aired on Sundays from 6:30 p.m. to 7:00 p.m. It featured musical and dance performances by Jamaican artistes. Later this slot became "Sunday Concert".

Status: Aired starting 1965.

Title: *Talent Hunt*

Description: This show aired at 8:50 p.m. on Saturdays. It brought together a variety of performers leading to a grand finale featuring the winners of all the parish-level competitions.

Status: Aired 1971.

Title: *Teenage Dance Party*

Description: A music and dance show based on the JBC radio show of the same name. The TV counterpart hosted by Roy Hall aired on Friday evenings. The show later merged with *Young World* and eventually became *Thru Tomorrow's Eyes*.

Status: On air from 1963 to 1965.

Title: *Tempo*

Description: This show aired at 9:30 p.m. on Fridays with Desmond Elliott.

Status: Aired 1967.

Title: *The E-Strip*

Description: Four hours of back-to-back music entertainment programming on CVM TV on Saturdays from 4:00 p.m. to 8:00 p.m., showcasing all aspects of the entertainment landscape.

Status: Unknown.

Title: *The Ity and Fancy Cat Show*

Description: A sketch and stand-up comedy show featuring Ity and Fancy Cat and a cast of other characters. The programme first aired on TVJ in 2008.

Status: First aired 25 April 2008; seasonal.

Title: *The Keith Stewart Show*

Description: This was a light entertainment series transmitted live from Studio B with Jamaican singer Keith Stewart.

Status: Aired 1975.

## APPENDIX 4

Title: *The Leslie Butler Show*

Description: This was a light entertainment series transmitted live from Studio B with Jamaican piano virtuoso Leslie Butler.

Status: Aired 1975

Title: *The Mike Thompson Show*

Description: This was a light entertainment series transmitted live from Studio B with entertainer Mike Thompson.

Status: Aired 1975.

Title: *The Party*

Description: A one-hour programme showcasing Jamaican popular music, parties and dance. Aired on CVM TV, it was hosted by Candace Buchanan, among others.

Status: Unknown.

Title: *The Richard Ace Show*

Description: A JIS TV programme that showcased Jamaican talent on Sundays at 6:00 p.m. The show featured singing and musical guests.

Status: Aired 1972 and 1973.

Title: *The Young Professionals*

Description: This featured classically trained musicians. The show was aired every first Sunday at 6:02 p.m. with Barry Davies.

Status: Aired 1972/1973.

Title: *This Sunday*

Description: This show appeared on Sundays at 6:00 p.m. and was produced by Pam Hickling and hosted by Carl Bradshaw and Patsy Ricketts. It involved a live studio audience, who shared their ideas during the programme, providing entertainment and important information on how viewers could develop themselves as citizens of a developing country.

Status: Aired 1978.

Title: *V Mix*

Description: A music video show with host "VJ Abnormal" that aired on Saturdays at 5:30 p.m.

Status: Aired from 2010.

TELEVISION PROGRAMMES PRODUCED AND AIRED IN JAMAICA

Title: *Video Alley*

Description: *Video Alley* is a one-hour reggae top ten music video chart show with producer and host Suzie Q, formerly of the radio station Irie FM. The programme, that has been streamed live online weekly, has been aired not only in Jamaica, but also in other countries including the United States and England.

Status: Aired starting in 2001.

Title: *Video Saturday*

Description: This is an hour-long compilation of music videos aired on Saturdays at 4:00 p.m.

Status: Aired 2004.

Title: *Where It's At*

Description: A music variety show hosted by Alphonso Walker and others including Elaine Wint. It began airing in 1971 on Fridays at 6:02 p.m. and was later shown at 7:00 p.m. By 1975, it was shifted to Saturdays at 6:02 p.m. In the early 1980s, the show returned to Fridays at 7:00 p.m.

Status: On air from 1971 to 1986.

Title: *Young World*

Description: This show first appeared in 1964 on Tuesdays at 6:15 p.m. with host Hu Gentles, and presented young Jamaicans engaged in folk dance and song. It was later merged with Teenage Dance Party in March 1965 and aired on Fridays at 6:00 p.m. The new half-hour show now provided discussion and dancing for young fans of both programmes with Hu Gentles and Roy Hall hosting. Beverley Anderson and Jeff Dixon hosted the show later.

Status: Aired 1964 to 1968.

Title: *Young, Gifted and Black*

Description: A one-hour musical entertainment show from JBC Studio B slated for transmission for the last Sunday each month.

Status: Aired 1972.

Title: *Youth and Music*

Description: Barry Davies presented this show on every third Sunday on JBC TV.

Status: Aired 1973.

– 189 –

**APPENDIX 4**

## Factual

Title: *A Day in the Life of . . .*

Description: This profile of prominent Jamaican figures showed them at home and work on a typical day. It aired on TVJ.

Status: Aired in 2004.

Title: *Bambu Tambu*

Description: This show highlighted aspects of the tourism industry and Jamaican heritage.

Status: Aired 1971.

Title: *Behind the Scenes*

Description: This show aired on alternate Wednesdays from 6:30 p.m. to 7:00 p.m. and gave an insider's view on various operations in Jamaica.

Status: Aired starting in 1965.

Title: *Campus Vybz*

Description: This series focused on lifestyle, entertainment, food, sports and all other aspects of school life in Jamaica. The show seen on CVM TV usually on Fridays at 9:30 p.m. is rebroadcast on Tuesdays at 6:30 p.m.

Status: Aired starting in 2012.

Title: *Country Calendar*

Description: A twice-weekly programme (Mondays and Thursdays from 6:15 p.m. to 6:30 p.m.) about agriculture and gardening with live material and filmed features. It was hosted by Carol Reckord, who did a similar show on radio.

Status: Aired in 1963.

Title: *Creative Cooking*

Description: Branded short cooking show where the host, sometimes with the help of a guest, prepared a meal and shared a recipe containing Grace products.

Status: Aired 1986 to 2011.

Title: *Doin' the T*

Description: Half-hour news magazine programme on tourism produced by David Ho of Mind's Eye Limited for the Jamaica Tourist Board.

Status: Aired 1998–1999.

TELEVISION PROGRAMMES PRODUCED AND AIRED IN JAMAICA

Title: *Expressions*

Description: The programme aired on Saturday nights. It featured Jamaican art and culture.

Status: Aired in the mid-1980s.

Title: *Feedback*

Description: The show featured written and telephoned comments on all aspects of JBC TV. At times, Dwight Whylie chaired this forty-five-minute show on Fridays at 8:15 p.m. aired simultaneously on JBC TV and JBC Radio 1.

Status: On air in 1974.

Title: *Health Forum*

Description: This show appeared on Tuesdays at 9:30 p.m. and was hosted by Pam Hickling and produced by Maxine Trotter.

Status: Aired 1978.

Title: *Health Watch*

Description: A short feature on health aired initially on JBC TV and later on TVJ. Hosted mainly by Shermaine Robotham, who also did *Alive and Well* on CVM TV for about five years.

Status: Started in the late 1980s.

Title: *Hidden Treasures*

Description: Travel programme on TVJ looking at places around Jamaica and exploring their cultural heritage. It was hosted by Alicia McCalla and aired on Sundays at 5:30 p.m.

Status: Started in January 2010.

Title: *Hill an' Gully Ride*

Description: A thirty-minute show that began airing on JBC TV. Narrated mainly by Carey Robinson, the show can be seen on Sundays at 6:00 p.m. on TVJ.

Status: Started in 1987 and still on air.

Title: *Homemaker*

Description: This show looked at domestic matters, such as the choice and making of clothing and laundry. It aired on alternate Thursdays from 6:30 p.m. to 7:00 p.m.

Status: Aired starting in 1965.

## APPENDIX 4

Title: *Hype Zone*

Description: Aired Saturdays at 9:00 p.m. and hosted by Susan Simes on TVJ, this show took viewers to various party spots and featured music videos, performances and interviews with artistes.

Status: Began in 1999 and lasted until about 2003.

Title: *In Focus*

Description: This JIS TV produced show aired on Mondays from 6:30 p.m. to 7:00 p.m. and focused on cultural and social topics such as independence festival celebrations and the National Insurance Scheme.

Status: Aired starting in 1965.

Title: *Inside Story*

Description: This programme involved an in-depth exploration of various topics of national interest. It was produced by JIS TV and aired on Thursdays.

Status: Aired in the mid-1980s.

Title: *Is the Customer Always Right?*

Description: This show looked at the commercial world and featured fashion and recreational activities.

Status: Aired 1971.

Title: *Island Dreams*

Description: This show originally aired on TVJ on Sundays at 5:30 p.m. This is an inspirational lifestyle magazine that explores Jamaican homes, design and architecture, and attractions. Hosted mainly by Kimberley Mais, it now airs on CVM on Sundays at 5:30 p.m. with an encore on Thursdays at 6:00 p.m. Rapid True Value has been the show's main sponsor.

Status: Eighth season aired in 2014.

Title: *Jamfit*

Description: This early morning fitness and exercise show with host Karelle Ashley-Jones aired on TVJ Mondays to Fridays at 6:00 a.m.

Status: Aired in 2003.

## TELEVISION PROGRAMMES PRODUCED AND AIRED IN JAMAICA

Title: *Jamicons*

Descriptions: Jamaican icons were featured in this five-minute feature that aired on Saturdays during Black History Month at 8:30 a.m., 12:30 p.m., 6:53 p.m., 8:30 p.m. and 10:30 p.m. on TVJ.

Status: Aired in 2005.

Title: *Landscape*

Description: This show aired every week for half an hour on Wednesdays starting at 6:00 p.m. to showcase the countryside, report on farming activities, and to interview agricultural experts and farmers at work. Vin Lumsden presented the show.

Status: Aired 1965 to 1966.

Title: *Let's Grow*

Description: This show aired fortnightly on Sundays at 5:30 p.m. It focused on the role of agriculture in the Jamaican economy. Vin Lumsden hosted the show that also featured interviews with people involved in agriculture.

Status: Aired 1971.

Title: *Living Treasures of Jamaica*

Description: A programme looking at the contribution Jamaicans have made to the arts, education and agriculture. It was produced by the CPTC.

Status: Aired in 1991.

Title: *Nation at Work*

Description: This was aired on Tuesdays from 6:30 p.m. to 7:00 p.m. and showed various activities and endeavours across Jamaica.

Status: Aired starting in 1965.

Title: *Nation on the Move*

Description: A magazine programme with useful information on Jamaican places, people and history. This was produced by JIS TV.

Status: Aired in 1972.

Title: *Nyammings*

Description: A show focusing on Jamaican food with a host who travelled around the island to interview individuals as they cooked.

Status: Started March 2010 and entered its seventh season in 2015.

## APPENDIX 4

Title: *On the Farm*

Description: This show aired on alternate Thursdays from 6:30 p.m. to 7:00 p.m. and featured agricultural topics with host Carol Reckord.

Status: Aired starting in 1965.

Title: *Police Calling*

Description: This programme was about the Jamaican police force and was broadcast from 6:30 p.m. to 7:00 p.m.

Status: Aired 1971.

Title: *Portraits*

Description: This aired on alternate Tuesdays and was a profile programme produced by JIS TV to showcase the lives of Jamaicans and Jamaican institutions that had a significant impact on Jamaican society.

Status: Aired in the mid-1980s.

Title: *Pulse*

Description: This was a weekly show about the "little man" in Jamaican society. The show highlighted the ingenuity and imagination of Jamaicans who went about their business without fanfare. It was produced by Pam Hickling and the JBC Film Unit and aired on Fridays at 8:00 p.m.

Status: Aired 1975 to 1976.

Title: *Ready for CFW*

Description: Hosted by former Pulse supermodels, Kimberley Mais-Issa and Romae Gordon, this series gave a weekly preview of upcoming Caribbean Fashion Week activities. There was also some post-event coverage.

Status: Aired starting in 2003.

Title: *Reflections*

Description: This was produced by JIS TV and chronicled the history of Jamaican institutions and their recent developments.

Status: Aired in the mid-1980s.

Title: *Seen*

Description: This was an award winning ten-minute feature on aspects of Jamaica that highlighted "things thought, heard and seen". It was aired mostly on Mondays on JBC TV.

Status: On air from 1987 to 1994.

Title: *Self Starters*

Description: A show produced by CPTC that featured Jamaicans who started small businesses.

Status: Aired 1991.

Title: *Spicy Hints*

Description: This JIS TV fortnightly series was hosted by Irma Parke, who gave hints on how best to make use of locally grown spices and their varied uses.

Status: Aired starting 1963.

Title: *Street Link*

Description: This magazine programme looked at Jamaican lifestyle including communities, schools, and artistes before they were famous. It was hosted by Kern Spencer at 6:00 p.m. on Saturdays.

Status: Aired in 2014.

Title: *Strong People, Stirring Times*

Description: This was a six-part series that explored the working class citizens of Jamaica from 1832 to 2000. It was produced by Cynthia Wilmot of Video for Change and aired on TVJ in October 2014.

Status: Aired 2014.

Title: *The Blackboard*

Description: This was an educational programme that featured careers and tertiary-level education.

Status: Aired 1971.

Title: *The Farmer*

Description: This agricultural show aired on Mondays from 6:30 p.m. to 7:00 p.m.

Status: Aired 1971.

Title: *The Health Report*

Description: Aired within *Prime Time News* on TVJ, health issues are covered in each edition with footage and an interview. The show is hosted by Shemala Mitchell. Previously, there was a feature called *Your Health* that began in 1998.

Status: Started in 2004.

Title: *The Purse Strings*

Description: This programme gave do-it-yourself hints along with money saving tips.

Status: Aired 1971.

Title: *Today in JA*

Description: This was produced by CPTC and hosted by Cathy Levy and then by Ruth-Ann Wynter. About twenty-five episodes were created before the run ended.

Status: 1987 to 1988.

Title: *Together We Learn*

Description: This adult literacy programme aired from 6:30 p.m. to 7:00 p.m.

Status: Aired 1971.

Title: *Trails*

Description: This thirty-minute upbeat programme showcased Jamaicans in a positive light and appeared on Sundays on JBC TV at 8:00 p.m. After four years as a broadcast journalist overseas, Roy Brown returned to Jamaica and, after a short stint in the JBC newsroom, he eventually conceptualized the programme and became the executive producer and host.

Status: On air from 1983 to 1987.

Title: *Update*

Description: This programme was produced by JIS TV and aired on Tuesdays and Thursdays at 8:05 p.m.

Status: Aired in the mid-1980s.

Title: *Vibes Cuisine*

Description: This show began as a five-minute cooking demo in 2006 and then became a thirty-minute food programme on CVM TV. It aired on Thursdays at 6:30 p.m. and was promoted as a Caribbean cooking show with international flavour. The presenter was Michelle Jones.

Status: Aired starting in 2006.

TELEVISION PROGRAMMES PRODUCED AND AIRED IN JAMAICA

Title: *Visions*

Description: A peek at interesting stories on the Jamaican landscape, shown on CVM TV at 6:30 p.m. on Sundays.

Status: On air in 2002.

Title: *Walk n' Talk*

Description: Produced by JIS TV as a five-minute feature including vox pops. It aired on Mondays, Wednesdays and Fridays, usually at 8:05 p.m.

Status: Aired 1986 to 1990.

Title: *West North West*

Description: This show focused on the people and culture in the west of the island. It was hosted by Vin Lumsden.

Status: Aired 1972.

Title: *Young Jamaica*

Description: This show aired on alternate Wednesdays from 6:30 p.m. to 7:00 p.m. and featured careers and young Jamaicans in action.

Status: Aired starting in 1965.

Title: *Yours Truly, Big J*

Description: Leonie Forbes hosted this half-hour show on Tuesdays at 7:00 p.m. that responded to audience questions and comments.

Status: Started airing in 1971.

## Magazine

Title: *CVM at Sunrise*

Description: Morning magazine programme with a mix of features, news and interviews on CVM TV.

Status: Started in 2003.

Title: *Evening Time*

Description: A magazine programme targeting a youth audience, with interviews and features in the early evening on JBC. The show's educational pieces included

**APPENDIX 4**

"Bankra Basket" with Laleta Davis, "World of Art" with Hope Wheeler, "World of Dance" with Sheila Barnett, "Music Corner" with Sam Wisdom and "Enter the Dojo" with Errol Lyn.

Status: Aired in the 1980s to 1990s.

Title: *In Town*

Description: This was a mid-week magazine on Wednesdays at 8:15 p.m. about local happenings, films, and entertainment, hosted initially by Fred Wilmot and then later by Gladstone Wilson.

Status: Began airing in 1973.

Title: *Impressions*

Description: Produced by Louis McLean at CPTC. A magazine show with features targeting a teen audience.

Status: Aired 1995 to 1997.

Title: *Mirror*

Description: This show initially aired on Tuesdays at 6:15 p.m. and eventually went to Wednesdays at 9:30 p.m. Cynthia Wilmot was associated with the show as host from its beginnings in 1963. Beverley Anderson also hosted. Fashion highlights, interviews and topics of interest to women formed most of the show's content.

Status: Started in 1963.

Title: *Morning Time*

Description: Magazine programme with a mix of features, interviews and news airing early morning on JBC TV. The show started when Gloria Lannaman was general manager of JBC TV between 1983 and 1985 and was hosted by Leonie Forbes and Lindy Delapenha. Other regular hosts included Erica Allen, Fae Ellington and Darcy Tulloch.

Status: Aired 1984 to 1997.

Title: *Rappin'*

Description: A discussion show by CPTC for young people featuring high schools and presented by young hosts. Aired on JBC TV it was shot mainly on location at the schools being featured, with special shows done in the CPTC studios. Some of the presenters continued in the television industry after getting their start here.

Status: Aired 1990 to 2001.

TELEVISION PROGRAMMES PRODUCED AND AIRED IN JAMAICA

Title: *Roundabout*
Description: This magazine show aired on JBC TV on Saturdays at 8:20 p.m.
Status: Aired 1971.

Title: *Smile Jamaica*
Description: A morning magazine programme aired initially Mondays to Fridays on TVJ. Later, Saturday mornings were added. The show's hosts have included Simone Clarke-Cooper, Neville Bell and Dahlia Harris, among others.
Status: Started in February 1998 and still on air.

Title: *Teen Seen*
Description: A programme of talk and features commissioned by Jamaica's National Family Planning Board using edutainment to deliver adolescent reproductive health information. Each series comprised twenty-four episodes shown initially on TVJ starting in 1999 and then aired on CVM TV from 2009.
Status: On air from 1999 to 2013.

Title: *This Is Sunday*
Description: An informative and entertaining magazine that looked at pertinent social issues, important aspects of national life and the people in and behind the news. It was shown at 8:00 p.m. on Sundays.
Status: Aired 1971.

Title: *The Vibe*
Description: This half-hour magazine programme covered current affairs and lifestyle issues with hosts Lauren Dunn and George Davis. It aired on Thursdays at 9:30 p.m.
Status: Aired starting in 2012.

Title: *Yow*
Description: A programme about adolescent reproductive health issues with drama, music and guests. Two series were produced for the "Youth.Now" project of the Ministry of Health and aired on TVJ and CVM TV.
Status: Aired 2003 to 2004.

**APPENDIX 4**

## Quiz and Game Shows

Title: *Brains Trust*

Description: Quiz show with host Bill Carr that started in November 1963 on JBC TV on Wednesdays at 8:30 p.m.

Status: Aired 1963 to 1964.

Title: *Bus Yu Brain*

Description: Host Ken Maxwell appeared on this show on Wednesdays at 7:00 p.m.

Status: Aired 1972 to 1973.

Title: *Claro Cash Cab*

Description: Passengers enter a taxi and become instant contestants on a game show which allows them to answer general-knowledge questions as they travel on their way to their destination. The first season was hosted by Felisha Lord and Wayne Whyte.

Status: First aired November 2010.

Title: *Deuces Wild*

Description: A dating game show hosted by Lisa Hanna that aired for one season.

Status: Aired in 1998.

Title: *Digicel's Deal or No Deal*

Description: A game show where individuals competed to win a briefcase full of money after successfully guessing which case contained the prize. Simon Crosskill presented the Jamaican version of this show whose original format was created by the UK independent production company Endemol.

Status: Aired for one season from 2009 to 2010.

Title: *Do You Follow Me?*

Description: This quiz show produced by Barry Davies aired on Sundays at 6:02 p.m. The show tested the knowledge of participants on the location of well-known places in Kingston and St Andrew. Viewers could participate by guessing the final destination of the host and mailing their answers to the station.

Status: Aired 1972.

## TELEVISION PROGRAMMES PRODUCED AND AIRED IN JAMAICA

Title: *Family Bonanza*

Description: A family quiz game show hosted by Karl Binger and produced by CPTC

Status: Aired 1991.

Title: *Family Quiz Show*

Description: James Verity was the host of this quiz show for families. After parish eliminations it aired on Tuesdays at 7:00 p.m. from 4 July to 5 September 1971.

Status: Aired 1971.

Title: *JAMAL JBC Quiz Show*

Description: A quiz for adults on JBC TV hosted, at times, by Desmond Elliott.

Status: Aired 1975 to 1982.

Title: *Jamaica Jigsaw*

Description: This quiz show aired on Tuesdays at 9:00 p.m. and was hosted by Desmond Elliott.

Status: Aired 1965 to 1966.

Title: *Junior Schools' Challenge Quiz*

Description: A spin-off from the senior quiz show, it follows the same format for a younger age group and includes the face-off round where individual students go up against one another to answer specialist questions.

Status: Seasonal and first aired in 2003.

Title: *KFC Junior Quiz*

Description: Jody-Ann Maxwell hosted this quiz show for ten- to thirteen-year-olds. School teams competed for the title.

Status: Aired 2002 to 2010.

Title: *Quest for Quiz*

Description: A preliminary round for *Junior Schools' Challenge Quiz* which allowed an additional thirty-two schools to vie for a chance to become part of the main show. As a result, the number of participating schools moved from sixty-four to ninety-six. It is a six-week series with thirty-two programmes.

Status: Seasonal mid-July to August. Started in 2015.

## APPENDIX 4

Title: *Round the World Quiz*

Description: A quiz show that aired on JBC on Thursdays at 8:30 p.m. Eventually, the show aired on a Wednesdays at 8:30 p.m. Fred Wilmot was the quiz master.

Status: Aired from 1963 to 1964.

Title: *Schools' Challenge Quiz*

Description: A thirty-minute quiz show for teams of high school students who respond to questions posed by a quizmaster. The show airs on TVJ at 6:30 p.m. Mondays to Fridays during its usual January to March season.

Status: Aired starting in 1970, seasonal, and still on air.

Title: *Take a Trip*

Description: This quiz show aired on Tuesdays at 9:30 p.m. with various hosts such as Fred Wilmot and Adrian Robinson. Contestants answered questions in chosen specialist areas and prizes included a tour of Kingston by plane and a trip abroad.

Status: Aired 1966.

Title: *Take Twenty*

Description: This was a programme with host Fred Wilmot that aired on Tuesdays at 9:15 p.m. Teams of two participated in this television version of a familiar parlour game "Animal, Mineral, Vegetable". Contestants were each given twenty clues to help them guess the identity of an object.

Status: Aired in 1973.

Title: *The Face is Familiar*

Description: This was a Jamaican quiz that premiered at 7:00 p.m. on a Wednesday in February 1973.

Status: Aired 1973.

Title: *Tic Tac Toe Quiz*

Description: This live quiz show aired on JBC TV on Mondays at 9:30 p.m. with questions from categories including sport, religion, current affairs, geography and history. The show was directed by Desmond Elliott and hosts included Morris Cargill and Neville Willoughby.

Status: Aired in 1967 and 1968.

Title: *Trace the Music*

Description: Barry Davies hosted this musical quiz show on Sundays at 6:02 p.m. giving music lovers the chance to show off their knowledge and win record albums to add to their collections. The show was directed by Julius McCalla.

Status: Aired 1971 to 1972.

Title: *TV I.Q.*

Description: This live quiz show aired in 1963 with teams competing for prizes while finding the answers to entertaining puzzles and questions. Viewers could participate. The show was swiftly replaced by *Brains Trust* after it did not find favour with viewers and one commentator described it as a failure.

Status: Aired in 1963.

## Reality

Title: *All Together Sing*

Description: A school choir singing competition in which schools compete in a live studio show. They are assessed by the judges, however, it is the audience votes that count when it comes to declaring the winner at the end of the season.

Status: First aired 2004 with its tenth season in 2014.

Title: *Caribbean Fashion Weekly*

Description: This was a fourteen-part series associated with the annual Caribbean Fashion Week shown on TVJ and other stations in the Caribbean. Before this there was *CFW Monthly* that aired on TVJ.

Status: Aired starting 2001/2002.

Title: *Caribbean Model Search Reality TV Show*

Description: In this show staged annually by model agency Pulse, supermodel hopefuls compete for various fashion titles and for an opportunity to become global supermodels. This was originally *The Search for the Caribbean's Next Supermodel*.

Status: Seasonal and started in 2006.

Title: *Dancing Dynamites*

Description: Shot on location with host Jenny Jenny and a panel of judges, each season of this talent show features twelve dance groups competing for the title. Viewer voting determines the winner.

## APPENDIX 4

Status: Seasonal and on air since 2006.

Title: *Digicel Rising Stars*

Description: The reality show genre came to Jamaica when *Digicel Rising Stars* came to TVJ. Contestants are mainly singers who move from location auditions to live shows, where they rely on audience voting to continue in the series until a winner is chosen.

Status: Started in 2004 and seasonal.

Title: *Guinness Sounds of Greatness*

Description: This show featured a sound clash competition among established selectors and sound systems to crown the best of the contestants.

Status: Unknown.

Title: *Heineken Green Synergy*

Description: This programme aired on TVJ and showcased the talent of aspiring DJs who competed in various performances to become the Heineken Green Synergy Champion.

Status: Aired 2009, 2010.

Title: *KFC on the Verge*

Description: A talent show series consisting of auditions and studio performances with the audience voting for the winner.

Status: Started in 2011 and seasonal.

Title: *Magnum Kings and Queens of Dancehall*

Description: A talent search for the male and female top dancehall deejays shot on location after a round of auditions held across Jamaica. Media personality Miss Kitty and producer Cordell "Skatta" Burrell, among others, have been judges on the show.

Status: First aired in January 2008 with its eighth season in 2015.

Title: *Magnum Vixens*

Description: This show featured a group of women fighting and cursing and behaving badly as they vied for the title Magnum Vixen.

Status: Started in 2014.

TELEVISION PROGRAMMES PRODUCED AND AIRED IN JAMAICA

Title: *Makeover Magic*

Description: This was a reality show that showcased the style and fashion makeover of a variety of Jamaicans. Hosted by Simone Clarke, the complete makeover transformations were executed by Novia McDonald-Whyte.

Status: Aired in 2006.

Title: *Mission Catwalk*

Description: On TVJ this show sees contestants vie for the top prize after undergoing a number of design challenges. It is hosted and executively produced by Keneea Linton-George, who is joined by other fashion experts as judges.

Status: Seasonal and started in 2011.

Title: *NCB Capital Quest*

Description: Business owners undergo a number of challenges in order to win and receive a substantial injection of funds for their business idea from NCB.

Status: First aired in 2015.

Title: *Star Search at Traxx*

Description: A talent show sitcom hybrid on CVM TV, featuring real auditions and comedy drama centred on the fictional Traxx club.

Status: Started in 2000 and seasonal.

Title: *Tastee Talent Trail*

Description: The Tastee talent show had been going on for over thirty years in venues across the island. In 2010 it came to television as a talent reality show on TVJ.

Status: First aired 2010.

Title: *Teacha's Pet*

Description: A group of young women compete for the attention of DJ Vybz Kartel, a.k.a. "The Teacha", in this show aired on CVM TV and available online. The show ended prematurely when Kartel was arrested and held on a murder charge.

Status: Started in 2011.

Title: *The Anchor*

Description: This reality series comprised half-hour shows that aimed to discover the next big television personality who could occupy the anchor's desk at CVM TV.

Status: Aired in 2010.

## APPENDIX 4

Title: *The Golden Nugget*

Description: A reality show on CVM TV where contestants completed challenges to win the top prize. The first season aired on Tuesdays at 9:00 p.m. The show moved to a Sunday night slot for its second season in 2005 with the third season being promoted for a 2006 start. It was hosted by Candice Buchanan.

Status: Started airing in November 2003.

Title: *The Innovators*

Description: Hosted by Yaneek Page and Gary Matalon, this show is an entrepreneurship and financial management competition show. Each season depicts the lives of twelve contestants (The Assignments) who receive advice on how to transform their businesses.

Status: First aired in 2012 with its fifth season airing in 2015.

Title: *TOK Taking Over*

Description: This is a series that followed the work and lives of Jamaican reggae and dancehall group TOK. The show depicted the challenges each group member faced with individual projects while trying to keep the group together.

Status: First season aired in 2014 on CVM TV.

Title: *Two Sisters and a Meal*

Description: Two sisters, Suzanne and Michelle Rousseau, travel the country cooking up meals and finding out about some of the history behind the dishes.

Status: Seasonal and first aired in January 2014.

Title: *Wray and Nephew Contender*

Description: This a TVJ reality show where a group of sixteen boxers from Jamaica and the Caribbean compete for the title in an elimination-style tournament.

Status: First aired April 2011 with its fifth season aired in 2015.

### Religious

Title: *A Question of Religion*

Description: This weekly panel discussion featured religious topics. It was moderated by Rabbi Bernard Hooker on Sundays at 2:00 p.m.

Status: Aired 1970.

## TELEVISION PROGRAMMES PRODUCED AND AIRED IN JAMAICA

Title: *Breakthrough*

Description: This was one of the first gospel programmes on Jamaican television. It appeared on Sundays at 6:02 p.m. with David Keane and the Teen Time Singers.

Status: Aired starting in 1973.

Title: *Catch the Fire*

Description: This was a gospel programme hosted by David Keane. It appeared on CVM TV at 9:30 p.m. on Sundays.

Status: Aired 2001.

Title: *Faith Deliverance*

Description: This show aired on Sundays at 6:00 a.m. on CVM TV.

Status: Unknown.

Title: *Gospel Report*

Description: This show aired on Saturdays at 6:00 a.m. on CVM TV

Status: Unknown.

Title: *Honest to God*

Description: The Reverend Clive Abdullah and three guests – clerical and lay – discussed social problems in Jamaica and the place of the church in society. This was aired on Sundays at 11:10 p.m.

Status: Aired 1967.

Title: *Living in the Sonshine*

Description: This programme was half an hour of gospel music with David Keane and the Sunshine Singers. It appeared on Sundays at 6:00 p.m. on JBC TV.

Status: Aired 1982 to 1983.

Title: *Profiles in Religion*

Description: This show aired at 2:00 p.m. on Sundays. Each week Rabbi Hooker conducted an in-depth interview with a leading religious personality.

Status: Aired in 1971.

Title: *Reformation Now*

Description: This show aired on Sundays at 6:30 a.m. on CVM TV.

Status: Unknown.

Title: *Revival Time*

Description: This show appeared on CVM TV on Sundays at 7:00 a.m.

Status: Started in April 2013.

Title: *Something More with Herro Blair*

Description: This is a morning showing of church services with Bishop Herro Blair.

Status: Started airing in 1984.

Title: *Soul*

Description: On Sundays at 1:00 p.m., members of the religious community talked about their issues.

Status: Started in 1972.

Title: *Today Is Sunday*

Description: This programme featured Sunday services from different churches around the country. It aired at 9:30 a.m.

Status: Aired 1970 to 1973.

Title: *Version*

Description: This focused on young people as they voiced their views on religion. It aired at 1:00 p.m. on Sundays.

Status: Started in 1973.

## Social Advocacy

Title: *A Ray of Hope*

Description: Part of the *Prime Time News* package on TVJ, the focus is on stories of help in the community and positivity in health and social issues.

Status: First aired in 1996 and still on air.

Title: *Inspire Jamaica . . . with Kerlyn Brown*

Description: Hosted by Kerlyn Brown, the feature shows how Jamaican children with health issues challenge their fears and face adversities. It airs on CVM TV on Sundays during *News Watch* at 8:00 p.m.

Status: First aired in 2011 and still on air.

TELEVISION PROGRAMMES PRODUCED AND AIRED IN JAMAICA

Title: *The Teller . . . Stories to Tell*

Description: A five-minute feature highlighting the corporate social responsibility activities of Scotiabank. The programme allows the beneficiaries to tell their stories.

Status: First aired 2007, seasonal and still on air.

## Sports

Title: *A Moment with Thoroughbreds*

Description: This show about horseracing aired on Mondays with hosts including Chris Armond and Howard Abrahams.

Status: Unknown.

Title: *Eye on Sports*

Description: This is an in-studio sports discussion programme with hosts and occasional guests and callers on the phone.

Status: Aired starting in 1998.

Title: *Football GPS*

Description: This sports call-in programme about football aired weekly for one hour on Tuesdays at 9:00 p.m. The show has been hosted by Wayne Walker and produced by Donald Oliver.

Status: Aired starting in 2011.

Title: *Just Bet Before the Whistle*

Description: This is a companion television feature to the Supreme Ventures Just Bet site. It is described as a sort of betting discussion segment that highlights upcoming sporting events in *Eye on Sports* on TVJ.

Status: First aired in November 2014 and still running.

Title: *Matters Arising*

Description: This show was hosted on Saturdays by Sydney "Foggy" Burrows, who addressed sports issues.

Status: Aired 1973.

Title: *Saturday Sports Special*

Description: Round up of sporting action locally and internationally.

Status: Unknown.

**APPENDIX 4**

Title: *Sports Commentary*

Description: Within the TVJ *Prime Time News* programme, Oral Tracey is the main host. He comments on sporting issues with ample use of a laugh track for emphasis.

Status: Started in 1998.

Title: *Sports Forum*

Description: This aired monthly at 6:02 p.m. on Sundays and was a discussion programme about sports.

Status: Aired 1972.

Title: *Sports Special*

Description: This aired on Saturdays at 7:10 p.m.

Status: Started in 1967.

Title: *Sports View*

Description: This show aired on Wednesdays from 11:25 p.m. to 12:25 p.m.

Status: Started in 1971.

Title: *Thursday Night at the Fights*

Description: This was a roundup of current boxing matches and a look at archived fights that aired on JBC TV. Presenters have included Patrick Anderson, Keith Brown, Hugh Crosskill and Ali McNab.

Status: Began airing around 1984.

Title: *Tuesday Night Sports*

Description: Sports discussion programme

Status: Unknown.

## Talk Shows

Title: *After Dark*

Description: This appeared on Thursday nights with host Jerry Benswick on TVJ at 9:00 p.m.

Status: Aired 2004.

Title: *Connection*

Description: Barbara Blake hosted this personality interview show on Fridays at

## TELEVISION PROGRAMMES PRODUCED AND AIRED IN JAMAICA

8:15 p.m. on JBC TV. The first interview was with Beverly Manley, the wife of the then-prime minister.

Status: Aired 1974.

Title: *Face-to-Face*

Description: This was an adult one-hour discussion programme on CVM TV about human sexuality. It featured three informed guests representing the spiritual, the medical and secular perspectives. The show had three seasons, each with thirteen to fifteen episodes.

Status: Started in 1993.

Title: *Face-to-Face*

Description: An interview show produced and aired on JBC TV on Wednesdays at 6:15 p.m. A programme with the same name appeared in 1983–1984 also on JBC at 9:05 a.m. on Thursdays.

Status: First aired 1963.

Title: *How's Life*

Description: An interview programme looking at the problems and pleasures of people from various sections of society. It aired from 2:00 p.m. to 2:30 p.m. on Sundays.

Status: Started in 1971.

Title: *In Person*

Description: This show was hosted by Dennis Hall on Sundays at 7:45 p.m. on JBC TV.

Status: Aired 1972.

Title: *Jamaican Woman*

Description: This was a radio show that began at 9:30 p.m. on Tuesdays.

Status: Aired 1967 to 1968.

Title: *Love Zone*

Description: This highlighted stories of people in love, exploring the challenges they encountered and how they triumphed. Hosted by Alrick McKenzie, it featured mostly couples talking about their relationships and aired on Sundays at 6:30 p.m. on CVM TV.

## APPENDIX 4

Status: Seasonal and started July 2009.

Title: *Man and Woman Story*

Description: A Sunday talk show on relationship issues with hosts Dr Leachim Semaj and Dr Carolyn Cooper in studio with guests.

Status: Started in 1998.

Title: *Man Talk*

Description: Talk show with a focus on issues related to men hosted by Christine Hewitt, among others. It aired on TVJ on Sundays at 9:00 p.m.

Status: Started in 2001.

Title: *My Guest*

Description: Hosted by John Akar, former ambassador of Sierra Leone to Jamaica, who interviewed many high-profile guests, including members of parliament, the diplomatic corps and government officials. The programme started on Saturdays after 9:00 p.m. in August. There was a rebroadcast on Sundays at 2:00 p.m. that was also heard on JBC radio.

Status: Aired 1972 to 1974.

Title: *Open House Reasoning*

Description: This discussion show appeared on JBC TV.

Status: Aired 1978.

Title: *Our Voices*

Description: A CVM talk show with female hosts, former Miss Jamaica World Lisa Hanna and Carlene "The Dancehall Queen" Smith, discussing a range of topics with guests. The show was produced by Angela Thame.

Status: May 2003 to August 2006.

Title: *Profile*

Description: A weekly thirty-minute talk show hosted by Ian Boyne and featuring the success stories of guests who appear on the programme. The show aired on Sundays on TVJ at 6:30 p.m.

Status: First aired 1987 and still on air.

## TELEVISION PROGRAMMES PRODUCED AND AIRED IN JAMAICA

Title: *Quest with Safa*

Description: A studio talk show with self-styled psychic Safa Asuntuwa responding to viewers' questions. This show aired on TVJ on Wednesdays at 11:00 p.m.

Status: Aired 2001 to 2002.

Title: *Religious Hardtalk*

Description: Religious issues are the focus of this weekly studio talk show with host Ian Boyne and guests. It is usually aired on Tuesdays on TVJ.

Status: Weekly show started in 2004.

Title: *Say It Loud*

Description: This show aired on Sundays at 6:02 p.m. and was hosted by Bobby Pickersgill, who introduced subjects and held discussions with a teenage panel. Produced by Alphonso Walker.

Status: Aired 1974 to 1978.

Title: *Simply Muta*

Description: This was a weekly one-hour show aired at 9:30 p.m. on Mondays on CVM TV, with dub poet Mutabaruka as host. The show featured guests and dealt with a range of issues such as the environment, religion and natural resources.

Status: First aired November 2009.

Title: *Talk Up Yout*

Description: This thirteen-episode talk show series was produced by Nadia Stanley and Emprezz Golding. It addressed stories of hope, love, success and triumph and broke the silence on unaddressed topics affecting young people.

Status: First aired in January 2011 with its fifth season released in 2015.

Title: *The Deiwght Peters Show*

Description: Night-time studio talk show which included commentary on celebrity fashion, personalities and topical issues, shown on TVJ in a six-episode series.

Status: First aired in 2014, with second season in 2015.

Title: *The Diana Wright Show*

Description: A studio talk show aired Thursdays at 9:30 p.m. on JBC TV and hosted by Diana Wright with guests and studio audience. Initially, it was produced at

## APPENDIX 4

the studios of CPTC before moving production fully to JBC TV, where the show ended its run. The original season consisted of eight episodes that began airing in December 1990. A second season returned in May 1991.

Status: Started airing in 1990.

Title: *The Naked Truth*

Description: An all-woman talk show featuring four women – Paula Kerr-Jarrett, Barbara Ellington, Terri Salmon and Shelly-Ann Weeks – sharing their perspectives on a wide range of topics.

Status: Debuted October 2012.

Title: *The Saudicka Diaram Show*

Description: The show was hosted by Saudicka Diaram and focused on lifestyle and entertainment. It premiered on TVJ on 22 August 2015 at 6:00 p.m.

Status: First aired 2015.

Title: *The Susan Show*

Description: A studio talk show produced and hosted by Susan Simes that debuted on CVM as *Susan* before moving to TVJ in 2010 as *The Susan Show*. The show has a studio audience and features a range of elements including talk, reuniting relatives and makeovers. The show is inspirational with the theme "Doing good in your neighbourhood" and highlighting acts of charity.

Status: First aired April 2005.

Title: *Thru Tomorrow's Eyes*

Description. An updated version of *Young World*, this JBC TV discussion programme for young people featured various hosts such as Uriel Aldridge, Radcliffe Butler and Dick Pixley.

Status: Aired 1968 and 1969.

Title: *Thwaites and Company*

Description: A JBC TV talk show with host Ronnie Thwaites and invited guests that started in March 1996 on Wednesdays at 9:00 p.m. It eventually aired on Thursdays at 9:00 p.m.

Status: Began airing in 1996.

## TELEVISION PROGRAMMES PRODUCED AND AIRED IN JAMAICA

Title: *Very Special People*

Description: An interview show hosted by Norman Rae on Saturdays at 9:20 p.m. This slot was later occupied after August 1972 by John Akar's *My Guest*.

Status: Debuted 1972.

Title: *We the Youth*

Description: This was a discussion programme targeting young Jamaicans that appeared on Fridays at 7:00 p.m.

Status: Aired 1978.

Title: *Wealth Magazine Business Access*

Description: A show featuring entrepreneurs aired on TVJ on Sunday afternoons before moving to its own cable channel Business Access TV. Each year would have three seasons of thirteen episodes each and there would be a break for a few weeks in between seasons.

Status: Aired from 2011 to 2014 on TVJ; continued after on Business Access cable channel in 2015.

## Other

Title: *The Bashco Shopping Show*

Description: An infomercial programme where hosts Elva "Queenie" Ruddock and Omar Azan tell people about the products in the Bashco store with the help of staff.

Status: Started in 2009 on CVM TV.

Title: *The Megamart Shopping Show*

Description: An infomercial programme with hosts, Christopher "Johnny" Daley and others, focusing on items available in the Megamart store.

Status: Started in 2010.

Title: *Wat a Gwaan*

Description: In this five-minute vox pop programme, aired on CVM TV the interviewer asks people "Wat a gwaan?" (translation: What is going on?) on a variety of issues.

Status: Unknown.

## APPENDIX 4

Title: *Weh Yuh Seh*

Description: This vox pop programme was known for ending with the phrase "Smile Jamaica TVJ, watch it every day", said to camera by a group of people. The host of this five-minute national vox pop programme that travelled the country was Bagga Brown. This show aired at various times including 6:40 a.m. and again at 6:58 p.m. on various days of the week.

Status: Started in 2001.

# Notes

## Preface

1. Karlene Salmon, "The Development Game Jamaican Broadcasting's Longest Running Show" (master's thesis, Queen's University, 1996); Livingston White, "Development Imperatives for Television Programming and Production in Jamaica: Identifying Appropriate and Feasible Alternatives" (master's thesis, Florida State University College of Communication, 2001); Nickesia Gordon, *Media and the Politics of Culture: The Case of Television Privatization and Media Globalization in Jamaica (1990–2007)* (Boca Raton: Universal Publishers, 2008).

## Chapter 1

1. Refer to appendix 4.
2. Rachel Beddow and Michael Sidwell, "Transparency International Annual Report 2011", accessed 4 September 2015. http://www.transparency.org/annual report/2011.
3. "Jamaica in Figures 2013", Bank of Jamaica, accessed 22 July 2015, http://www.boj.org.jm/uploads/pdf/jam_figures/jam_figures_2013.pdf.
4. Nancy Rytina, "Estimates of the Legal Permanent Resident Population in 2011", accessed 23 July 2014, https://www.dhs.gov/xlibrary/assets/statistics/publications/ois_lpr_pe_2011.pdf.
5. Relating to the BBC's first director general Lord Reith, who believed that broadcasting should not be commercial but should be dedicated to high-quality products rather than to those with popular appeal.
6. Carey Robinson, *Memoirs of a Jamaican Media Man* (Kingston: LMH, 2012), 173.
7. Martin Mordecai "State: Policy, Global Trends and Regulation in Broadcasting: The Case of Jamaica", in *Globalization Communications and Caribbean Identity*, ed. Hopeton Dunn (Kingston: Ian Randle, 1995), 202.
8. Robinson, *Memoirs*, 174; "JBC-TV Opening Day", *Gleaner*, 4 August 1993, 4.
9. W. Stanley-Moss, "Teleview", *Gleaner*, 6 August 1963, 7.
10. Ibid.

11. Ibid.
12. "Emil George a Specialist in National Fact-Finding Missions", *Gleaner*, 14 August 2015, B8; Harry Milner, "Television 1963", *Gleaner*, 29 December 1963, 18; W. Stanley-Moss, "Teleview", *Gleaner*, 6 August 1963, 7; Wycliffe Bennett, "Questions of Identity, Democracy and Broadcasting: The Case of Jamaica", *Caribbean Quarterly* 4, no.2 (1994), 29; "Top 40 Local TV Shows", Birth of a Nation, *Gleaner* special feature, *Gleaner*, 31 July 2002; Tony Robinson, "TV or not TV", *Observer*, 29 April 2012, http://www.jamaicaobserver.com/lifestyle/TV-or-not-TV_11341836; Harry Milner, "Television 1963", *Gleaner*, 29 December 1963, 18; "Round the World Quiz", *Gleaner*, 7 August 1964, 18; Alma Mock Yen, *Rewind: My Recollections of Radio Broadcasting in Jamaica* (Kingston: Arawak, 2002), 236; see also Silvera Castro, "Remembering Teenage Dance Party", *Gleaner*, 12 April 2012, http://jamaica-gleaner.mobi/20090412/ent/ent3.php. *Teenage Dance Party* was originally a radio programme for teenagers that later became a television show.
13. "The Jamaica Broadcasting Corporation August 1964 Weekly Television Programme Schedule", *Gleaner*, 7 August 1964, 18; Harry Milner, "Television 1963", *Gleaner*, 29 December 1963, 18; JBC, "Programme Schedule for the Months of August and September 1970"; "The Jamaica Broadcasting Corporation August 1964 Weekly Television Programme Schedule", *Gleaner*, 7 August 1964, 18. On Sundays in 1964 JBC broadcast from 4:00 p.m. to 5:30 p.m.
14. In 1956 the Government Public Relations Office was established. In 1957 it was merged with the Government Broadcasting Service and the Jamaica Film Unit. In 1963 it was renamed the Jamaica Information Service and the television unit was formed.
15. "The Jamaica Broadcasting Corporation August 1964 Weekly Television Programme Schedule", *Gleaner*, 7 August 1964, 18.
16. Jean Barnes, former executive director of CPTC, discussion with the authors, 20 May 2015.
17. Robinson, *Memoirs*, 182.
18. Ibid.
19. Ibid.
20. Bryan Cummings, "$135,000 Saved by JIS-TV", accessed 3 September 2015, Norbertthomas.webs.com/JIS-TV.pdf.
21. Aggrey Brown, "Mass Media in Jamaica", in *Mass Media and the Caribbean*, ed. Stuart Surlin and Walter Soderland (New York: Gordon and Breach, 1990), 27.

22. Vernon Davidson, "Good Evening and Welcome to TVJ", *Observer*, 30 October 1998, 6.
23. Claire Forrester, "Crosskill's Departure from TVJ Marks End of an Era", *Observer*, 23 May 2012, http://www.jamaicaobserver.com/columns/Crosskill-s-departure-from-TVJ-marks-end-of-an-era_11519019.
24. "Radio Jamaica Limited Annual Report and Financial Statements 31 December 1998", 16.
25. "Chase Equips Archive and Records Dept", Jamaica Information Service, 4 May 2010, http://jis.gov.jm/chase-equips-archives-and-records-dept/; Denise Norman, "Government to Purchase US$200,000 State-of-the-Art Digital Archival System", Jamaica Information Service, 12 November 2015, http://jis.gov.jm/government-to-purchase-us200000-state-of-the-art-digital-archival-system. In some cases, JBC tapes had been recorded over with material and not relabelled to reflect this. In one example, a tape labelled as 1991 when viewed was revealed to contain material from 1992.
26. "About Us", CVM TV, accessed 1 September 2015, http://www.cvmtv.com/about.php.
27. "CVM's First Day", *CVM 10th Anniversary Supplement*, 30 March 2003, X.
28. Arnold Kelly, discussion with the authors, 8 June 2015.
29. "Television and Sound Broadcasting Regulations 1996", BCJ, accessed 11 September 2015, http://www.broadcastingcommission.org/images/TV_Sound_Broadcasting_Regs.pdf.
30. Clifton Segree, "Cable Television Developing Local Shows", *Gleaner*, 23 April 2000, 2C; White, "Development Imperatives", 75.
31. Claire Grant, general manager of TVJ, discussion with the authors, 26 February 2015.
32. "Public Broadcasting Corporation Begins Operations Next Financial Year", Jamaica Information Service, 22 December 2005, http://jis.gov.jm/public-broadcasting-corporation-begins-operations-next-financial-year/.
33. Mock Yen, *Rewind*, 148.
34. Ibid., 315.
35. "Ministry Paper No. 61: Establishment of Television Services", National Library of Jamaica, accessed 10 September 2015, http://www.nlj.gov.jm/MinistryPapers/1962/No.61.pdf.
36. "CPTC Productions: About Us", CPTC, 21 January 2017, http://cptcjamaica.com/about-us. CPTC offers training through the Media Technology Institute. However, before the institute was established CPTC offered training in areas of radio, voice and speech, and video.

37. Colin Hoskins, Stuart McFadyen and Adam Finn, *Global Television and Film: an Introduction to the Economics of the Business* (Oxford: Clarendon, 1997), 9.
38. "About the Film Commission", Film Jamaica, accessed 30 August 2015, http://www.filmjamaica.com/.
39. "Reviving Jamaica's Film Industry", *Star*, 2 September 1999, 6–7.
40. "Survey of Radio, TV", *Gleaner*, 2 January, 1966, 10; "Who Listens to What and Why", *Gleaner*, September 1965, 10.
41. "RJR's Listenership Survey", *Gleaner*, 10 September 1967, 8.
42. "Party to Announce Fourth Listenership Survey", *Gleaner*, 9 September 1967, 17.
43. "Results of Research into the Television Audience", CRAM International, December 1970, 1–20.
44. Don Anderson, CEO, Marketing Research Services Limited, discussion with the authors, 11 March 2016.
45. "Nielsen Estimates More Than 116 Million TV Homes in the US", Nielsen, 29 August 2014, retrieved 7 July 2016 from http://www.nielsen.com/us/en/insights/news/2014/nielsen-estimates-more-than-116-million-tv-homes-in-the-us.html.
46. "Number of TV Households in Canada from 2010 to 2014 (in Millions)", Statista, accessed 11 July 2017, https://www.statista.com/statistics/507043/number-tv-households-canada.
47. Supported by sponsorship and advertising these television stations are offered free to the public and are received via antenna or via cable providers.
48. Don Dobson, information officer, BCJ, email to the authors, 25 July 2016.

## Chapter 2

1. Salmon, "The Development Game".
2. Keeble Macfarlane, "Canada's Early Contribution to Local Broadcasting". *Observer*, 22 January 2011. Retrieved 3 September 2015, http://www.jamaicaobserver.com/columns/Canada-s-early-contribution-to-local-broadcasting_8308542.
3. Norman Stolzoff, *Wake the Town and Tell the People* (London: Duke, 2000), 65.
4. Lloyd Bradley, *Bass Culture: When Reggae Was King* (London: Viking, 2000), 88.
5. Harry Milner, "Television 1963", *Gleaner*, 29 December 1963, 18; W. Stanley-Moss, "Teleview", Gleaner, 6 August 1963, 7.

6. Bennett, "Questions of Identity", 29.
7. Everold Hosein, "The problem of imported television content in the Commonwealth Caribbean", *Caribbean Quarterly* 9, no. 4 (1976), 8.
8. Aggrey Brown and Roderick Sanatan, *Talking with Whom* (Kingston: Caribbean Institute of Mass Communication, 1987), 129.
9. Aggrey Brown, *Television Programming Trends in the Anglophone Caribbean in the 1980s*, Occasional Paper no. 2 (Kingston: Caribbean Institute of Mass Communication, 1987) 9.
10. Livingston White, "Reconsidering Cultural Imperialism", *Journal of Transnational Broadcasting Studies*, no. 6 (Spring–Summer 2001), http://tbsjournal.arabmediasociety.com/Archives/Spring01/whiteref.html.
11. Stanley Baran, *Introduction to Mass Communication Media Literacy and Culture* (Boston: McGraw-Hill, 2006).
12. Aggrey Brown, "Caribbean Culture and Mass Communication Technology: Re-examining the Cultural Dependency Thesis", in *Globalisation, Communications and Caribbean Identity*, ed. Hopeton Dunn (Kingston: Ian Randle, 1995), 53.
13. Ibid., 40–54.
14. "Telecommunications: The Experience of Hurricane Gilbert", *Caribbean Disaster News*, June 1989, 1, www.islandvulnerability.org/docs/PCDPPP1989CDN18.pdf.
15. Government of Jamaica, "An Act to Amend the Jamaica Broadcasting Corporation Act. 31 October 1991 (Jamaica)".
16. Claude Robinson, former director general of JBC, discussion with the authors, 24 March 2016.
17. Gordon, *Media and the Politics of Culture*, 2008, 83.
18. Lucille Burbank, *Secrets from Sesame Street's Pioneers: How They Produced a Successful Television Series* (Bradenton, FL: Booklocker.com, 2013).

## Chapter 3

1. Laurence Stewart, former assistant general manager at JBC, discussion with the authors, 8 May 2015. In "The Early Years", *Schools' Challenge Quiz* supplement, *Gleaner*, 11 May 2004, iv, it is noted that the first show aired on 27 February 1970, but checks with several other sources indicate that the show first aired on 26 February 1970. On page 4 of Ian Boyne and Glendon Smith's *Profile of Excellence*, it is said that *Schools' Challenge Quiz* began in 1972. However, the show started in 1970.

2. Robinson, *Memoirs*, 305–6.
3. Tandy Lewis, "Hope Stewart: Brains Behind Schools' Challenge Quiz", *Gleaner* supplement, 11 May 2004, ii.
4. Stewart, discussion.
5. Lewis, "Hope Stewart", ii.
6. "The Early Years", iv.
7. Lewis, "Hope Stewart", ii.
8. Bill Cummings, retired engineer at JBC TV, discussion with the authors, 7 May 2015.
9. Stewart, discussion.
10. Mark Taylor, Jamaica College *Schools' Challenge Quiz* team member, discussion with the authors, 10 July 2015; James Moss-Solomon, *Schools' Challenge Quiz* team member, discussion with the authors, 3 September 2015.
11. Stewart, discussion.
12. Carole Ivey, former producer at JBC TV, discussion with the authors, 13 May 2015.
13. Michael Gonzales, *Schools' Challenge Quiz* executive producer, discussion with the authors, 22 July 2014.
14. Suzanne Francis-Brown, historian, discussion with the authors, 8 May 2015.
15. Ruth Ho Shing, former producer at JBC TV, discussion with the authors 2 June 2015; see also "The Winners Circle", *Gleaner* supplement, 11 May 2004, xi.
16. Ruth Chisholm, "Behind the Scenes: Michael Gonzales", *Schools' Challenge Quiz Souvenir Magazine*, 2014, 20.
17. Gonzales, discussion.
18. Reverend Glen Archer, letter to the editor, *Observer*, 19 August 1997, 8.
19. Stephen Vasciannie, letter to the editor, *Gleaner*, 20 January 1997, A4; "When the JBC is swallowed up by RJR, there will be major changes in the programming line-up at the station. For my two cents worth, I could live with the passing of *Perspective* and *Tuesday Forum* in their current formats, but please, let me have the *Schools' Challenge Quiz* for years to come." Gonzales, discussion.
20. "RJR Annual Report 2004/2005", RJR, 2005.
21. Stephen Vasciannie, "TVJ's Quizzical Timing", *Gleaner*, 13 June 2005, A8.
22. "New Changes for *Schools' Challenge Quiz*", *Star*, 13 December 2005.
23. Ibid.
24. "The Quamps Double", *Schools' Challenge Quiz Souvenir Magazine*, 2015, 21–22.

25. Robert Lalah, "We Are the Champions", *Gleaner*, 11 April 2010, F1–F2; Gareth Davis, "Titchfield's *Schools' Challenge Quiz* Team Home Town Heroes", *Gleaner*, 16 April 2011, A2.
26. Michael Gonzales, *Schools' Challenge Quiz* executive producer, discussion with the authors, 25 May 2014.
27. "Schools' Challenge Launched", *Star*, 6 January 2004. See also *Schools' Challenge Quiz*, forty-fifth anniversary DVD (Kingston: TVJ, 2014).
28. Ruth Chisholm, "Quizmasters", *Schools' Challenge Quiz Souvenir Magazine*, 2014, 15. Marlene Stephenson-Dalley was the main host of the programme at the time of this publication.
29. Grant, discussion.
30. "Program History", *College Bowl*, accessed 4 September 2015, http://collegebowl.com/arch/history.asp/. *College Bowl* started in 1953 on radio in the United States. It began on television in 1959 on CBS which aired it until 1963. From 1963 to 1970 it was on NBC; *It's Academic*, http://itsacademicquizshow.com/, accessed 22 July 2015. *Guinness World Records* has acknowledged *It's Academic* as the longest-running quiz show. In 2015 it entered its fifty-fifth season. It began on NBC Washington in 1961.
31. *The Price Is Right*, Internet Movie Database, accessed 4 September 2015, http://www.imdb.com/title/tt0068120/. *The Price Is Right* is a game show in the United States featuring contestants trying to guess the price of consumer items to win prizes. It has been on air since 1972; *Wheel of Fortune*, Internet Movie Database, accessed 14 August 2015, http://www.imdb.com/title/tt0072584/?ref_=nv_sr_1. 2015. *Wheel of Fortune* has been on the air in the United States since 1983; *Jeopardy*, Internet Movie Database, accessed 14 August 2015, http://www.imdb.com/title/tt0159881/?ref_=nv_sr_2. This US general-knowledge quiz programme has been on the air since 1984. *University Challenge* was produced by the College Bowl Company in association with Granada Television. It ran on the Independent Television Network up until 1987. It was later revived on the BBC.
32. "Promotional Package: Launch of *Schools' Challenge Quiz* 2001", TVJ, 3 January 2000.
33. "Thieves Strip JBC Archives", *Gleaner*, 5 January 2008, http://old.jamaica-gleaner.com/gleaner/20080105/lead/lead1.html. Attempts to view programmes which had been aired before 1988 proved futile while conducting the research for this book.
34. Gonzales, discussion, 24 May 2014.

35. Ibid.
36. *KFC Quiz*, Internet Movie Database, accessed 14 August 2015, http://www.imdb.com/title/tt2594058/?ref_=fn_al_tt_2. This quiz ran from 2002 to 2010.
37. H.A. Blair, letter to the editor, *Gleaner*, 22 July 1997, A5; O'Neil Richards, letter to the editor, *Gleaner*, 26 January 2013, A6.
38. Barry Robinson, letter to the editor, *Gleaner*, 12 March 2012, A8.
39. Media watcher, letter to the editor, *Gleaner*, 12 May 2004, A5.
40. Sonia Mitchell, letter to the editor, *Gleaner*, 4 April 2009, A5.
41. H.A. Blair, letter to the editor, *Gleaner*, 22 July 1997, A5; Richards letter, January 26, 2013, A6; Jacqueline Wright, letter to the editor, *Gleaner*, 26 January 2004, A5; Robinson letter 12 March 2012, A8; Media Watcher letter, 12 May 2004, A5; J. McPherson, letter to the editor, *Gleaner*, 13 May 2002, A5; Henley Taylor, letter to the editor, *Gleaner*, 17 May 2012, A8; Mitchell letter 4 April 2009, A5.
42. W.M. Thompson, letter to the editor, *Gleaner*, 18 February 2011, A6; see also Vasciannie. "TVJ's Quizzical Timing", 13 June 2005, A8.
43. McPherson, letter to the editor.
44. Francis-Brown, discussion.
45. "Roll of Honour Winners", *Schools' Challenge Quiz Souvenir Magazine* 2015, 24–25. Kingston College would go on to redeem itself by winning eleven titles in the first forty-five years of the show.

## Chapter 4

1. Carlton Alexander, interview with Ian Boyne, *Profile*, aired 22 February 1987, JBC TV, Kingston.
2. Ibid.
3. Ian Boyne and Glenford Smith, *Profile of Excellence* (Kingston: Ian Randle, 2013).
4. Lois Gayle, former public relations manager at JBC, discussion with the authors, 4 June 2015.
5. Boyne and Smith, *Profile*, 266.
6. "Profile Now Number One TV Talk Show", *Gleaner*, 5 February 1995.
7. Boyne and Smith, *Profile*, 5.
8. Ibid., 30–31.
9. Patrick Foster, "Profiling the Indefatigable Ian Boyne: The Longest Programme of Its Kind on Local Television", *Observer*, 19 February 2012, 12–13.
10. Ibid.

11. "Boyne Now Hosting Religious Talk Show on RJR", *Observer*, 16 June 2002, 45.

## Chapter 5

1. "Sunday Special" and "Friday Special" were programme slots on JBC TV devoted to programmes and features made by CPTC. Public service programmes developed by CPTC for Public Broadcasting Jamaica were shown during these slots. The first episode of *Hill an' Gully Ride* appeared during the "Friday Special" slot on 13 January 1989. The next episode aired on 5 February 1989 during "Sunday Special". Thereafter, the show aired on Sundays.
2. Monica Johnson, former *Hill an' Gully Ride* producer, discussion with the authors, 21 February 2015.
3. Other features in *Sunday Special* included *Currents* which focused on community activity or people trying to solve their problems and *Fine Arts* which showcased Jamaican art.
4. Mock Yen, *Rewind*, 315; see also "Public Broadcasting Corp Launched", *Gleaner*, 7 September 1988, 3 and "PBJ not Launched", *Gleaner*, 9 September 1988, 2. PBJ or the Public Broadcasting Jamaica was set up by the Office of the Prime Minister to facilitate transmission of local public service programming. The arrangement started in September 1988, though the exact date is uncertain. The *Gleaner* reported on 7 September 1988 that the PBJ was launched on 6 September 1988, but later reported, on 9 September, that the launch was really a meeting to acquaint advertisers and public relations executives with the new entity. In 1989, the name PBJ was changed to the Cultural Broadcasting Facility. In 1990, that was subsumed into the JBC. The programmes created by this entity continued to be produced by CPTC and aired on JBC TV.
5. "New Local Programmes for JBC TV", *Gleaner*, 5 January 1989, 6. The name was actually printed in a *Gleaner* article.
6. Mona Macmillan, *The Land of Look Behind: A Study of Jamaica* (London: Faber, 1957).
7. B.W. Higman and Brian Hudson, *Jamaican Place Names* (Kingston: University of the West Indies Press, 2009), 35.
8. *Land of Look Behind*, Internet Movie Database, accessed 3 September 2015, http://www.imdb.com/title/tt0157918/; Michelle Cliff, *Land of Look Behind: Prose and Poetry by Michelle Cliff* (Ithaca, NY: Firebrand Books, 1985).
9. In a film production of the *Music and Youth* series, students from Marcus Garvey Secondary School are seen walking along the Dunn's River Falls with

"Hill an' Gully Rider" heard in the background. It is not clear whether it is the children of St Catherine High School or those of Marcus Garvey High School who can be heard singing on the track.

10. Olive Lewin, *"Rock It Come Over": The Folk Music of Jamaica* (Kingston: University of the West Indies Press, 2000), 82 (for full lyrics).
11. "Unusual Place Names in Jamaica", Keepitjiggy.com, accessed 6 September 2015, http://keepitjiggy.com//?s=fat+hog+quarter&x=0&y=0.
12. Higman and Hudson, *Jamaican Place Names*, 4.
13. "Some Place Names in Westmoreland", National Library of Jamaica, accessed 25 October 2017, http://www.nlj.gov.jm/rai/place-names/Place Names of Westmoreland.pdf.
14. Gary Neita, former manager of Jamvision, discussion with the authors, 18 March 2015.
15. Ibid.
16. Ibid.
17. Ibid.
18. Market Research Services Limited, *MRSL All Media Survey 2012*.
19. Claude Robinson, former director general of JBC, discussion with the authors, 8 July 2015.
20. This is the actual text from the tweet. The spelling does not conform to any standard Jamaican spelling.
21. Ross Sheil, "Prince Charles to Visit Jamaica Next Month". *Observer*, 21 February 2008, 5.
22. *Hill an' Gully Ride, Port Royal*, directed by Carey Robinson. Kingston: CPTC, 2003.
23. Robinson, discussion, 8 July 2015.

## Chapter 6

1. JBC Television, *Nightly News*, 15 November 1991.
2. Mark Thomas, former JBC news producer, discussion with the authors, 20 May 2015.
3. Anthony Miller, producer of *Entertainment Report*, discussion with the authors, 16 March 2013.
4. Gayle, discussion.
5. Chester Dowdy, telephone call to authors, 20 July 2015. The *Star* (25 March 1993, 14) indicated in the JBC TV programme schedule that *ER* would be aired from 8:45 p.m. to 9:45 p.m. suggesting it was now a longer programme.

6. "TV Spotlight", *Star*, 25 March 1993, 14.
7. Annie Paul, social commentator, discussion with the authors, 10 February 2013.
8. Bev Brammer, CPTC librarian, discussion with the authors, 13 July 2015.
9. Vernon Davidson, "Good Evening and Welcome to TVJ", *Observer*, 30 October 1998, 6.
10. Miller, discussion.
11. *ER* twenty-first anniversary documentary, directed by Yvette Rowe (Kingston: TVJ, 2013).
12. In 2001 the links for the show were recorded on location at James Bond Beach, St Mary, during the Sashi stage show.
13. O.C. Powell, *Entertainment Report* editor, discussion with the authors, 12 January 2013.
14. Jomo Kato, marketing manager, Red Stripe, discussion with the authors, 26 December 2012.
15. "Entertainment Report for CIN." *Gleaner*, 6 June 1999, 11.
16. "TVJ's ER to Debut in UK", *Gleaner*, 17 September 2006, J2.
17. "Report on the Commission of Enquiry into Extradition Request for Christopher Coke", 6 June 2011, Government of Jamaica, http://japarliament.gov.jm/attachments/641_REPORT%20OF%20THE%20COMMISSION%20OF%20ENQUIRY%20INTO%20THE%20EXTRADITION%20REQUEST%20FOR%20MR.%20C.%20COKE.pdf.
18. Yasmin Peru, entertainment writer, discussion with the authors, 26 December 2012.
19. Donna Hope, cultural analyst, discussion with the authors, 16 March 2013.
20. Ibid.

## Chapter 7

1. Herbert Zettl, *Television Production Handbook* (Belmont, CA: Wadsworth, 2003), 421.
2. Dan Weaver and Jason Siegel, *Breaking into Television and Film: Proven Advice from Veterans and Interns* (Princeton, NJ: Peterson's, 1998), 234–36; Gerald Millerson, *Video Production Handbook* (London: Focal Press, 2004), 3.
3. Joseph Straubhaar, "Distinguishing the Global, Regional and National Levels of World Television", in *Media in Global Context: A Reader*, ed. Annabelle Sreberny-Mohammadi, Dwayne Winseck, Jim McKenna and Oliver Boyd-Barrett (New York: Oxford University Press, 1997), 286.

4. Ian Boyne, discussion with the authors, 28 December 2000; see also Boyne and Smith, *Profile of Excellence*, 25.
5. John Ellis, "Television Production", in *The Television Studies Reader*, ed. R.C. Allen and A. Hill (London: Routledge, 2004), 281.
6. "Rising Stars: Case Study in Branded Entertainment", *Gleaner*, 14 August 2005, C10.
7. Rebecca Rowell, *YouTube: The Company and Its Founders* (Edina, MN: ABDO, 2011), 78.
8. Claude Robinson, *Let's Do It*, dir. Basil Jones Jr (Kingston: CARIMAC, 2011).
9. Aggrey Brown, "Caribbean Cultures and Mass Communication in the 21st Century" (paper presented at the Caribbean Studies Association Conference, Trinidad, 22–27 May 1990), ufdcimages.uflib.ufl.edu/CA/00/40/00/66/00001/PDF.pdf.
10. Millerson, *Video Production Handbook*, 9.
11. Ibid., 279.
12. Ellis, "Television Production", 275–91.
13. Millerson, *Video Production Handbook*, 192.
14. Shaun Walker, editor of *Entertainment Report*, discussion with the authors, 15 January 2013.
15. Brian McNair and Ben Goldsmith, "Local Content and the ABC", *The Conversation*, accessed 21 March 2015, http://theconversation.com/local-content-and-the-abc-36128.
16. Salmon, "The Development Game"; White, "Development Imperatives"; Gordon, *Media and the Politics of Culture*.
17. Patrick Barwise and Andrew Ehrenberg, *Television and Its Audience* (London: Sage, 1988), 34–35.
18. Jean Chalaby, "Producing TV Content in a Globalized Intellectual Property Market: The Emergence of the International Production Model", *Journal of Media Business Studies* 9, no. 3 (2012): 19–40.
19. Ellis, "Television Production", 275–91.
20. Ibid.
21. Gerald Millerson, *Effective TV Production* (London: Focal Press, 1993), 90.
22. "The Shorter Seasons on Cable Have Been Influencing More Shows on TV to Follow Suit", *New York Daily News*, 7 July 2013.
23. Landon Palmer, "Just What Is a Television 'Season' Anyway?", Film School Rejects, accessed 3 September 2015, https://filmschoolrejects.com/just-what-is-a-television-season-anyway-5dfc30fb48b7/.
24. Ibid.

25. George Barnett, Hsiu-Jung Chang, Edward Fink, William Richards Jr. "Seasonality in Television Viewing: A Mathematical Model of Cultural Process", *Communication Research* 18, no. 6 (1991): 756.

## Chapter 8

1. Giannalberto Bendazzi, Animation: A World History, vol. 3: *Contemporary Times* (London: Focal Press, 2015), 313.
2. George McBean, "Illustrations and Animation for Development", accessed 11 July 2017, http://georgemcbean.com/1982-89-nepal-animation/caribbean-album/the-workshop-in-jamaica.html.
3. Bendazzi, *Animation*, 314.
4. Howard Campbell, "Icon: Miss Lou – 'Ring Ding! Concert Time!'", *Gleaner*, 1 August 2006, A8.
5. Mervyn Morris, *Miss Lou: Louise Bennett and Jamaican Culture* (Kingston: Ian Randle, 2014), 31.
6. Leonie Forbes, actress and former JBC TV producer, discussion with authors, 11 June 2016.
7. Campbell, "Icon: Miss Lou"; Marjorie Whylie, musician, in discussion with the authors, 22 December 2016.
8. "New Show Challenges Idea That 'Nobody Cares about the Caribbean'", National Public Radio, 20 February 2014, http://www.npr.org/2014/02/20/280172732/new-show-challenges-idea-nobody-cares-about-the-caribbean.
9. Simone Morgan, "CVM Rolls Out Live@Seven", *Observer*, 10 July 2010, 16.
10. Dionne Jackson-Miller, journalist, in discussion with authors, 13 January 2017.
11. "Jamaica's Premier Entertainment Television Show", Onstage TV, accessed 25 August 2015, http://www.onstagetv.com/about/145-winford-williams-host-creator; "OnStage Is Now on FLOW TV Channel 100", Youtube.com, 11 February 2014, https://www.youtube.com/watch?v=i7-9OVe12iI.
12. Nackeshia Tomlinson, "Famous House Stands Tall in Pullet Hall", *Gleaner*, 28 July 2012, C4.
13. "The Blackburns of Royal Palm Estate", Mediamix Limited, accessed 24 June 2015, http://www.mediamix-palm.com/Royal%20Palm%20Estate_%20Blackburns.htm.
14. Richard Johnson, "Royal Break", *Observer*, 7 May 2015, http://www.jamaicaobserver.com/entertainment/Royal-break-_18880002.
15. Melita Samuels, scriptwriter, email to the authors, 4 July 2017.

16. Pablo Hoilett, *Lime Tree Lane* producer/director, discussion with the authors, March 2017.
17. Laura Tanna, "On Trails with Roy Brown", *Flair Magazine*, 21 May 1985, 11.
18. "Sponsor Yanks 'Trails' from TV; Host Angry", *Gleaner*, 10 December 1987, 2.
19. "Grace through the Years", *Gleaner*, 19 April 2009, 14.
20. Carmeta Tate-Blake, television producer, discussion with the authors, 9 February 2016.
21. Jeremy Tunstall, *BBC and Television Genres in Jeopardy* (Berne: Peter Laing, 2015).
22. Glen Creeber, *The Television Genre Book* (London: Palgrave, 2015); "About Us", CPTC, accessed 13 September 2015, http://www.creativetvjamaica.com/index.php/home/about-us.
23. "How I Ripped Off TV Quiz Viewers", Technology Marketing Corporation, 25 March 2007, http://www.tmcnet.com/usubmit/2007/03/25/2441422.htm.
24. Owen Gibson, "ITV Scraps Its Scandal-Hit Late Night Quiz Show Phone-ins", *Guardian*, 13 September 2007.
25. "Digicel's Deal or No Deal to Premiere on TVJ", Gleaner, 17 September 2009, http://mobile.jamaica-gleaner.com/20090917/ent/ent3.php; see also "Digicel Deal or No Deal", Internet Movie Database, accessed 22 August 2015, http://www.imdb.com/title/tt2594086/.
26. "CPTC Annual Reports 1989 and 1992 Combined", 1.
27. "Dating Show Affected by Identity Crisis", *Gleaner*,, 25 October 1998, 8E.
28. Hasani Walters, "Cash Cab Heads to Jamaica", *Gleaner*, 11 November 2010, D1–D2.
29. "The KFC Quiz Show", vpag.org, accessed 22 August 2015, http://www.vpaj.org/anyhoo-productions/kfc-quiz-show; see also "The KFC Quiz Show", Internet Movie Database, accessed 22 August 2015, http://www.imdb.com/title/tt2594058/.
30. "York Castle Wins!", *Observer*, 18 April 2015.
31. Gonzales, discussion, 4 July 2017.
32. Sadeke Brooks, "Kurt Campbell Is 'Mission Catwalk' Winner", *Gleaner*, 19 November 2014, http://jamaica-gleaner.com/article/entertainment/20141119/kurt-campbell-mission-catwalk-winner-0.
33. Sharon Schroeter, television producer, discussion with the authors, 12 March 2017.
34. "David Keane Foundation", David Keane Foundation, accessed 10 July 2017, http://www.davidkeanefoundation.com/programs/biography/.

35. Yvonnie Davis, Faith Cathedral Deliverance Centre, discussion with authors, 3 August 2015.
36. "Broadcasting and Media Rights in Sport", WIPO, accessed 11 September 2015, http://www.wipo.int/ip-sport/en/broadcasting.html.
37. "2014 FIFA World Cup Brazil Media Rights Licensees", FIFA, accessed 11 September 2015, http://www.fifa.com/mm/document/affederation/tv/01/47/76/00/2014_fifa_world_cup_brazil™_media_rights_licensee_list_0909.pdf.
38. "2015 ISSA Boys and Girls Champs Launched", *Gleaner*, 11 March 2015, http://jamaica-gleaner.com/article/sports/20150311/2015-issa-boys-and-girls-champs-launched.
39. CPTC Annual Reports 1989 and 1992, 1.
40. Olivia Leigh Campbell, "Lisa and Carlene Team in Our Voices", *Observer*, 31 March 2003, 14.
41. "CVM Unveils the 'Naked Truth' ", *Gleaner*, 14 October 2012, D11.
42. "Wealth Magazine Launches TV Programme", *Observer*, 3 October 2012, http://www.jamaicaobserver.com/business/Wealth-magazine-launches-TV-show_12672296.
43. Karena Bennett, "Wealth Magazine to Launch Business Access TV", *Observer*, 15 February 2015, http://www.jamaicaobserver.com/business/Wealth-Magazine-to-launch-Business-Access-TV_18402627.
44. Susan Simes, television producer, in discussion with the authors, 23 March 2016.
45. Ibid.
46. Ibid.
47. Corey Robinson, "Bagga Brown: Linstead's Colourful Hero Laid to Rest", *Observer*, 6 February 2011, 13; see also "Media Colleagues Mourn 'Bagga' Brown", *Observer*, 30 January 2011, 13.
48. "Ity and Fancy Cat Show: Mega Shopping Show [with Diego and Pablo]", YouTube, 13 October 2010, https://www.youtube.com/watch?v=iQrA6aKAgxc. The hosts of the show were well enough known to be characters in a skit by comedians Ity and Fancy Cat but the show ended in 2010 after someone associated with it was held on sex-related charges; "Leave Our Town Now: Colombian Salesman Accused of Assaulting Boy Residents Want Trade Show to Leave Mandeville", *Star*, 7 June 2010, 3.
49. Curtis Campbell, "Teacha's Pet to Be Replaced", *Star*, 17 September 2012, http://jamaica-star.com/thestar/20120917/ent/ent1.html. The show aired on CVM Fridays in 2011 before the arrest of Kartel. The programme had also been shown on Lime's mobile TV. It was launched in September 2011.

50. Campbell, "Lisa and Carlene", 14.
51. Emprezz Golding, television producer, email to the authors 27 July 2015.
52. Straubhaar, "Distinguishing", 293.

## Chapter 9

1. Stanley Baran, *Introduction to Mass Communication: Media Literacy and Culture* (New York: McGraw-Hill, 2006), 213–15.
2. Casper Llewellyn Smith, "Ellen DeGeneres' Oscars Selfie beats Obama Retweet Record on Twitter", *Guardian*, 3 March 2014, http://www.theguardian.com/film/2014/mar/03/ellen-degeneres-selfie-retweet-obama.
3. Countries in the Caribbean where there have been Rising Stars competitions are Haiti, Guyana, Grenada, St Lucia, Barbados, St Kitts and Nevis, Antigua and Barbuda, and Anguilla.
4. Joseph Dominick, Fritz Messere and Barry Sherman, *Broadcasting, Cable, the Internet, and Beyond: An Introduction to Modern Electronic Media*, Sixth Edition (New York: McGraw-Hill, 2007), 61. The digital switchover is the process of replacing analogue television signals with digital signals. After the switchover broadcast would no longer be available to be received through antennae and analogue television. Sets will not be able to receive digital signals without a set-top converter box. Some countries have subsidized the cost of these boxes to consumers. Digital signals provide better quality.
5. John Plunkett, "Why British TV Producers Are Going Global", *Guardian*, 29 March 2013, http://www.theguardian.com/media/2013/mar/29/international-production-drama-actors; Paige Albiniak, "Necessity Is Mother of All Co-productions", *Variety*, 19 March 2013, http://variety.com/2013/tv/features/tv_summit_hannibal_mr_selfridge-1200325314.
6. Jovan Johnson, "TVJ Gave Notice of 'The Voice' Rights Acquisition: Broadcasting Commission", *Gleaner*, 8 October 2013, http://jamaica-gleaner.com/power/48495.
7. Grant, discussion.
8. "TOK Dabbles in Journalism", *Gleaner*, 16 December 2013, C6.
9. BCJ, "Television and Sound Broadcasting Regulations 1996". According to Section 17-(1)(g) of the Television and Sound Broadcasting Regulations 1996, cable operators are required to carry at least two free-to-air TV channels or stations and one channel for public service and educational programmes.
10. Peter Applebombe, "Selling Caribbean TV Network from the Island of Newark", *New York Times*, 28 March 2010, http://www.nytimes.com/2010/11/29/nyregion

/29towns.html?_r=0; Tempo is a Caribbean music channel launched in 2005, available in the region and in parts of the United States via satellite and cable.
11. "Lime Launches Mobile TV and It's Free for Now", *Observer*, 10 December 2010, 16; Julia Richardson, "Lime Suspends Mobile TV", *Observer*, 5 June 2013, B3.
12. "New Regional News App Scores Well in App Stores", *Observer*, 2 July 2014, B13.
13. "RJR, Gleaner Announce Merger", *Gleaner*, 5 August 2015, B8.
14. Hopeton Dunn, "Jamaican Media: Ringing the Changes – 50 Years and Beyond", BCJ, 8 April 2012, available at http://www.broadcastingcommission.org/resources/speeches-presentations/item/download/17_1114cde0a37ffb36e-90082d396e034ed.
15. "JAFTA", Jamaica Film and Television Association, accessed 9 September 2015, https://jafta.wildapricot.org/. In June 2015 the association was established to support Jamaica's film and television practitioners.
16. Julian Richardson, "MJK Productions Sets New Height for Local TV, Boxing", *Observer*, 20 February 2011. Mark Kenny of MJK Productions is behind *Digicel Rising Stars*, based on *Pop Idol*, *Claro Cash Cab*, and *Wray and Nephew Contender*, based on the original *Contender* show produced in the United States in the mid-2000s by Sylvester Stallone and Mark Burnett.
17. "Romper Room and Friends", Internet Movie Database, accessed 15 January 2015, http://www.imdb.com/title/tt0190196/plotsummary?ref_=tt_ov_pl.
18. "Man Who Brought the Big Event to the Small Screen", *Sydney Morning Herald*, 29 July 2005, http://www.smh.com.au/news/obituaries/man-who-brought-the-big-event-to-the-small-screen/2005/07/28/1122143959885.html.

## Chapter 10

1. Mike Gasher, "Media Convergence", 5 September 2011, revised by Andrew McIntosh 13 March 2014, Canadian Encylopedia, http://www.thecanadianencyclopedia.ca/en/article/media-convergence/.
2. "The Reality TV Business: Entertainers to the World", *Economist*, 5 November 2011, http://www.economist.com/node/21536602.
3. Lynn Gross, Brian Gross and Phillippe Peribinossoff, *Programming for TV Radio and the Internet: Strategy, Development and Evaluation* (Burlington, MA: Focal Press, 2013), 14.
4. Albert Moran, Copycat TV: Globalisation Program Formats and Cultural

Identity (Luton, UK: University of Luton Press, 1998); see also Cynthia Littleton, "Blighty Yucks Save Mighty Bucks", *Variety*, 12–18 April 1999; and Elizabeth Guider, "Croisette Was Frothy with Hybrid Formats", *Variety*, 11 October 1999, 88.

5. "TV/Internet Convergence Measurement", Nielsen, last modified 2008, accessed 11 September 2015, http://www.nielsen.com/content/dam/nielsen/en_us/documents/pdf/White%20Papers%20and%20Reports/TV%20Intenet%20Convergence%20Measurement.pdf.

# Selected Bibliography

## Newspapers and Periodicals

*Economist*
*Entertainment Weekly*
*Forbes*
*Gleaner* (Jamaica)
*Guardian*
*New York Daily News*
*New York Times*
*Observer* (Jamaica)
*Star* (Jamaica)
*Sydney Morning Herald*
*Telegraph*
*Variety*
*Washington Post*

## Books and Articles

Baran, Stanley. *Introduction to Mass Communication: Media Literay and Culture*. New York: McGraw-Hill, 2006.

Barnett, George, Hsiu-Jung Chang, Edward Fink and William Richards Jr. "Seasonality in Television Viewing: A Mathematical Model of Cultural Process". *Communication Research* 18, no. 6 (1990): 755–72.

Barwise, Patrick, and Andrew Ehrenberg. *Television and Its Audience*. London: Sage 1988.

Bendazzi, Giannalberto. *Animation: A World History*. Volume 3, *Contemporary Times*. London: Focal Press, 2015.

Bennett, Wycliffe. "Questions of Identity. Democracy and Broadcasting: The Case of Jamaica". *Caribbean Quarterly* 4, no. 2 (1994): 23–32.

Boyne, Ian, and Glenford Smith. *Profile of Excellence*. Kingston: Pelican 2013.

Bradley, Lloyd. *Bass Culture: When Reggae Was King*. London: Viking, 2000.

# SELECTED BIBLIOGRAPHY

Brown, Aggrey. "Caribbean Cultures and Mass Communication in the 21st Century". Paper presented at the Caribbean Studies Association Conference. Trinidad, 22–27 May 1990. ufdcimages.uflib.ufl.edu/CA/00/40/00/66/00001/PDF.pdf.

———. "Mass Media in Jamaica". In *Mass Media and the Caribbean*, edited by Stuart Surlin and Walter Soderland, 11–28. New York: Gordon and Breach, 1990.

———. "New Communication Policies and Communication Technologies in the Caribbean". In *Democratizing Communication? Comparative Perspective on Information and Power*, edited by Mashoed Bailie and Dwayne Winseck, 159–72. New Jersey: Hampton Press, 1997.

———. *Television Programming Trends in the Anglophone Caribbean: The 1980s*. Occasional Paper no. 2. Kingston: Caribbean Institute of Mass Communication, 1987.

Brown, Aggrey, and Roderick Sanatan. *Talking with Whom? A Report of the State of the Media in the Caribbbean*. Kingston: Caribbean Institute of Mass Communication, 1987.

Burbank, Lucille. *Secrets from Sesame Street's Pioneer: How They Produced a Successful Television Series*. Bradenton, FL: Booklocker.com, 2013.

Chalaby, Jean. "Producing TV Content in a Globalized Intellectual Property Market: The Emergence of the International Production Model". *Journal of Media Business Studies* 9, no. 3 (2012): 19–40.

Creeber, Glen. *The Television Genre Book*. London: Palgrave, 2015.

Dominick, Joseph, Fritz Messere and Barry Sherman. *Broadcasting, Cable, the Internet, and Beyond: An Introduction to Modern Electronic Media*. 6th ed. New York: McGraw-Hill, 2007.

Dunn, Hopeton. "Jamaican Media: Ringing the Changes – 50 Years and Beyond". BCJ. 8 April 2012. Available at http://www.broadcastingcommission.org/resources/speeches-presentations/item/download/17_1114cde0a37ffb36e-90082d396e034ed.

Ellis, John. "Television Production". In *The Television Studies Reader*, edited by R.C. Allen and A. Hill, 275–92. London: Routledge, 2004.

Gordon, Nickesia. *Media and the Politics of Culture: The Case of Television Privatization and Media Globalization in Jamaica (1990–2007)*. Boca Raton: Universal Publishers, 2008.

Gross, Lynn, Brian Gross and Phillippe Peribinossoff. *Programming for TV Radio and the Internet: Strategy, Development and Evaluation*. Burlington, MA: Focal Press, 2013.

Higman, B.W., and Brian Hudson. *Jamaican Place Names*. Kingston: University of the West Indies Press, 2009.
Hosein, Everold. "The Problem of Imported Television Content in the Commonwealth Caribbean". *Caribbean Quarterly* 9, no. 4 (1976): 7–25.
Hoskins, Colin, Stuart McFadyen and Adam Finn. *Global Television and Film: An Introduction to the Economics of the Business*. Oxford: Clarendon, 1997.
Lewin, Olive. *"Rock It Come Over": The Folk Music of Jamaica*. Kingston: University of the West Indies Press, 2000.
Macmillan, Mona. *The Land of Look Behind: A Study of Jamaica*. London: Faber, 1957.
Millerson, Gerald. *Effective TV Production*. London: Focal Press, 1990.
———. *Video Production Handbook*. London: Focal Press, 2004.
Mock Yen, Alma. *Rewind: My Recollections of Radio Broadcasting in Jamaica*. Kingston: Arawak, 2002.
Moran, Albert. *Copycat TV: Globalisation Program Formats and Cultural Identity*. Luton, UK: University of Luton Press, 1998.
Mordecai, Martin. "State: Policy, Global Trends and Regulation in Broadcasting: The Case of Jamaica". In *Globalization Communications and Caribbean Identity*, edited by Hopeton Dunn, 198–214. Kingston: Ian Randle, 1995.
Morris, Mervyn. *Miss Lou: Louise Bennett and Jamaican Culture*. Kingston: Ian Randle, 2014.
Robinson, Carey. *Memoirs of a Jamaican Media Man*. Kingston: LMH, 2012.
Rowell, Rebecca. *YouTube: The Company and Its Founders*. Edina, MN: ABDO, 2011.
Salmon, Karlene. "The Development Game: Jamaican Broadcasting's Longest Running Show". Master's thesis, Queen's University, 1996.
Schimmel, Howard, and Justin Rosen. "Six Ways TV Networks Can Drive Viewership Through Effective Marketing". Nielsen, 6 June 2012. http://www.nielsen.com/us/en/insights/news/2012/six-ways-tv-networks-can-drive-viewership-through-effective-marketing.html.
Stolzoff, Norman. *Wake the Town and Tell the People*. London: Duke, 2000.
Straubhaar, Joseph. "Distinguishing the Global, Regional and National Levels of World Television". In *Media in Global Context: A Reader*, edited by Annabelle Sreberny-Mohammadi, Dwayne Winseck, Jim McKenna and Oliver Boyd-Barrett, 284–98. New York: Oxford University Press, 1997.
Tunstall, Jeremy. *BBC and Television Genres in Jeopardy*. Berne: Peter Laing, 2015.
Weaver, Dan, and Jason Siegel. *Breaking into Television and Film: Proven Advice from Veterans and Interns*. Princeton, New Jersey: Peterson's, 1998.
White, Livingston. "Development Imperatives for Television Programmes and

Production in Jamaica: Identifying Appropriate and Feasible Alternatives". Master's thesis, Florida State University College of Communication, 2001.

———."Reconsidering Cultural Imperialism". *Journal of Transnational Broadcasting Studies*, no. 6 (Spring–Summer 2001). http://tbsjournal.arabmediasociety.com/Archives/Spring01/whiteref.html.

Zettl, Herbert. *Television Production Handbook*. Belmont, CA: Wadsworth, 2003.

# Index

*Unless otherwise noted in parentheses, entries in italics are Jamaican television programmes.*

Abdullah, Reverend Clive, 207
Abrahams, Howard, 209
adult channels, 8
adult literacy programme, 196
advertisers, 12, 21, 22, 29, 107; contra-deals, 83, 100; as revenue source, 13, 20, 220n47. *See also* sponsors
advertisements: animation in, 91; commercial breaks, 86; by Jamaican production houses, 9; live production of, 16; online, 19, 73, 134; product placement, 71, 101; revenue through, 13
*After Dark*, 210
*A Graders*, 166–67
agriculture and farming programmes, 193, 194, 190, 195
*Ah ZuzuWah*, 182
Airey, Carlene, 60
Akar, John, 212, 215
Alberga, Judith, 60
Alcyone Animations Productions, 92
Aldridge, Uriel, 214
Alexander, Carlton, 37
*Alive and Well*, 191
*All Angles*, 42, 97–98, 123, 170
Allen, Erica, 5, 26, 29, 167, 198
*All Media Survey*, 12, 53–54, 152
*All Together Sing*, 34, 123, 131, 203
alternative media platforms. *See* distribution platforms

Alpha Omega Band, 182
Amiel, Rohan, 52, 60
analogue broadcasting, 75, 126, 232n4
*Anansi Stories from an Island*, 167
*Anchor, The*, 205
Anderson, Beverley, 5, 189, 198
Anderson, Don, 152
Anderson, Patrick, 118, 210
Anderson, Sonia, 169
Animae Caribe Animation Festival, 92
animation: 3D, 91–92; *Cabbie Chronicles*, 92–93, 166; commercials, 91–92; featured in *Watch n' Win*, 170; genre and subgenres of, 143; Jamaican television content, 91–93; music videos, 91–92
Armond, Chris, 209
arts and culture: *Expressions*, 191
Ashley-Jones, Karelle, 192
Asuntuwa, Safa, 213
audiences, 67–68; consumption habits, 124–25; market research of, 11–12; participation, 114; trends in, 137
audience, live. *See* studio audience
Azan, Omar, 121, 215

Bailey, Dr Margaret, 112
*Bambu Tambu*, 190
*Bandana Boat*, 167
*Bandstand*, 182

– 239 –

# INDEX

"Bankra Basket" (feature on *Evening Time*), 198
Barnes, Jean, 47, 56
Barnett, George, 87
Barnett, Sheila, 198
Barrow, Frank, 5
Barwise, Patrick, 81
*Bashco Shopping Show, The* (infomercial), 120–21, 215
*Bashment Granny* (comedy theatre show), 100, 181
Bay C (dancehall musician), 128, 174
BBC, as model for JBC, 15
*BBC and Television Genres in Jeopardy* (book), x
Beckman, Hertha, 60
*Behind the Scenes The*, 190
Belafonte, Harry, 49
Bell, Neville, 110, 199
Bennett, Louise (Miss Lou), 5, 94, 95, 96, 169; as subject of documentary, 106
Bennett, Wycliffe, 17, 25, 48, 182
Bent, Rupert, 25
Benswick, Jerry, 210
Berbick, Dwayne, 171
Berbick, Trevor, 118
Berry, Russhaine Jonoy, 128
*Best of Live @ Seven, The*, 97, 177
Bidwell, Andre, 47, 52, 60
*Big Brother* (international TV programme), 126
Binger, Karl, 111, 201
Black History Month, 193
*Blackboard, The*, 195
*Blackburns, The*, 100, 181
Blair, Bishop Herro, 115, 208
Blair, Toni "Bella", 128
Blake, Barbara, 210
Blake, Celia, 50

bleaching, as topic on *All Angles*, 98
Bowen, Wenty, 175
Boyne, Ian: awards, 42; host of *Profile*, 37–44, 45, 68, 69, 81, 82, 132, 212; host of *Issues and Answers*, 43, 174; host of *Religious Hardtalk*, 43–44, 131, 213
Boyne, Ian, interviews on *Profile*: Shelly-Ann Fraser-Pryce, 40–41; Una James, 43; Peter Muir, 38
Bradley, Lloyd, 16
Bradshaw, Carl, 188
Bradshaw, Sonny, 5
*Brains Trust*, 5, 200, 203
*Breaking into Television and Film* (book), 67
*Breakthrough*, 207
broadcast channels (free-to-air broadcasting stations), 6, 13
Broadcasting Commission of Jamaica (BCJ), 8, 130
Brown, Aggrey, 18, 173
Brown, A.J., 113
Brown, Basil "Bagga", 120, 216
Brown, Doreen, 109
Brown, Erica, 102, 178
Brown, Keith, 118, 210
Brown, Kerlyn, 208
Brown-Lindo, Jodi, 97, 174
Brown, Roy, 106–7, 196
Brown, Vashan, 98
Browne, Chris, 181
Bryan, Erica Crawford, 173
Buchanan, Candace, 188, 206
Buchanan, Kirk, 109
Bucknor, Donat (Don), 27, 102, 108, 185
budget for production, 71
Burford, Garfield, 172
Burger King, 168

– 240 –

# INDEX

Burger King's National Secondary Schools' Debating Competition, 111
Burke, Jonathan, 50
Burke, Louis, 41, 108
Burrell, Cordell "Skatta", 204
Burrows, Sydney "Foggy", 209
Burton, Zahra, 96, 170
Business Access TV, 119, 215
*Business Day*, 170–71
*Business Review*, 171
*Business Watch*, 171
*Bus Yu Brain*, 200
Butler, Calvin, 179
Butler, Leslie, 188
Butler, Radcliffe, 186, 214
*Buzz*, 7, 182

*Cabbie Chronicles* (animated television show), 92–93, 166
cable channels, 8, 13, 130
cable operators (subscriber service providers), 8
cable subscription service licenses, 19
Campbell, Glen, 99, 181
Campbell, Paul, 181
Campbell-Brown, Nadine, 29
Campbell-Williams, Carol, 100
Campion College, 112
*Campus Vybz*, 190
*Capital Quest*. See *NCB Capital Quest*
Carby, Vanessa, 171
Cargill, Morris, 202
Caribbean Fashion Week, 194, 203
*Caribbean Fashion Weekly*, 203
Caribbean International Network (CIN), 44, 63, 130, 173
*Caribbean Model Search Reality TV Show*, 203
Caribbean Research Limited, 11

Caribbean School of Media and Communication, 10, 91
Carr, Bill, 5, 200
Carter, Reggie, 100
cartoonists, training of, 92
cartoons, 91. See *also* animation
*Catch the Fire*, 7, 114, 207
categories of television programmes, 143–47. See *also* genres; specific category names
cell phone technology, 76
census, TV sets in Jamaican households, 13
*CFW Monthly*, 203
*Chameleon Series, The*, 181
*Children's Corner*, 5, 167
children's television programmes, 93–96, 166–70; *Ring Ding*, 93–96
*Children's Special*, 167
Chin, Bernie, 25
Chin, Tami, 60
Chin, Tessanne, 127
Chin, Yvonne, 29
CIN (Caribbean International Network), 44, 63, 130, 173
*Claffy*, 6, 99, 178
Clarke, Richard "Shrimpy", 118
Clarke, Sydney, 47
Clarke-Cooper, Simone, 110, 199, 205
*Claro Cash Cab*, 111, 122, 200, 233n16
classical music programmes, 188
Cliff, Michelle, 48
*Close Up*, 182
Coley-Nicholson, Helene, 29
*College Bowl* (US TV programme), 32, 223n30
Collins, Mary, 167
comedy, *Shebada in Charge*, 181; in *The Ity and Fancy Cat Show*, 104; *Uppers and Downers*, 182

– 241 –

# INDEX

*Commentary*, 171
commercial model of production, 90–91, 122
commercials. *See* advertisements
Community Television Systems, 7, 107
content of television programmes, 80
cooking shows, 107–9, 196; *Two Sisters and a Meal*, 206
Cooper, Dr Carolyn, 212
Cooper Research and Marketing International, 12
*Copycat TV: Globalisation Program Formats and Cultural Identity* (book), 134–35
*Connection*, 210–11
*Controversy*, 171
Cooke, Aston, 178
copyright issues, 6, 128, 135, 137; and illegal distribution, 125–26
costs of production, 71–72
*Countdown*, 183
*Country Calendar*, 5, 190
*Country Time* (pilot for *Pullet Hall*), 180
*Cover Stories*, 171
CPTC. *See* Creative Production and Training Centre
Craigie, Valton, 93
*Creative Cooking*, 6, 107–8, 109, 123, 190
Creative Production and Training Centre (CPTC), x, 2, 9, 10, 108, 109, 111, 167, 180, 181, 182, 193, 195, 196, 198, 201, 219n36, 225n1, 225n4; *Entertainment Report*, 58–59, 62, 65; establishment of, 47; *Hill an' Gully Ride*, 46–50, 52, 54, 56, 72; *Ring Ding Again*, 93, 169; *The Diana Wright Show*, 118, 214–15; *The Play's the Thing*, 100
Creeber, Glen, 110

Crooks, Emily, 173
Crosskill, Hugh, 118, 210
Crosskill, Simon, 110, 111, 174, 200
Cultural Broadcasting Facility (CBF), 10, 225n4; and JBC/CBF, 47, 54
cultural programmes, 192
Cummings, Bill, 25
Cunningham, Dorothy, 102
current and public affairs programmes, 96–99, 170–78; *All Angles*, 97–98; *Listen Mi News* as commentary on, 128; *On Stage*, 98–99
*Currents* (feature programme on *Sunday Special*), 225n3
*CVM Gospel Report*, 115
*CVM at Sunrise*, 197
CVM TV, establishment of, 2, 7, 8, 19, 107; government based programmes aired, 6; programmes aired on, 97, 98, 99, 100–101, 108, 109, 111, 114–15, 118, 119, 120, 121, 122, 167, 171, 172, 173, 174, 175, 176, 177, 179, 180, 181, 182, 183, 185, 187, 188, 190, 191, 192, 196, 197, 199, 205, 206, 207, 208, 211, 212, 213, 214, 215; *Inspire Jamaica*, 116; sports on, 117; YouTube shows transferred to, 128

DaCosta, Harvey, 5
DaCosta, Leighton, 47
DaCosta, Tony, 186
Daley, Christopher "Johnny", 102, 121, 215
dancehall music, 58, 174
*Dancing Dynamites*, 203–4
Darien, Martin, 25
*Day in the Life of . . ., A*, 190
Davies, Barry, 5, 29, 167, 184, 188, 189, 200, 203

## INDEX

Davis, Cameal, 114
Davis, Carlene, 60
Davis, George, 199
Davis, Laleta, 198
Dawkins, Toni-Kay, 112
Dawkins, Zed, 41
*Dear Mama*, 6, 99, 178
Deer, Sakina, 110
*Deiwght Peters Show, The*, 213
Delapenha, Lindy, 198
*Deuces Wild*, 7, 111, 122, 200
*Dialogue*, 172
*Diana Wright Show, The*, 42, 118, 213–14
Diaram, Saudicka, 171, 214
Digicel (Jamaican telecommunications provider), 113
*Digicel Rising Stars*, 71, 113–14, 126, 131, 204, 233n16
*Digicel's Deal or No Deal*, 200
Digital Liquid Light Studio, 91–92
digital technology, 75; access to, 19; switchover from analogue, 126, 128, 232n4
Dillon, Joseph, 47
*Direct*, 172
*Disco Jam*, 183
discussion programmes, 172, 173, 175
distribution platforms, 122, 136–37
Dixon, Jeff, 189
Dixon, Rochelle, 116
documentation of television programmes, 138–40
*Doin' the T*, 190
*Double Take*, 10, 172
Douglas, Eric, 186
*Do You Follow Me?*, 200
drama. *See* dramatic television programmes
dramatic television programmes, 99–103, 178–82; *Lime Tree Lane*, 102–3; *Royal Palm Estate*, 100–101; theatre productions, 99–100
*Duckunoo*, 183
Dunn, Lauren, 199
duppy stories, 167
"DuttyBerry" (television character), 128
*D'Wrap*, 104, 171

Eddy Thomas Dancers, 182
Educational Broadcasting Service, 9
educational programmes, 9; *The Blackboard*, 195
Edwards, Al, 173
Edwards, Lucie, 51
Edwards, Michael, 60
Ehrenberg, Andrew, 81
*18 Degrees North*, 96–97, 170
Ellington, Barbara, 214
Ellington, Fae, 198
Elliott, Desmond, 183, 187, 201, 202
Ellis, Aston, 104
Ellis, Hall Anthony, 99, 178
Ellis, Ian "Ity", 104
Ellis, John, 70, 77–78, 82, 84
Ellis, Owen "Blakka", 104
Ellis International Jamaica Limited, 104
Eluwemi-Ennis, Romke, 110
Endemol (UK production company), 200
entertainment journalism, 58
entertainment news, 174
entertainment news magazine programme, 171
*Entertainment Prime*, 172
entertainment programmes, 104–6, 182–89; *The Ity and Fancy Cat Show*, 104; *Where It's At*, 104–5

# INDEX

*Entertainment Report*, xii, xiii, 57–65, 130, 133, 150, 172, 226n5; Miller, Anthony, 57–61, 64; and music videos, 63, 86; Manatt Enquiry, 63–64; market research figures on, 164–65; Paul, Annie, 64; sponsorship, 63
"Enter the Dojo" (feature on *Evening Time*), 198
E-Prime. See Entertainment Prime
ER2, 172
*The E-Strip*, 183, 187
Ethiopian Zion Coptic Church, 185
*Evening Time*, 197–98
exclusivity deals, 127
exercise and fitness programmes, 192
*Exposure*, 172
*Expressions*, 191
*Eye on Sports*, 209

Facebook, 33, 92, 125; *All Angles*, 97; *Entertainment Report*, 63; *Hill an' Gully Ride*, 54; *Schools' Challenge Quiz*, 132; *The Susan Show*, 120; *The Teller*, 117
*Face Is Familiar, The*, 202
*Face-to-Face*, 5, 7, 211
factual programmes, 190–97; *Creative Cooking*, 107–8, 109; documentaries, 106; genre and subgenres of, 106–9; *Hidden Treasures*, 109; *Island Dreams*, 109; *Nyammings*, 109; *Time of Fury* (docu-drama), 106; *Trails*, 106–7, 109; *Two Sisters and a Meal*, 109; *Walk n' Talk*, 109
Faith Cathedral Deliverance Centre, 115
*Faith Deliverance*, 207
*Family Bonanza*, 201
*Family Quiz Show*, 201
*Farmer, The*, 195

farming and agriculture programmes, 193
fashion show, 182
Fashion Week, Caribbean, 194, 203
*Feedback*, 191
Ferguson, Gary, 47
*Festival* (documentary film), 4
*Feya Daughter of Zion*, 184
film industry of Jamaica, 10–11
finance, as stage of production, 77
financial journalism programme, 175
*Financially Focused*, 173
*Financial Week*, 172–73
*Firing Line*, 173
fitness and exercise programmes, 192
*Fi We Choice Top Ten*, 104, 183
Flow (telecom and subscription television provider), 92, 99, 104, 130, 166
*Focus*, 173
food programmes, 193, 196; *Nyammings*, 109; *Two Sisters and a Meal*, 206
*Football GPS*, 209
Foote, Khadene, 112
Forbes, Leonie, 94, 179, 182, 185, 186, 197, 198
foreign programming, reliance on, 8, 18, 19–20
foreign TV shows, 5
format, and genre, 141
format exporting, 134–35
Foster, Sandra, 57
Fox Network, 127
franchises, 134–35
franchised shows, 131, 169
Fraser-Pryce, Shelly-Ann, 40–41
free-to-air broadcasting stations. See broadcast channels
free of charge programmes, 174

– 244 –

# INDEX

"Friday Special" (JBC TV programme slot), 225n1
Fuller, Ann-Marie, 178
funding models for free-to-air stations, 70, 71; product placement, 101

gardening programme, 190
Gascho, Denese, 60
Gayle, Kaneal, 98
Gayle, Kathy, 167
Gayle, Lois, 26, 27
Gayle, Noel, 186
game shows. *See* quiz and game shows
Gauron, Marguerite, 107
Geister, Michelle, 110
genres: concept and use of in television production, 20–21, 141–42; influence of in small markets, 123; in Jamaican television, 90; definitions of, 141–47; as factor in sustainability of programmes, 90–91, 135–36
Gentles, Hu, 176, 189
George, Emil, 5
Ghisays, Bobby, 173, 185
*Gleaner*, 38
Gleaner Company's Spelling Bee Competition, 111
Gloudon-Nelson, Anya, 93
*God's Way*, 100, 178
*Golden Nugget, The*, 7, 206
Golding, Emprezz, 110, 184, 213
Gonzales, Michael, 27, 34, 68, 111
Gordon, Archibald, 98, 112
Gordon, Dannielle, 60
Gordon, Nickesia, 20, 80
Gordon, Romae, 194
gospel programmes, 114–15, 141; *Breakthrough*, 207; *Catch the Fire*, 207; *Gospel Report*, 207; *Living in the Sonshine*, 207

*Gospel Report*, 115, 207
government based programmes, 6
Government Broadcasting Service, 218n14
government information programme, 174
Government Public Relations Office, 218n14
government-sponsored programmes, 174
Grace products, 190
Grace Vienna Sausage, 112
GraceKennedy, 37, 54, 101, 107, 108
Graham, Neville, 110
Grange, Olivia "Babsy", 38
*Great Junction*, 178, 180
Greenberg, Allen, 48
Green, Cordel, 29
*Groove Music*, 183
*Guinness Sounds of Greatness*, 204
Guthrie, Ian, 60, 113, 116

Hackett, Mario, 93
Hall, Dennis, 37, 211; moderator for *Question Time*, 176; quizmaster for *Schools' Challenge Quiz*, 5, 26, 29, 69
Hall, Roy, 5, 182, 187, 189
Hanna, Lisa, 111, 118, 123, 200, 212
Hardware, Alton "Fancy Cat", 104
Harriott, Karen, 100
Harris, Dahlia, 100, 110, 178, 181, 199
Harrow, Everald, 41
Hart, Reverend Philip, 26, 29
Haughton, Jackie, 110
Haughton, Nicole, 110
health, *The Health Report*, 195; *Teen Seen*, 199; *Yow*, 199
*Health Forum*, 191
*Health Report, The*, 195–96
*Health Watch*, 6, 191

## INDEX

Hearne, John, 171
*Heineken Green Synergy*, 204
*Hello World Jamaica*, 167
Hendricks, Tony, 179, 185
*Here and Now*, 5, 173
Hewitt, Christine, 212
Hickling, Deborah, 60, 167
Hickling, Pam, 188, 191, 194
*Hidden Treasures*, 53, 109, 132, 191
Higgins, Steve, 167
Hill, Phillip St J., 185
Hill, Sheila, 169
"Hill an' Gully" (Jamaican folk song), 48
*Hill an' Gully Ride*, xii, xiii, 46–56, 133, 151, 191; a CPTC Production, 47, 52; hosts, on-camera vs. narrator, 50; interview with Connie Webster, 55; market research figures on, 162–63; origins of, 47–49, 225n1; ownership controversy, 54; Robinson, Carey, 49–52, 55–56; sponsorship, 54; stand-up links, 50
*Hit List*, 183
Ho, David, 190
Hogan, Michael, 113
Hoilett, Pablo, 102, 103
Holman, Sonia, 50
*Homemaker*, 191
*Honest to God*, 207
Hooker, Rabbi Bernard, 206, 207
Hope, Donna P., 64
*How's Life*, 211
Hughes, Cliff, 96, 173
human-interest content, 115. *See also* social advocacy genre
Hunt, Denise, 59, 65, 69, 113, 121
Hussey, Dermot, 184
Hutchinson, Joan Andrea, 167
Hyde, Beth, 100
Hylton, Khadine "Miss Kitty", 173
Hype, Benzly, 179
*Hype Zone*, 119, 192

*Impact with Cliff Hughes*, 96, 173
*Impressions*, 198
*In Focus*, 192
infomercial programmes, 120–21, 215
Innerarity, Daphne, 178
*Innovators, The*, 206
*In Person*, 5, 211
*Inside Story*, 6, 192
inspirational programmes. *See* religious programmes
*Inspire Jamaica...with Kerlyn Brown*, 10, 116, 208
Instagram, 92
Institute of Mass Communication, UWI, Mona (Caribbean School of Media and Communication), 10
*Intense*, 104, 174
International Monetary Fund (IMF), influence from, 17
*In the Dance*, 183–84
*In Town*, 198
investigative new magazine television programme, 170
investigative news programme, 175, 176
Irons, Stan, 178
Irving, Sean, 60
*Island Dreams*, 109, 192
Issa, Paul, 100
*Issues and Answers*, 43, 174
*Is the Customer Always Right?*, 192
*It's Academic* (US TV programme), 32, 138, 151, 223n30
*It's a Smart World*, 96, 168
Ity and Fancy Cat (Jamaican comedians), 104, 231n48

# INDEX

*Ity and Fancy Cat Show, The*, 104, 105, 187

Ivey, Carol, 31

*Jack Mandora*, 6, 184

Jackson, Anika, 29

Jackson-Miller, Dionne, 97, 170

Jamaican Animation Nation Network, 92

Jamaica Biscuit Company, 112

Jamaica Broadcasting Corporation Television (JBC TV): acquired by RJR, 19, 58–59; establishment of, 4, 15–17, 18; first broadcast, 4–5; becomes TVJ, 6–7; JBC history, x; JBC/CBF, 47, 54; *Ring Ding*, 94–96; and Public Broadcasting Jamaica, 225n4. *See also* JBC TV

*Jamaica Daily News*, 38

*Jamaica DWL*, 123, 184

Jamaica Film Producers Association, 11, 130

Jamaica Film and Television Association, 11, 130, 233n15

Jamaica Film Unit, 218n14

Jamaica Folk Singers (music group), 182

Jamaica Information Service (JIS), 4, 174, 218n14

*Jamaica Jigsaw*, 201

*Jamaica Magazine*, 174

*Jamaica Observer* (newspaper), 167

Jamaica Promotions Corporation, 130

Jamaica Tourist Board, 190

Jamaican heritage, 190

"Jamaicanizing" television content, 186

*Jamaican Woman*, 211

"Jamaican Showcase" (showcase of Jamaican dramas), 180, 181

Jamaican television: cable television, 8, 130; definition of, xi–xii, 13; early programmes, 4–5; future trends in, 124–32; history of, 2–10, 15–20; free-to-air stations, 7–9; as national institution, 15; small market issues, 20; success in, 21–22. *See also* CVM TV; Love TV; JBC TV; TVJ

Jamaican television programmes, 166–216. *See also* names of individual programmes; specific genres

*JAMAL JBC Quiz Show*, 201

James, Greg, 60

James, Owen, 175, 177

James, Una, 43

*Jamfit*, 192

*Jamicons*, 193

Jankee, Bernard, 47, 56

JBC Act, amended, 19

JBC archives, 223n33

JBC Film Unit, 194

JBC Radio, x, 173, 179

*JBC's National Song Competition*, 184

JBC tapes, 219n25

JBC TV, 167, 168, 169, 170, 172, 173, 177, 179, 180, 185. *See also* Jamaica Broadcasting Corporation Television

Jebbinson, Andre, 98

Jenny Jenny (reality TV host), 203

*Jeopardy* (US TV programme), 32, 223n31

JIS staffers, 178

JIS TV, 179, 180, 184

"Johnny Sad Boy" (cartoon addressing child abuse), 91

Johnson, Bari, 93–94

Johnson, Brian "Johno", 52

Johnson, Monica, 46, 47, 50, 56

Johnson, Sheena, 110

Johnson, Trevor, 100

# INDEX

Johnson, Volier, 99, 178
*Joint Tenants*, 178
Jones, Dwayne "Gully Queen", 97–98
Jones, John, 100
Jones, Michelle, 196
Jose Marti School, 184
*Junior Schools' Challenge Quiz*, 34, 111–12, 123, 131, 201
Juno, Warren, 47
*Just Bet Before the Whistle*, 209

Kartel, Vybz, 122, 205, 231n49
Keane, Pastor David, 7, 114, 207
*The Keith Stewart Show*, 187
Kennedy, Shawn, 47
Kenny, Mark, 113, 233n16
Kerr, Michael, 60
Kerr-Jarrett, Paula, 214
*KFC Junior Quiz*, 111, 201
*KFC on the Verge*, 71, 113, 204
*Kids Say . . .*, 96, 120, 168
Kingston College, 28, 35, 224n45
Kirlew, Denise, 41
Konshens (reggae artiste), 61

Laidley, Teddy, 47, 48, 50
*Landscape*, 193
Lannaman, Gloria, 38, 107, 185, 198
Largie, Tebel, 100
Latchman, Alison, 92
Latchman, Aneiph, 92
Laughton, Alaine, 113
*Layers of Soul*, 184
Lazarus, Pat, 169
Lee, Errol, 29
Lee, Keri-Ann, 171
*Leslie Butler Show, The*, 188
Levy, Cathy, 196
Levy, Ivan, 23
Levy, Tallawah, 60

Lewis, Garnet, 52
Lewis, Gary, 42
Lewis, Kathryn, 112
Lewis, Kerry-Ann "Kiki", 50, 172
*Life with the Littles*, 47, 99, 179
*Lime Tree Lane*, 6, 102–3, 108, 123, 179
Linton-George, Keneea, 113, 205
*Listen Mi News*, 128, 174
literacy programmes, 196
Little-White, Heather, 107–8
Little-White, Lennie, 100, 101
*Live @ Seven*, 96–97, 174, 177
"live-to-tape", 85
live TV, advertising as, 16
*Living in the Sonshine*, 207
*Living Treasures of Jamaica*, 50, 193
Lloyd, Peter, 179
local television, 129
Lodge, J.C., 170
long-running television programmes: analysis of, ix, 66–89, 90–91, 131–32, 133; content factor, 80–81; definition of, 13; funding factor, 70–74; genre factor, 90–91, 122–23; international programmes, 149–51; people factor, 66–70, 122; production factor, 77–79, 122; relevance factor, 81–84; routine factor, 84–87; sponsorship, 122; technology factor, 74–77. *See also* time on air
Lopez, Adrian, 91
Lopez, Vernon, 184
Lord, Felisha, 200
Love TV (National Religious Media Television Service), 3, 6, 7, 8, 19, 114
*Love Zone*, 211–12
Lue, Oval, 25
Lumsden, Vin, 193, 197
Lyn, Errol, 198

## INDEX

Mackie (television character), 181
magazine programmes, 104, 197–99; genre and subgenres of, 109–11; *Smile Jamaica*, 109–10; *Weekend Smile*, 110
*Magnum Kings and Queens of Dancehall*, 71, 113, 204
*Magnum Vixens*, 204
Mais-Issa, Kimberley, 109, 192, 194
*Makeover Magic*, 205
Malcolm, Dervan, 29
*Man and Woman Story*, 7, 42, 212
Manley, Beverly, 211
Manley, Norman, 106
Manning, Orville, 49
Manning's School (Savanna-la-Mar), 23, 24, 25
*Man Talk*, 42, 212
Marcus Garvey Secondary School, 225n9
market research, 11, 13; *Entertainment Report*, 164–65; *Hill an' Gully Ride*, 162–63; *Profile*, 160–61; *School's Challenge Quiz*, 153–59
Market Research Services Limited, 12
market size, TV access in Jamaica, 12–14
marketing: departments of, 71, 133; hidden costs of, 72; and media convergence, 133–34; as stage of production, 78
Marketing Counselors Limited, 108
Marley, Bob, 184
Martin, Chris, 114
Matalon, Gary, 206
Matherson, Ruddy, 41
*Matters Arising*, 209
Maxwell, Jody-Ann, 34, 111, 201
Maxwell, Ken, 185, 200
McBean, Radcliffe, 41, 100

McCalla, Alicia, 191
McCalla, Julius, 185, 186, 203
McDonald-Radcliffe, Sabrena, 100
McDonald-Whyte, Novia, 205
McFarlane, Doreth, 112
McGlashan, Sharon, 178
McGregor, Margery, 168, 169
McIntosh, Myrnelle, 48
McKenzie, Alrick, 211
Mckenzie, Clyde, 113
McLean, Louis, 198
McMillan, Mona, 48
McNab, Ali, 118, 210
McPhail, Gregory "Asha", 60
*Me and Mi Kru*, 103, 179
Media Association of Jamaica, 130
media convergence, 124–25, 129–30; and distribution, 136–37; regulation of, 130; as strategy for success, 133–34
Mediamix Limited, 7, 9, 101, 119
Media Technology Institute, 10, 219n36
Meeks, Amina Blackwood, 93, 169
*Megamart Shopping Show, The* (Jamaican infomercial), 120–21, 215
*Mega Shopping Show* (TV trade programme), 120, 231n48
*Memoirs of a Jamaican Media Man* (book), x
Menou, Jean-Paul, 29
Mercy and Truth Ministries Television, 115
*Mike Thompson Show, The*, 188
Miller, Anthony: *Digicel's Rising Stars*, 113, 131; *Double Take*, 172; *Entertainment Report*, 57–61, 65, 68, 69, 80, 99, 172; Manatt Enquiry, 63–64
Miller, Donald, 107

# INDEX

Miller, Mazie, 108
Miller, O'Neil C., 60
Millerson, Gerald, 67, 74, 76, 78, 84–85
Milner, Harry, 107
Mind's Eye Limited, 190
*Mini Matters*, 168
Ministry of Education (Jamaica), 168
*Miranda Hill*, 179
*Mirror*, 5, 198
*Mission Catwalk*, 113, 205
Miss Kitty (media personality), 204
Miss Lou. *See* Bennett, Louise
Mitchell, Shemala, 196
Mitchell, Tafanyah, 53
Mock Yen, Alma, x, 182
*Moment with Thoroughbreds, A*, 209
Mona Preparatory, 112
Monk, Mr (television character), 178
Moo Young Butler and Associates, 107
Moran, Albert, 134
Morant, Jean, 47
Morant Bay Rebellion, 106
*Morning Time*, 6, 7, 109–10, 198. *See also Smile Jamaica*
Moss, Richard, 110
Moxam, Earl, 97
*Music and Youth*, 168, 225n9
"Music and Youth" record, 48
"Music Corner" (feature on *Evening Time*), 198
*Music My Hobby*, 184
music videos, 9, 10, 63, 86, 92; animation in, 91; *Fi We Choice Top Ten* (TV chart show), 104; as part of entertainment genre, 183, 188–89; as part of factual genre, 192; in religious programmes, 114;
Mutabaruka (dub poet), 213
*My Guest*, 212, 215

*Naked Truth, The*, 118, 214
national public radio station (Jamaica), 4
National Religious Media Television Service (Love TV), 7. *See also* Love TV
*National Schools' Debating Competition*, 168
*National Song Competition, JBC's*, 184
*Nation at Work*, 193
*Nation on the Move*, 193
*NCB Capital Quest*, 71, 113, 205
NCB's Omni Educator, 112
Neale, Ken, 48
Netflix, 125, 129
Nettleford, Rex, 171
news commentary, 144
newspapers, as source of information on Jamaican television, 139
news programmes: *Cover Stories*, 171; *Double Take*, 172; *Here and Now*, 173; and social advocacy genre, 116; *News Watch*, 208
Nicholson, Hilary, 106
Nicholson, Michael, 100
nightclub show, *Duckunoo* as, 183
*Nightview*, 6, 174
*Nommo*, 184–85
Norman, Floyd, 91
Northern Caribbean University, training in media and communication, 10
Nunes, Tahnida, 113
*Nyammings*, 53, 109, 193

*Oliver*, 6, 99, 180
*Oliver at Large*, 6, 99, 179
Oliver, Donald, 209
*On Assignment*, 175
*On a Personal Note*, 175

INDEX

on-demand viewing. *See* video on demand (VOD)
1Spotmedia, 33, 73, 77, 98, 110, 127
*On Stage*, 7, 98, 123, 175
*On Stage Encore*, 99
*On the Farm*, 194
*Onstage*, 180
*Open House Reasoning*, 212
*Our Voices*, 42, 118, 123, 212
Owen, Kathy, 182
*Owen James Report, The*, 177
ownership issues. *See* copyright issues

Page, Yaneek, 174, 206
*Paleface Point of View*, 185
Palmer, Landon, 87
Parke, Irma, 195
Parkinson, Elon, 174
*Party, The*, 188
Patterson, Richard Sven, 93
Paul, Annie, 64
PBCJ Act, 3, 9
*Peradventure*, 185
Perkins, Wilmot, 175, 176
Peru, Yasmin, 64
*Perspective*, 6, 175
Phase Three Productions, 9, 107, 167, 178
Phillips, Yendi, 113
Pickersgill, Robert "Bobby", 29, 213
Pinnock, Melissa, 41
Pixley, Dick, 214
*Play Pen*, 168
*Point Counterpoint*, 175
*Police Calling*, 194
*Portfolio*, 176
*Portraits*, 6, 194
post-production, as stage of production, 78–79
Powell, Debbie, 60

Powell, O.C., 60
Prendergast, Patrick, 102
pre-production, as stage of production, 77–78
*Press Conference*, 96, 176
*Price Is Right, The* (US TV programme), 32, 223n31
*Prime Time News* (TVJ), 172, 195, 208, 210
Prince, Richard, 41
privatization, 6
*Probe* (1960s), 176
*Probe* (1990s), 96, 176
production: changing patterns, 126–27; as factor of success, 77–79; five stages of, 77–78; models of, 90; ownership issues, 128; people involved in, 67
production houses, 7, 9
*Profile*, xii, xiii, 37–45, 133, 151, 212; host Ian Boyne, 37–44, 45, 69; market research, 160–61; post-production, 79; production crew, 41; set of, 39–40; sponsors, 41; viewer connection and response, 42, 67–68
*Profile*, guests on: Carlton Alexander, 37; Shelly-Ann Fraser-Pryce, 40–41; Una James, 43; Peter Muir, 38
*Profiles in Religion*, 207
Public Broadcasting Corporation of Jamaica (PBCJ), x, 3, 7, 9, 19, 103, 115; *Entertainment Report* archived, 59; JBC archived, 33–34
Public Broadcasting Jamaica (PBJ), 225n4
public broadcasting model of production, 90–91, 122, 133
public broadcasting via television, 9–10
public service programming, 9–10

INDEX

*Pullet Hall*, 99, 180
*Pulsation*, 185
*Pulse*, 194
Pulse (modeling agency), 203
puppets, 167
*Purse Strings, The*, 196

QUAMPS double, 28
*Quest for Quiz*, 112, 201
*Quest with Safa*, 213
*Question of Religion, A*, 206
*Question Time*, 176
quiz and game shows, 111–12, 200–203; *KFC Junior Quiz*, 111; *Junior Schools' Challenge Quiz*, 111–12; *Schools' Challenge Quiz*, 111–12

Rae, Norman, 215
radio, format exporting, 134
Ragga Boo Boo (puppet character), 167
Rainford, Leavan, 60
Ramanand, Sanjay, 113
Ramsey, Keith "Shebada", 99, 181
*Rappin'*, 6, 10, 109, 123, 198
*Ray of Hope, A*, 10, 116, 208
*Ready for CFW*, 194
*Real Friends*, 180
reality programmes, 113–14, 203–6; *Digicel Rising Stars*, 113–14; *KFC on the Verge*, 113; *Magnum Kings and Queens of Dancehall*, 113; *Mission Catwalk*, 113; *NCB Capital Quest*, 113; *Tastee Talent Search Competition*, 113
Reckord, Carol, 5, 190, 194
Reckord, Michael, 102, 103
Reel Rock GSW Animation, 92
*Reflections*, 6, 194
*Reformation Now*, 115, 207
*Reggae Trail TV*, 185

regulations of media, 130
Reid, Carol, 100
Reid, Noel, 92
Reid, Sheldon, 112
Reid, Terri-Karelle, 113
Reith, Lord John, 4, 217n5
Reithian Model, 4
*Religious Hardtalk* (Jamaican radio programme), 43
*Religious Hardtalk*, 123, 130, 131, 213
religious programmes, 114–15, 206–8; *Catch the Fire*, 114; *Faith Deliverance*, 114–15; *Something More*, 115
Renae, Lady, 113
revenue generated through advertising, 13
*Revival Time*, 208
*Rewind: My Recollections of Radio Broadcasting in Jamaica* (book), x
*Richard Ace Show, The*, 188
Richard Ace and the Youth Band, 184
Ricketts, Patsy, 188
*Ring Ding*, 5, 93–96, 123, 169
*Ring Ding Again*, 93, 169
Rising Stars competitions, 232n3
Robinson, Adrian, 5, 202
Robinson, Carey, x, 6, 49–52, 54, 55–56, 68, 69, 81, 106, 191
Robinson, Claude, 7, 177
Robinson, Sadie, 53
Robotham, Shermaine, 191
Rodney, George, 25
*Romper Room*, 5, 131, 169
Rose, Sandra, 110
*Roundabout*, 5, 199
*Round Table Talk*, 6, 42, 96, 123, 176
*Round the World Quiz*, 5, 202
Rousseau, Michelle, 206
Rousseau, Suzanne, 206
Rowe, Yvette, 60, 172

## INDEX

Rowell, Rebecca, 73
*Royal Palm Estate*, 7, 100–101, 103, 123, 180; spin-off shows from, 181
Ruddock, Elva "Queenie", 121, 215
*Run di Track*, 100, 180

Salmon, Karlene, 80
Salmon, Terri, 214
Samuda, Milton, 34
Samuels, Doraine, 121
Samuels, Melita, 102, 103
Samuels, Oliver, 99, 179, 180
*Sarge in Charge*, 99, 180
satellite dishes, 8, 18
*Saturday Night Sit-In*, 185
*Saturday Sports Special*, 209
*Saudicka Diaram Show, The*, 214
*Say It Loud*, 213
*Scan*, 176
Schiller, Herbert, 18
*Schools' Challenge Quiz*, xii, 23–36, 79, 133, 151, 202, 222n19; critiques of, 34–35; first season, xiii, 23–26, 221n1; format of, 32–33; grand final shows, 32; market research, 153–59; popularity of, 28–29; prizes awarded, 27, 29; production team and studio set, 30–31, 126; quizmasters, 29–30, 36, 69; seasons in the 1980s to 1990s, 26–27; sponsors, 27, 29; St George's College vs Wolmer's Boys' School, 31; success factors, 33–34, 67–68; TVJ scheduling, 27–28
*Schools' Challenge Quiz Access*, 169
*Schools' Challenge Quiz Preview*, 169
*Schools' Challenge Quiz Souvenir Magazine*, 223n28, 224n45
Schroeter, Sharon, 60, 113
Scotiabank, 209

Scotiabank Jamaica Foundation, 116
Scott, Marlo, 92
*SCQ Beat*, 169
*Search for the Caribbean's Next Supermodel, The*, 203
*Seen*, 6, 194–95
*See Tyah*, 186
*Self Starters*, 195
Semaj, Dr Leachim, 212
*Sesame Street* (children's US TV programme), 94
*Seven O'Clock Wrap*, 186
Sharpe, Michael, 178
Shaw, Nadine, 152
*Shebada in Charge*, 99, 181
Shing, Ruth Ho, 26
*Showcase*, 186
Shuga (reggae artiste), 114
Siegel, Jason, 67
Silburn, Carlington, 116
Simber Productions Limited, 119
Simes, Susan, 119, 168, 192, 214
*Simply Muta*, 213
*Sing Along with Sweet and Lovely*, 186
*Sing n' Learn*, 170
*Six O'Two (6:02 p.m.) Wrap*, 186
SkyRes (animation studio), 92
Small, Verlando, 114
Smikle, Althea, 103
*Smile Jamaica*, 30, 108, 199. See also *Morning Time*
Smith, Bobby, 100
Smith, Cameka, 41
Smith, Carlene "The Dancehall Queen", 118, 123, 212
Smith, Ernie, 182
social action television. *See* social advocacy genre
social advocacy genre, 147; television programmes, 115–17, 208–9; *Inspire*

# INDEX

social advocacy genre *(continued)*
  Jamaica, 116; *A Ray of Hope*, 116; *The Teller*, 116–17
social media networks, 77, 125, 127
*Something More with Herro Blair*, 208
Sommerville, Gail, 110
*Soul*, 208
*Sounds of the Seventies*, 186
*Spectrum*, 186
Spence, Neville, 60
Spencer, Kern, 195
*Spicy Hints*, 195
sponsors, 8, 71, 220n47; Burger King, 168; Courts Jamaica Limited, 63, 104; Digicel, 29, 63, 71, 101, 104, 111, 113; Flow, 104; KFC, 104, 111; lack of, 122, 129; Red Stripe beer, 101; Sherwin Williams paints, 101. *See also* individual corporations
sponsorships: for *Entertainment Report*, 63; for *Hill an' Gully Ride*, 54; lack of, 122, 129; for *Schools' Challenge Quiz*, 29; for *The Ity and Fancy Cat Show*, 104; for *Trails*, 107; for *Weekend Smile*, 110
*Sports Commentary*, 210
sports events: exclusivity deals, 127; live broadcasting of, 9
*Sports Forum*, 210
sports programmes, 117–18, 209–10; *Thursday Nights at the Fights*, 117–18; *Wray and Nephew Contender*, 206
*Sports Special*, 210
*Sports View*, 210
Sportsmax (cable TV channel), 117
St Catherine High School, 225n9
St Juste, François, 29
stand-up comedy: *Paleface Point of View*, 185
Stanley, Nadia, 213

Stanley-Moss, William, 4–5
*Star Search at Traxx*, 205
Stephenson-Dalley, Marlene, 29, 223n28
Stewart, Dean, 41
Stewart, Hope McIntyre, 23, 82
Stewart, Keith, 187
Stewart, Laurence "Laurie", 23, 25
Stolzoff, Norman, 16
Straubhaar, Joseph, 68, 123
*Street Link*, 195
*Strong People, Stirring Times*, 195
studio audience, 42, 95, 177, 183, 184, 185, 188; and talk shows, 42, 147, 213, 214; *School's Challenge Quiz*, 30, 31
Sullivan, Leo, 91
"Sunday Concert", 187
*Sunday Report*, 177
*Sunday Theatre*, 187
*Sunday Special* (JBC TV programme slot), 225n1, 225n3
Sunshine Singers, 207
Supreme Ventures Just Bet, 209
*Susan Show, The*, 42, 119–20, 123, 214
Sutherland, Nadine, 113
Suzie Q (music video host), 189
Swaby, Kevin "Kevin2wokrayzee", 184

*Take a Trip*, 202
*Take Twenty*, 202
*Talent Hunt*, 187
talking-head format, 40
talk show programmes, 42, 118–20, 210–15; genre and subgenres of, 42; *Kids Say...*, 120; *Our Voices*, 118; *The Diana Wright Show*, 118; *The Naked Truth*, 118–19; *The Susan Show*, 119–20; *Wealth Magazine Business Access*, 119
*Talk Up Yout*, 213

# INDEX

*Tastee Talent Trail*, 205
Tate, Carmeta, 109
*Teacha's Pet*, 122, 205, 231n49
technology, 74–77; digital, 75; cell phone, 76; new, 124–27; social media networks, 77
*Teen Seen*, 199
teen shows, 198
*Teenage Dance Party*, 5, 187, 189, 218n12
Teen Time Singers, 207
Television and Sound Broadcasting Regulations (1996), 232n9
television genres. *See* genres
television programming, elements of success in, 1, 21–22, 66–89; content and storytelling, 80–81; funding, 70–74; human element, 67–70; lack of success, 122; production, 77–79; relevance factor, 81–84; routinization, 84–88; technology, 74–77
television studies, research questions for, 121
television viewers. *See* audience
*Teller, The*, 116–17, 209
*Tempo*, 187
terrestrial broadcasters, 12
Thame, Angela, 212
*Thicker Than Water*, 100, 181
*This Is Sunday*, 199
*This Sunday*, 188
Thomas, A.G., 47
Thomas, Moya, 97
Thompson, Daisy, 47
Thompson, Judith, 102
Thompson, Mike, 188
Thompson, Tyrone, 177
*Thru Tomorrow's Eyes*, 187, 214
*Thursday Night at the Fights*, 117–18, 210

*Thwaites and Company*, 6, 42, 96, 214
Thwaites, Ronnie, 173, 176, 214
*Tic Tac Toe Quiz*, 202
*Time of Fury* (docu-drama), 106
time on air, assessment of, 138
Tiger (dancehall artist), 57
*Titus*, 6, 99, 181
*Today in JA*, 10, 196
*Today is Sunday*, 208
*Together We Learn*, 196
TOK (Jamaican music group), 174
*TOK Taking Over*, 206
Tomlinson, Cyrene, 100
Toon Boom/World Bank/Jamaica Promotions Corporation, 92
*Topic for Today*, 177
tourism industry, 190
Townsend, Silton, 102, 103
*Trace the Music*, 203
Tracey, Oral, 210
*Trails*, 6, 106–7, 109, 132, 196
training institutions (in media and communication), 10
travelogue format programmes, 53; *Hidden Treasures*, 191
*Traxx*, 7, 181
Trotter, Maxine, 191
*Tuesday Forum*, 6, 42, 96, 177, 222n19
*Tuesday Night Sports*, 210
Tuff Gong, and Bob Marley, 184
Tulloch, Darcy, 198
Tunstall, Jeremy, x, 110
*TV I.Q.*, 203
TVJ, 166, 167, 168, 169, 170, 171, 172, 173, 174, 178, 179, 185
*TVJ Prime Time News*, 210
"TV Kindergarten" (Romper Room), 169
Twitter, 33, 42, 63, 97, 120, 125, 132
*Two Sisters and a Meal*, 53, 109, 206

# INDEX

underwriting of programmes, 71
*University Challenge* (UK TV programme), 32, 82, 223n31
University of Technology, training in media and communication, 10
*Update*, 6, 196
*Uppers and Downers*, 182

*Variety Showcase*, 5
Vasciannie, Stephen, 222n19
*Verdict Is Yours, The*, 5, 96, 177
Verity, James, 201
*Version*, 208
*Very Special People*, 215
*Vibe, The*, 199
*Vibes Cuisine*, 196
*Vibrations*, 6, 96, 170
video: emergence of, 17; by production houses, 9
*Video Alley*, 104, 189
*Video Production Handbook*, 67
video-on-demand (VOD), 124, 129, 33
*Video Saturday*, 189
*Videos for Change*, 195
Virgo, Romain, 114
Virtue, Noddy, 114
*Visions*, 197
VJ Abnormal (music video host), 188
*V Mix*, 104, 188
*Voice, The* (US TV programme), 16, 126, 127, 232n6
vox pop programmes, 53, 97, 104, 120–21, 197, 215–16
Vybz Kartel. *See* Kartel, Vybz

*Wadup*, 177
*Walk n' Talk*, 6, 109, 197
Walker, Alphonso, 5, 105, 189, 213
Walker, Cleo, 93
Walker, Milton, 97, 171
Walker, Shane, 60
Walker, Shaun, 60, 61
Walker, Wayne, 209
Wallace, Ed, 180
Wan, Dianne, 93
*Wat a Gwaan*, 53, 120, 132, 215
*Watch n' Win*, 7, 170
*We the Youth*, 215
*Wealth Magazine Business Access*, 119, 128, 215
Weaver, Dan, 67
Webley, Herman, 93
Webster, Connie, 55
Weeks, Shelly-Ann, 214
*Weh Yuh Seh* (vox pop programme), 53, 120, 132, 216
Welsh, Zoe, 116
*West North West*, 197
*What's My Line* (US and UK TV programme), 134
*Wheel of Fortune* (US TV programme), 32, 223n31
Wheeler, Hope, 198
*Where It's At*, 5, 105–6, 123, 189
White, Livingston, 80
*Who Wants to Be a Millionaire* (international TV programme), 16, 126
Whylie, Dwight, 191
Whylie, Marjorie, 93, 94, 95, 169
Whyte, Wayne, 200
Williams, Dennise, 173
Williams, Karl, 110
Williams, Ranny, 5
Williams, Winford, 98–99, 175
Williams, Winston, 29
Willoughby, Neville, 186, 202
Wilmot, Cynthia, 5, 106, 195, 198
Wilmot, Fred, 198, 202
Wilmoth, Kalando, 29

# INDEX

Wilson, Clevans, 41
Wilson, Conroy, 113
Wilson, Erica, 60
Wilson, Gladstone, 198
Wilson, Scott, 60
*Win Some, Lose Some*, 182
Windward Road Primary, 112
Wint-Leslie, Elaine, 105, 177, 189
Wisdom, Sam, 198
women's programmes, 198
"World of Art" (feature on *Evening Time*), 198
"World of Dance" (feature on *Evening Time*), 198
*Wray and Nephew Contender*, 118, 206
Wright, Diana, 213
Wynter, Ruth-Ann, 196

Yetman, Devon, 29
*Young, Gifted and Black*, 189
*Young Jamaica*, 197
*Young Professionals, The*, 188
*Young World*, 187, 189, 214
*Your Health*, 196
*Your Issues Live*, 96, 178
*Yours Truly, Big J*, 197
*Youth and Music*, 184, 189
"Youth.Now" project, 199
youth programmes, 198
YouTube, 73, 92, 128, 174
Yow, 199

Zacca, Munair, 100

www.ingramcontent.com/pod-product-compliance
Lightning Source LLC
Chambersburg PA
CBHW021138230426
43667CB00005B/170